PSYCHEDELICACIES

BREAKING CONVENTION: PSYCHEDELICACIES

Lead Editor: Nikki Wyrd
Co–Editors: David Luke, Aimée Tollan, Cameron Adams & Dave King

A CIP catalogue record for this book is available from the British Library.

ISBN: 978–1–907222–88–7

Distributed by the MIT Press, Cambridge, Massachusetts. and London, England.
Printed and bound in Great Britain by TJ International Ltd. Padstow.

Strange Attractor Press
BM SAP, London, WC1N 3XX, UK
www.strangeattractor.co.uk

PSYCHEDELICACIES: MORE FOOD FOR THOUGHT FROM BREAKING CONVENTION

LEAD EDITOR: NIKKI WYRD

CO–EDITORS: DAVID LUKE, AIMÉE TOLLAN, CAMERON ADAMS & DAVE KING

PSYCHEDELICACIES:
MORE FOOD FOR THOUGHT
FROM BREAKING CONVENTION

PSYCHEDELICACIES –
INTRODUCTION

Breaking Convention began in 2011. I turned up, not quite knowing what to expect, and was greeted enthusiastically by David Luke, one of the conference's co-founders. As the years have gone by, I progressed from delegate to speaker, and from volunteer co-ordinator to director of what is now a fully-fledged charity. Its three stated missions are to hold a biennial conference, to promote, support and disseminate the useful results of research on psychedelic substances—and disseminate the useful results of such research—and to publish an academic book based upon each conference. Little did I know, at that first shouted 'hello' across a crowded room, that I myself would be the lead editor of that book, a mere seven years later!

In July 2017, the sun shone down on more than a thousand people who had gathered at the University of Greenwich in London, for three days of presentations about psychedelic consciousness. Lecture theatres were filled with keen attentive faces, the grass outside buzzing with circles of folk exchanging tales and opinions. Friends old and new, from a vast variety of backgrounds, came together to share, to argue, to find out things they never knew. Of the over two hundred speakers, many submitted essays on their field of interest, and twenty-two of these have been selected for this volume of essays. Ranging widely across the ways in which psychedelics have influenced culture through art, literature, philosophy, and ritual, these essays take us on journeys across time and space, into dark spaces, places of deep healing, and poetic ponderings.

In a moment of epiphany, I recently realized that culture is made of people, and we really ought to be cognisant of this fact when discussing and describing wider currents within our social structures. As individuals, none of us exist in isolation (no man is an island) and we do well to remember this, especially when looking to the distant past or to other lands. Broadly categorising movements, fashions and cultures has a utility, but hides much of the detail of the way tropes emerge from the sums of actions and behaviours.

Psychedelics are all about the loss of boundaries. As such, trying to speak of how x causes y seems somewhat laughable, it is all a play of matter forming itself into complex standing waves that, to the time-bound awareness, appears to comprise separate identities and linear causal relationships. Yet as we lose our verbal processing we watch in awe as the world makes itself happen. The flow state of the universe arises and we react with emotion. Reasoning is applied only after the fact, and rightly so, because the human animal uses intellect and storytelling to bring the distant into the present. Stripping us of the power of verbiage though, at least on the higher end of dosages, psychedelics return us to a state of Here and Now. We see the world in all its overwhelming spontaneity.

Visions reveal our internal worlds, our conceptual frameworks, our otherworlds. The kaleidoscope of psychedelic consciousness mixes these in novel ways, a sensitive state which we should be wary of entering into without good companions. Over time humans have created a variety of settings constructed to deal with this issue. From the earliest known sites to today's festivals, we have made physical constructions whose semiotic influences on behaviours have been foundational to the experience. Saharan cave paintings of mushroom figures, the carved animals of Gobekli Tepe, are direct antecedents of the Tribe of Frog wall hangings at a Welsh psytrance rave. The material cultures of today's psychedelic environments are the living legacy of distant lineages that are ever present with us, even if we are oblivious to precise knowledge of their sources.

We make spaces to contain the process of this eternal awakening, this escape from who we thought we were. This process is not without its challenges, and from early times writers have tried to make sense of precisely what this hyperpresent state is like, and what it does. Ironically, we present our research here in the form of words, and written words at that, in an attempt to paint pictures of this most non-verbal of states!

The title of this book, *Psychedelicacies*, indicates the treats in store for you, gentle reader. This introduction is intended to be your menu, to make your mouth water with anticipation at what lies within. A selection box of the bitter and the sweet, nourishing morsels concocted in the crucible of our gathering in Greenwich. I hope you find some food for thought here, something worth digesting. Here I would like to describe, for your delectation and delight, the treats that contained within these pages, and to outline some of the thoughts they prompted in me:

We start at the beginning, with a masterful piece from Tim Hardwick about Plato, writing, and the Eleusinian Mysteries, an annual ceremonial gathering held near ancient Athens. Tim identifies the widespread teaching of writing to children at this point in history as perhaps having informed Plato's concept of Forms as somehow existing separately to the physical, a moment in history we shall return to.

Whilst there is some value to the commonly recited adage of all Western philosophy being a footnote to Plato, I would direct the reader's attention towards a slightly earlier philosophical view. Heraclitus' ever-changing style of imagery may suit the psychedelic state more aptly— everything is in a state of flux: "The fairest universe (κάλλιστος κόσμος kállistos kósmos) is but a heap of rubbish (σάρμα sárma, lit. 'sweepings') piled up (κεχυμένον kechuménon, i.e. 'poured out') at random (εἰκῇ eikê 'aimlessly')." A fluid, unbounded view of the universe offers more familiar "ground" for the psychonaut, rather than the fixed world of Platonic solids etc. which has preoccupied so much of European ontological reality, and has colonized so much of the globe.

In return, from far away have come those exotic substances we are so familiar with in contemporary psychedelic usage, such as the various brews we collectively refer to as ayahuasca (typically a mix of *Psychotria viridis* and *Banisteriopsis caapi*, with a range of other herbs added for flavour and effect; including not uncommonly small amounts of toé, or datura.) Looking further back in time and towards the east from Europe, we find tales of similar compound potions, and Matthew Clark has researched in some depth a vast swathe of evidence to try and identify what may have been used by cultures in the Old World. Whilst we can only speculate, it seems likely they would have made use of these sacraments to power lengthy communal ceremonies which enabled them to share the embodied knowledge these entheogens produce.

So, just what can the experience of psychedelic consciousness teach us? Two writers present different aspects of this question. An epistemological essay follows, asking us to consider what forms of knowledge psychedelics might be said to provide us with. Christopher Letheby leads us by the hand through a potentially tricky area and keeps us on track with this well-referenced chapter, in which he lays out the value of understanding (information gained by experience) compared to intellectual knowledge. Next, Lindsay Jordan asks whether psychedelic experiences can be educational: do they, intrinsically, prompt us to be led out of our preconceived paradigms? Or does this depend largely upon the accompanying setting; the rituals, the people, the environmental furniture of an experience?

One of my favourite chapters in this book is Nadia VE's piece, challenging us to consider the psychedelic experience and community using the lessons we can learn from feminist theory. I strongly resonate with her statement that "not only should intersectional diversity issues be a central concern in the community, but...it is a central component of the very purpose of the community". By postulating the status quo as a kyriarchy—"best theorized as a complex pyramidal system of intersecting multiplicative social structures of superordination and subordination, of ruling and oppression" (Fiorenza, 2001, Glossary)"— we can address issues of ensuring inclusion, identify just how the psychedelic community has an intrinsic need to break the conventional top-down systems of power-over that characterize so many aspects of our failing cultures.

Psychedelics also work as medicinal and therapeutic agents, often used as such by those suffering from mental health issues caused in large part by the inequalities of kyriarchy. Nikla Serning provides us with a paradigm of therapists who behave not as priests, but as people who "promote joy", By reminding sufferers of the astonishment of raw existence, psychedelic therapists work alongside their clients, encouraging them to heal themselves with the help of the drug.

Joy, in particular the joy conjured by comedians, is the focus of Oli Genn-Bash's chapter. Sometimes the worthiness of psychedelic converts needs countering with a good laugh, which accompanies the falling into place of a new idea or revelation, or a witty pun, or a contrast to the over-the-top views mainstream media presents to society of the wacky world of psychedelic experience. (Some have conjectured that Plato, as shown in his crazy tale of early humans as cartwheeling creatures, was not averse to a bit of comedy; might we then regard all of Western philosophy as the footnotes to a massive trolling of the original Academy with the apparently ridiculous concept of an objective realm of Forms?!). Much as "visions" on mushrooms can frequently consist of nothing more startling than subtly shifting patterns of colour or wobbly-edged walls, insights might be as simple as realising that we are deeply connected to all living beings by dint of familial relationships. The garish multicoloured psychedelic monstrosities so beloved of our predominantly visual media are products of commercially orientated artists who seem to have a) never taken any psychedelics or b) only encountered the full-on high dose range.

Some of the people who encountered this high high are the heroes of Eli Lee and Nina Lyon's essay. Derrida, Deleuze, Foucalt, le Guin et al. all mention wordlessness in relation to psychedelic consciousness, and how important it can be to see the thing, not the name of the thing. In the 1960s and 1970s, this revolutionary approach to reviving the world around them by escaping the baggage of verbiage from previous generations was a contributory factor in the whole postmodernist artistic and social endeavour.

The postmodernists' extensive use of spatial mapping when considering the world at hand, instead of placing themselves primarily in a historical context, prepares us for the next chapter. Escaping from the mechanistic perception of time as a linear reality was the motif of many writers of the twentieth century. Luke Goaman-Dodson introduces several of them, puts them in relation with each other, and quotes a few nice excerpts. Having a sense of events allows escape from the standard straight trajectory portrayed as the march of time. As he says, "if the present-day psychedelic movement is to withstand the ever-more-turbulent shifts generated by technological and social upheavals, a sense of temporal perspective could prove invaluable".

The countercultural descendants of the literary set, the hippy movement who likewise rejected those "gimcrack values" of society, as Priestley described them, went all out to create a new aesthetic, introducing world-making changes to how things looked on the most fundamental of levels (which to a tripper, become synonymous with the most superficial aspects). This creation of a distinctive psychedelic look, originally created to produce eye-catching posters, is the subject of Michael Montagne's chapter, and has influenced perceptions of the psychedelic state ever since. It is not too strong to say that psychedelic consciousness has ever after been associated, in the mind's eye of the general population, with swirly, near incomprehensible lettering, garish colours and rock music concerts. By laying their trips upon the world (however innocently) the poster artists of the 1960s drafted a style from which we still struggle to differentiate ourselves.

Today, much of the psychedelic research discourse is centred upon medicinal usage, presently in the form of assisting with therapeutic interventions, although other, more physiologically based trials and treatments are appearing. Authorised clinical therapy trials are taking place in several countries, all with promising results; approval is imminent. Tharcila Chaves makes a case for ketamine clinics being the first legitimate, authorised psychedelic clinics for those suffering from treatment-resistant depression. Used as a pharmacotherapy one wonders if combining therapy alongside it might prove even more effective?

In this approach to psychedelic experience as a state of deep relaxation and calm, as contrasted with the standard model of excitatory consciousness, we venture now into the realms of dreaming, the dark, and the silence. Josie Malinowski and her colleagues have compared the dream state with psychedelic consciousness, with some intriguing results. Regina U. Hess relates how her dark retreats allowed contact with the deeper feminine archetype. David Luke and colleagues put volunteers into an anechoic chamber, and drew further parallels to the psychedelic state. These three chapters postulate commonalities between naturally occurring ways of perceiving and constructing interior worlds, and those we find when tripping. This area of research offers insights into the way the different modalities of our senses create our worlds, our emotional states, and our internal narratives of self.

Poets have long played with the sounds of syllabic susurrations to effect alterations in attention. Rhythmic patterns alter feeling, one word at a time. George Erving focusses on that master of the craft, William Blake, whose works "suggested that such heightened states of awareness are not the exclusive preserve of saints, mystics, shamans, or madmen" but could be accessed by anybody. As part of the English Romantic movement, this notion that all people could access the sublime took issue with hierarchical authorities of all types, and there was also an egalitarian aspect to their emotional connection with nature-consciousness that was inherited by the hippies of the 1960s on. Luke Walker broadens our concept of Romanticism by suggesting the term Psychedelic Romanticism, linking areas of literary endeavour, from Blake to Ginsberg, with the powerful immanence of nature, emotion, and awareness revealed in the apocalyptic manner of the classic psychedelic substances.

Sam Knot is a poet of no small talent, as evidenced in his style of writing where waterfalls of words tumble and arrange themselves into sculptural phrases to depict pictures. He writes:

We return to a state of namelessness, both in the psychedelic experience and as be-mused poets, when we see beyond language as merely the habit of thinking we already know what it is we are talking about. In tripping we encounter language alive, as something that emerges in and as experience itself, being the many ways existence says itself.

Knot investigates metaphorical space, with words as relationships; as carriers of emotional objective realities, as indicators, objects to puzzle and delight in their many solutions. Thus we return to the Aristotelian roots of how we intellectually conceive of words as metaphors, carriers of meaning transferring characteristics between material stuffs: the use of words as not-what-they-seem-to-say. This chapter asks us to consider our psychedelically enhanced embodied cognition as a precious resource from which we can extract the treasure of better awareness of perceptual and conceptual processes.

The shamanic storyteller Eric Maddern is the next to take on the mantle of narratologist, relating some poems from his native tradition. Spanning a spectrum from cultural to sacred, heightened speech can induce strange states in the hearers, as well as express the otherworldliness of a transported speaker. Rituals, prayers, chanting, prophesying, and enchanting spells happen as we transcend our individualities, relating to an eternal (outside time) awareness in some form or other. Rituals and ceremonial activities are common to humans throughout time and space, we seem to enjoy and seek out such gatherings, often travelling for days to join our fellows to make movements, sounds, and create our lived experiences in concert with each other.

The shadow-side to certain recent explorations of this behaviour is addressed by Elizabeth Joyce. Cults "governed by closed, isolating, hierarchical power structures, and exclusive totalising ideologies" may, at first glance, seem antithetical to psychedelic consciousness, with its fundamentally connective mechanism. But the destabilising moments, the uncertainty of comprehension, the wiping away of supporting structures which, in circumstances of camaraderie, might appear as funny, as freedom to make anew, can be upended and turned into fear-inducing mechanisms by those that would try to exert power-over. Ayahuasca tourism, with its surplus of young, vulnerable (and mostly well-off) seekers, cast adrift in a (Brave?) New World with little to anchor them, where the leader tells the participant what to make of their experience, removes that vital self-determination so key to a healthy personality. All of life is like this, but especially so when psychedelics are thrown into the mix. Whilst this chapter takes ayahuasca misuse as its model, any other substance could potentially be abused in similar fashion. This is another reason why it is so important to bear in mind why we must constantly strive to increase our communities' intrinsic inclusivity, diversity, connectedness and openness, as Nadia VE so carefully elucidates in her chapter on stepping away from the kyriarchy.

The magic of ceremony makes its appearance next, as Julian Vayne's exemplars of good practice in preparation, divination, prayer, tending the fire, and suchlike activities, bestow upon simple acts the meaningful engagement with our own personal mythos that is so often neglected in one's lives. We are the heroes of our own lives, and to feel this as lived experience makes everything change.

Psychedelic consciousness can also change our attitude towards death. Utilised for decades in modern society, to varying degrees of formal intention, the history of this therapeutic/spiritual preparation is recounted by Sam Gandy. Work continues in the research and evaluation of such techniques, as for those who find themselves terminally ill and overwhelmingly anxious, their anxiety can often steal away potential enjoyment of their precious last months.

In other chapters we have heard mention of the word 'imaginal'; but what does it mean? According to William Rowlandson, tarot divination spells out

> . . . *mythic narratives of essential aspects of life, germane to all people, translatable into languages and cultures across time and geography. This is the mythic power, but it is not necessarily the imaginal power.*

> *There are times that the Tarot winks back. That peculiar resonance again, that uncannily conscious response. This is the imaginal. The layers are blurred.*

And:

> *This is why psychedelic therapy can be so effective. The imagination can be animated by the particular medicine, by the set and setting, and the explorer can enter landscapes of such realness that the important*

work of healing can take place. Memories, dreams, events, people and beings can be encountered and engaged with. Knotty traumatic blocks may be untangled. Fragmented aspects of the self, visible and tangible in this radically altered state of consciousness, may be harmonised and integrated. Destructive patterns of behaviour may be modified.

It is this tangible encounter with the ineffable fact of being present in the world, the intimate superpositioning of the physical and the imaginal, which so often characterises psychedelic consciousness.

I leave you with one final observation. Looking back at the educational system of ancient Athens, we see that prior to the mid fifth century BCE, two strands of education existed. One was to teach and practise physical prowess, fitness, athleticism, strength, all the skills required of a warrior. The other was what today we might collectively conceive of as the Arts; music, dancing, rhythmic activities. Only subsequently do we find higher education in topics such as rhetoric, logic, and what came to be called science. The difference is clear; these higher education subjects are the teachings of words.

A conceptual split between mind and body as contrasting states was inevitable following this compartmentalisation of the practical and the theoretical. The subject of our book, psychedelic consciousness, unmakes this divide, making manifest the contents of our psyche so that we can walk through our emotional landscapes, meet the remarkable in everyday environments, and behold the possibility of meaning-making for ourselves. Whilst this can be achieved through other methods, nothing is as reliable in inducing the perceptions of a well-examined life as a pinch of the psychedelic.

Nikki Wyrd
Devon, 2019

VISION AT ELEUSIS: PLATO'S THEORY OF FORMS

TIM HARDWICK

Contemporary scholars still debate the exact nature of the Eleusinian Mystery rituals of Ancient Greece, but the fact that they were performed regularly for almost two millennia and witnessed by thousands of participants sworn to secrecy is testament to their cultural importance. According to the available evidence, the rites at Eleusis involved a reenactment of the sacred death–rebirth mythos of Demeter and Persephone, as recounted in the Homeric Hymns of the Olympian pantheon, and were said to provide initiates with a vision of the afterlife that changed the way they saw the world and their place within it. Both Socrates and Plato are believed to have attended the Mysteries, as did many important thinkers of antiquity. Plato likely alludes to his own experience at Eleusis in the *Phaedo*, in which Socrates reflects on the immortality of the soul: "Our mysteries had a very real meaning: he that has been purified and initiated shall dwell with the gods."[1] In the same dialogue, Socrates claims that those who genuinely follow a philosophy of wisdom "pursue the study of nothing else but dying and being dead."[2] Elsewhere, in the later *Symposium*, Plato even draws an analogy between philosophy and the Mysteries, suggesting that both end with a similar divine revelation, although it is only the philosopher who is truly changed by the experience and continues to seek in life the knowledge bestowed upon him.[3]

Clearly, initiates revered the rituals as a wellspring of spiritual wisdom, but how their experiences were charged with such reliably consistent potency remains a topic of considerable debate. Insofar as scholars have granted psychedelics not only philosophical import but historical significance, readers of entheogenic literature will recognise the debt owed to the work of Wasson, Hofmann, and Ruck, whose *The Road to Eleusis* (1978) remains the most sustained argument in support of the theory that an LSD-like psychoactive tincture played a pivotal role in the mysteries. To give a brief outline, the book explores the possibility that a ritual drink known as the *kykeon*, imbibed at the culmination of the ceremony, provided the intoxicating trigger for the mystical visions beheld by participants when they entered the darkened inner chamber of the *telestrion* or initiation hall. Given Plato's participation in the rituals, the possible implications of the entheogenic theory for Western philosophy are touched upon in the book and perhaps best summarized in the following passage, courtesy of Wasson:

> *It is clear to me where Plato found his "Ideas"; it was clear to those who were initiated into the Mysteries among his contemporaries too. Plato had drunk of the potion in the Temple of Eleusis and had spent the night seeing the great Vision.*

Before considering this bold assertion, we will briefly summarize Plato's theory of Ideas or Forms, which will allow us to understand its 'cash value' for the Greek philosopher and ultimately help us to appreciate the accuracy of Alfred North Whitehead's famous assessment that most of Western philosophy has consisted of "footnotes to Plato".[4]

The theory first appears in the *Phaedo*, where, having been present at Socrates' death bed, one of his students recounts his teacher's attempt to establish the immortality of the soul by describing its transmigration from one life to the next. He explains that only when the soul is unhinged from the body can it ponder the eternal Forms and pure qualities like the Good, the True and the Beautiful. In the later *Meno* dialogue, Plato offers an extensive mythological account of how a transmigrating soul contemplates this realm of unchanging, abstract Forms beyond the senses, and suggests that when we seem to be learning about things in this world, we're in fact recollecting the Forms we contemplated before we were born. An example he gives of how the Forms function in the world of appearances is the sight of two equal sticks: when you look at them, you're reminded of the Form of the Equal, but they're also unlike the Form of the Equal because in other ways they're unequal. In this way, appearances are always inferior and subject to decay, being imperfect copies of the Forms.

In pre-Socratic philosophy, the desire to discover the essence of reality (metaphysics) was generally given priority over the problem of how such a fundamental substance might be known (epistemology). Parmenides claimed that reality *is*—meaning by which to say it that is timeless, uniform and unchanging—whereas Heraclitus believed that the only constant in the cosmos was absolute flux. Plato's genius was to synthesize the two opposing views in such a way that allowed him to answer the call of both metaphysics and epistemology. Since the Forms have eternal being or true essence, this enables them to explain the properties things have in common. A beautiful flower is only perceived as beautiful because the Form of Beauty causes it to be beautiful (just as the soul is the cause of the body being alive). This is the Form's metaphysical or causal role. As for epistemology, if you can discover the thing that explains why all beautiful things are beautiful, then you can claim to have discovered the definition of beauty. Using that absolute standard to check if your beliefs about other things being beautiful are true, you may thereby come to knowledge. Taken as such, orthodox scholars typically regard the Forms as purely theoretical concepts, and the soul's recollection of them as being Plato's creative solution to the problem of universals (how one thing in general can be many things in particular). Similarly, the mythological narrative he employs as an explanatory framework is usually interpreted as a series of metaphors and allegories which serve the philosopher's political motives.[5]

Short of unambiguous archaeological proof, one way to begin testing Wasson's alternative claim that Plato beheld the Forms in a vision at Eleusis is to reconcile the Ideas with the definition of psychedelic experience as direct revelation in the classical mystical sense. The word "mystical" refers to an experience of which one cannot speak, originating from the Greek *muein*, "to keep silent". We have noted that initiates of the Mysteries were bound by inviolable oaths to preserve the secrecy of the ceremonies. This requisite to "keep silent" also suggests their ineffability or resistance to reason, a defining characteristic of mystical experience first noted by William James.[6] Here we arrive at a paradox, however, for in Plato's theory of Ideas, reason exists as intercessor by way of the *logistikon*—the ruling, thinking part of the soul which discerns truth from falsity and reality from appearance. To be sure, psychedelic rhetoricians commonly appeal to some notion of an ordering entelechy or logos at the heart of their visionary experiences. Yet this appeal to reason highlights an oddly recurring co-incidence of logos and aporia: parallel lines, one of which proclaims epistemic insight, the other a simultaneous end-state of perplexity or impassable doubt.

At this juncture, we might do well to consider Richard Doyle's suggestion that psychedelics work as "adjuncts to eloquence" in their being a "provocation to language", despite claims that the experiences are at heart inexpressible. To underline this point, it is worth noting the principal result of Aldous Huxley's "unspeakable yet self-evident" mescaline experience: an encounter with that numinous Other World that the author nonetheless went on to speak about for the rest of his life. Arthur Koestler's own "gratuitous grace" unearthed the same dilemma: it was "meaningful though not in verbal terms". Of his attempts to describe it: "to express the inexpressible one must somehow put it into words, and so one moves in a vicious circle."[7]

Plato may have faced the same linguistic predicament when attempting to give a logical account of his own mystical experiences, as reflected in his awareness of the apparent incommensurability between an eternal realm of archetypal Forms maximally removed from the material world of change. Plato refers to the problem of their interaction as "the great difficulty" in the dialogue with Parmenides, whose character offers the following counterargument to the theory: if the Forms are separate, then they may relate to one another, but they won't relate to the things of this world. The example he gives is that a human master is master of a human slave, not of the Form of Slavery. Likewise, the eternal Form of Mastery is not master of some particular earth-bound slave. Indeed, if it has mastery over anything then it must be mastery over the eternal Form of Slavery. Ultimately, if nothing in this world relates to the Forms, asks Parmenides, then how can we ever have knowledge of them? Socrates' character is unable to defend against the Eleatic's sustained critique.[8] However, in a surprise about-turn, Parmenides nevertheless advocates the theory of Forms by insisting that it should be possible for a "very gifted man" to defend their existence and hence the possibility of dialectic. He then goes on to prescribe a method of logical training that focuses in detail on the consequences of the existence and non-existence of Forms, which he claims would lead us to understand that sometimes Forms wander and may even take on contradictory properties.

Scholars have struggled to adequately characterise this complex and puzzling dialogue since antiquity, but some believe Parmenides' counterarguments serve an aporetic purpose.[9] In other words, their aim is to perplex—to erect problems that must be solved by philosophers further down the line, either by rejecting some of the premises that lead to contradiction in the theory, or by finding fault with the reasoning. Whatever the case, any lingering doubts about the Forms that Plato may have harboured seldom arise in the other dialogues, and the theory is used as the basis for many of his arguments, with myth and allegory stepping in to support it as required.

If Wasson is correct and Plato apprehended these objects of knowledge in a visionary state, then the depth of feeling that accompanied this revelation may have been considered reason enough for myth to act as handmaid to the philosopher's new metaphysical idealism. William James was first to define the curious sense of authority or "noetic quality" that infuses all mystical experiences.[10] In coining the latter term, the psychologist borrowed from Plato's concept of noesis or nous—the eternal aspect of the psyche/soul which was said to bring it into immediate contact with the Forms. Drawing on decades of experience administering LSD, Stanislav Grof identified this noetic character in the reports of his patients, who would often describe "complex revelatory insights into the nature of existence, often accompanied by a sense of certainty that this knowledge is ultimately more relevant and 'real' than the perceptions and beliefs we share in everyday life."[11] Likewise, Shanon notes how ayahuasca drinkers often claim that "what is seen and thought during the course of intoxication defines the real, whereas the world that is ordinarily perceived is actually an illusion."[12]

We have already pushed back against the notion that the "ineffable" mystical state is perfectly incommunicable. Likewise, the "noetic quality" of a mystical insight is on its own an insufficient guarantor of truth. Given that Plato associates the act of knowing with rationality and linguistic propositions, his certainty about the existence of the Forms, despite their logical inconsistencies, may betray the legacy of a particular way of thinking about nature. Prior to the Athenians, what exists was overwhelmingly the major issue at stake among philosophers: Thales concluded that everything is ultimately made of water, while others suggested air and fire. Once it is believed that things are in fact different from the way they appear, then there follows a number of questions about the senses. As Mortley notes, Parmenides' contrast of logos or reason with the "heedless eye, sounding ear and tongue" was a striking statement of the new consciousness that was unfolding in Plato's time; one in which reality was eternal and intelligible, and beyond the ken of sense perception.[13]

This inherited metaphysics would no doubt have influenced how Plato framed an experience of breaking through to a more authentic realm or state of consciousness. Indeed, metaphors of "lifting the veil of illusion" and "awakening to reality" are clearly alluded to in Plato's allegory of the cave, which is often referenced by psychedelic enthusiasts as a prototypical metaphor for spiritual transcendence. However, it should be clear by now that for metaphysical idealism to hold, there must be two different substances and a privileging of one of them, which leads us back to the question all philosophies of transcendence face: how does interaction between the two occur? In the absence of a reasonable answer, some scholars have wondered whether the real problem lies in the linguistic premises that make the question seem reasonable to begin with.

Commenting on early accounts of language, John Dewey puts forward the case that the Greeks:

...took the structure of discourse for the structure of things, instead of for the forms which things assume under the pressure and opportunity of social cooperation and exchange. They overlooked the fact that meanings as objects of thought are entitled to be complete and ultimate only because they are but a happy outcome of a complex history... They overlooked the fact that the import of logical relations and rational essences is the consequence of social interactions, mutual assistance, direction and concerted action. Hence they conceived of ideal meanings as the ultimate framework of events, in which a system of substances and properties corresponded to subjects and predicates of the uttered proposition.[14]

Dewey's conclusion stems from his understanding that language is a development out of prior biological activities and exists as part of a wider cultural matrix. Within this matrix a reciprocity occurs, in which language is mutually conditioned by culture in its functioning as an agent of cultural transmission and retention.[15] On this basis, language is not just a simple tool for communicating our ideas, but also shapes and sculpts the thoughts we have about ourselves and the world.

Acknowledging this reciprocity, Eric Havelock identifies the transition from orality to literacy as a major turning point in Greek culture, with the result that thought patterns were also altered (and have remained altered ever since). Indeed, the classicist singles out the Greek alphabet as the primary innovation that facilitated the activity of abstraction and the method of reflection we call Western philosophy.[16] Many writing systems were used by humans prior to the alphabet, which emerged in Semitic civilisations around 1500 BC, but the Greeks were the first to establish specific letters for vowel sounds, which effectively completed the literal representation of oral speech. The initial consequence of this innovation was to record orality itself on a scale never before attained (we might think of Homer and Hesiod's works as unique cases of "written orality"). This entailed a gradual removal of pressure to memorize acoustic speech and the composer's corresponding pressure to narrativize, which allowed them to replace agents, or persons, with impersonal ideas and abstractions. Once the use of "topics" for discourse became an accepted habit, pressure mounted for predicates which, having previously supplied an "always action" (by defining personalities in oral narrative by what they do), could instead furnish an "always condition" or relationship. In this way, claims Havelock, static "facts of the case" began to replace the mobile presence of oral narrative, while in the language of philosophy, being (as a form of syntax) began to replace becoming.[17]

Although the Greek alphabet was developed around 700 BCE— several centuries before Plato's time—it was only between the late fifth and early fourth century BC that it was assimilated in Athenian life. As Ivan Illich and Barry Sanders note, "Plato stands on the threshold between the oral and written cultures of Greece...The earliest indications of young boys being taught to write date from Plato's childhood."[18] It is therefore possible, and perhaps even likely, that Plato's ideal Forms are in fact hyper-imaginative reifications of verbalized concepts, which in a world of unstable appearances, had recently achieved a mysterious new changelessness by dint of the written word. As David Abrams notes, to a culture previously steeped in the fluidity of an orally narrated universe, a sequence of written words—symbols that appeared to "speak themselves" when seen—would have had a profound magic, as fixed and eternal in their significance as the stars.[19] Representing words like "tree" or "table" are ideas that belong to the same abstract realm as moral truths such as justice and honesty, and don't exist in the world of ordinary vision. The impact of contemplating these symbols within the timeless, noetic vacuum of psychedelic experience must have made their otherworldly nature appear self-evident. Indeed, Plato's contempt for poetry suggests a rejection of traditional oral modes of awareness in favour of a psychedelicised, yet at base, literary mode of thinking.

Accounting for Plato's Forms in terms of hyper-visionary symbolic abstraction does not detract from their extraordinariness or philosophical import. They remain one of the finest examples of the imaginative power of intellection, and no doubt helped Plato rationalize the emerging

Athenian political culture of his time. It also supports the suggestion that the recourse to language, to logos, is the sine qua non of psychedelic use, and even that this desire to "language" the experience often begins during the experience itself. Indeed, Stanley Krippner refers to this reflexivity as "a release of the semantic function", in which timeworn and impoverished signs take on visionary significance. Such visions can appear "not so much as a symbolisation of another reality [but], as the very act of symbolisation; not precisely to mean something, but actually to mean meaning as such."[20] (The coming together of knower and known may even dissolve these very distinctions in the moment of contact, resulting in a merging of ontological and epistemological categories.)

However, Plato's ultimate division between the intelligible and the sensible runs counter to Dewey's pragmatic principle of continuity, in which "all of our rational abstracting operations grow out of organic activities, without being identical with that from which they emerge."[21] As Merleau-Ponty notes, the body enacts a "meaning before logic", which discloses what is revealed in our "perceptual openness to the world" and "pronounces itself silently in each sensible thing"; this "bodily logos" is silent because it is "the Logos of the natural, aesthetic world, on which the Logos of language rests."[22] Our embodied experience is therefore freighted with significance from the very outset, "presupposed from the set groupings with which we have become familiar in dealing with the world", so that meaning is everywhere carnal and "every human use of the body is already primordial expression."[23] Contemporary theories of embodied cognition underline the fundamental role which the flesh plays in generating meaning. Following Merleau-Ponty, modern research supports the theory that verbal utterances have their origins in gestures, whose meanings are inseparable from their occurrence as events, and implicitly expressed by virtue of their situated, embodied performance.[24] In other words, thinking, insofar as it results in speech, may have its beginnings in visual/kinetic images of gestural expression.

These investigations into the corporeal origins of language indicate that Plato's encounter with an intelligible realm outside of space and time was very likely a felt connection to his earthbound body—a synaesthetic, affective apprehension of his inner gestural activity, mediated and elevated by a visionary symbolism made possible by his literary inheritance. (Indeed, the decidedly visual nature of this encounter appears to have been guided by the subconscious assumption that writing is identical to language, rather than merely a visual artefact designed to trigger the memory of a series of linguistic noises by symbolic association.) But in separating the sensible from the intelligible, Plato exiled the implicit meaning of the body, with tremendous consequences for the direction of Western philosophy. Thereafter, meaning was either imprisoned in a transcending spirit realm, or—beginning with Descartes and culminating in Kant—an equally isolated transcending subjectivity.

In contrast, the above linguistic analysis disconfirms the belief that thought is a purely analytical affair or the sole product of speculative reasoning, and instead preserves a continuum between thought's bodily meaning and its reflective, linguistic conceptions. At the same time, it does not overlook the possibility that our awareness is regularly constrained through an increasingly habitual staccato-like process of abstraction, for, the more ingrained an act of representation, the more transparent it is and the less truly representative it will be, as evidenced by the fact that we often fail to distinguish abstraction from the variegated multiplicity that constitutes our immediate, felt experience. Ultimately, however, psychedelics appear to be capable of disrupting this formal aspect of thought that has in some sense run amok, and may thereby allow us to once again, in Alan Watts's words, "see the world as the whole body sees it".[25]

NOTES

1. Plato, *Phaedo*, (New York: Liberal Arts Press, 1951), trans. F. J. Church, 69:d.

2. Ibid., 75:d.

3. For an exhaustive analysis, see Barbara Sattler's "The Eleusinian Mysteries in Pre-Platonic Thought: Metaphor, Practice and Imagery for Plato's Symposium" in *Greek Religion, Philosophy and Salvation*. (de Gruyter, 2013), Vishwa Adluri (ed.), pp. 151-190.

4. Whitehead, *Process and Reality* (Free Press, 1979), p. 39.

5. In the *Republic*, for example, Socrates' character claims that the rulers of an ideal or just society would have to be wise philosophers, because only they can have true knowledge, and by implication, know what is truly just.

6. James, *The Varieties of Religious Experience* (Longmans: New York, 1917), p. 381.

7. Stace, W T. *Mysticism and Philosophy*. London: Macmillan Press Ltd; 1961, p. 278.

8. The criticisms of the theory within this dialogue are in fact numerous.

9. Allen, R. E., *Plato's Parmenides*, revised edition (New Haven: Yale University Press, 1997), p. 96.

10. James, *The Varieties of Religious Experience* (Longmans: New York, 1917), p. 381.

11. Bennett, Stanislav Grof with Hal Zina, *The Holotropic Mind: The Three Levels of Human Consciousness and How They Shape Our Lives* (Harper: San Francisco, 2006), p. 38.

12. Shanon, Benny, *The Antipodes of the Mind: Charting the Phenomenology of the Ayahuasca Experience* (Oxford University Press: New York, 2002), p. 205.

13. Mortley, Raoul, *From Word to Silence* (Hanstein: Bonn, 1986), p. 20.

14. Dewey, John, *Experience and Nature* (Dover Publications: New York, 1958), pp. 170–171.

15. That culture is a condition of language is attested to by the fact that meanings and the significance of certain phenomena differ between cultural groups. – Tesconi Jr, Charles, "John Dewey's Theory of Meaning", *Educational Theory*, Vol. 19 (1969), p. 157.

16. Havelock, Eric, The Muse Learns to Write (Yale University Press: London, 1986), p. 98.

17. Ibid., pp. 104–105.

18. Illich, Ivan., Sanders, Barry, *ABC: The Alphabetization of the Popular Mind* (North Point Press: London1988), p34. The continuing partnership between orality and literacy required Plato to reassert the primacy of speaking and hearing even as he wrote, as indicated by the spoken format of his dialogues.

19. Abram, David, "On the Ecological Consequences of Alphabetic Literacy: Reflections in the Shadow of Plato's PHAEDRUS" Available at: www.aislingmagazine.com/ aislingmagazine/articles/TAM32/ethical/davidabram.html [Accessed: 15 May 2018]

20. Krippner, S., 'The Effects of Psychedelic Experience on Language Functioning', *Psychedelics: The Uses and Implications of Hallucinogenic Drugs*, eds. B. Aaronson & H. Osmond, New York: Doubleday & Company (1970). Available at: http://druglibrary.org/ schaffer/lsd/krippner.htm [Accessed 12 May 2018].

21. Dewey, J., *Logic: The Theory of Inquiry* (1938), p. 26.

22. Quoted in Hamrick, S. & Van der Veken, J., *Nature and Logos: A Whiteheadian Key to Merleau-Ponty's Fundamental Thought* (2011), p. 119.

23. Ibid., p. 124.

24. The first speech acts of children reflect this affective continuum, mimicking the gestural spontaneity of the body in its felt expression and sensual responsiveness to environmental changes. Such speech acts are not yet arbitrary signs coupled with particular meanings, but rather *directly meaningful* gestural sounds, such as cooing and wailing. For an excellent analysis, see David McNeill's *Hand and Mind: What Gestures Reveal About Thought* (University of Chicago Press: Chicago, 1992).

25. Watts, A., *The Joyous Cosmology*, New York USA: Vintage Books (1962), p. 83.

ANCIENT AYAHUASCA ANALOGUES FROM CENTRAL ASIA: SOMA, HAOMA AND KYKEŌN

MATTHEW CLARK

INTRODUCTION

The hypothesis presented in this article is that by the late Bronze Age (c. 1600 BCE) in Central Asia (in the Upper Oxus region and in what is now Turkmenistan) there was sufficient botanical knowledge to manufacture analogues of ayahuasca from a variety of plants. It is well known that the main formula for making ayahuasca necessarily comprises at least one plant containing *N-N* dimethyl-tryptamine (DMT) and another containing a monoamine-oxidase inhibitor (MAOI). Orally consumed DMT is rapidly broken down by enzymes in the human gut, and ineffective unless combined with an MAOI, which inhibits the breakdown by enzymes.

It is now known that around seventy plants contain DMT (in various amounts) and that around another sixty plants contain MAOIs, in one form or another; these plants are globally distributed. The effects of the 4200 possible combinations of these plants are very similar (Ott 1997; 2011:109ff.). More plants containing these chemicals are being discovered almost every year (Ott 2001).

In the indigenous traditions of the Amazon region, besides the plants usually used to manufacture ayahuasca, namely the *Banisteriopsis caapi* vine (which contains the MAOIs harmine, harmaline and tetrahydroharmine), and *Psychotria viridis* (usually known as *chacruna*, a relative of the coffee plant, which contains DMT), many other plants may be added to the mixture as boosters or enhancers (Ott 2006:19). It is suggested that through trial and error the same kinds of formulas were developed in antiquity in Central Asia.

THE TRANSMISSION OF THE SOMA/AMṚTA CULT TO INDIA

Around 1615 BCE, there was a massive eruption of the volcanic mountain in the midst of the Santorini islands, which lie around 110 kilometres north of the island of Crete in the Mediterranean. This was the largest explosion on Earth since the last ice age, about 10,000 years ago. Magma fell 200 kilometres from the epicentre, the tsunami went twice around the world, and Indigenous Australians heard the explosion in Alice Springs; seven inches of volcanic ash covered the ground in South Africa, and the skies went dark in China for seven years, causing crop-failure and famine (Friedrich 2009).

It is known by scholars of ancient Asian history that around 1600 BCE there were extensive human migrations throughout Central Asia. People would have moved around as a consequence of the volcanic catastrophe, looking for food and sustenance, and taking with them, I suggest, a certain degree of knowledge about potentially psychoactive plants. 1600 BCE was also the time of the collapse of all the highly developed Late Bronze Age city states, which stretched from the Mediterranean to India. It is now believed that these city states knew about each other, and various artifacts such as jewelry and pottery items found at different sites illustrate that there was also trade between them (Sarianidi 1999; Possehl 2002; Witzel 2003:31).

While the sudden demise of the Minoan civilization on Crete is now recognized as a consequence of the eruption of the Santorini volcano, the non-violent collapse of the Indus Valley civilization, which probably, at its peak, numbered around a million people, has never been satisfactorily explained; various theories have been proposed, including climate change or disease as possible causes. I suggest that the collapse of the Indus Valley culture was also probably due to the eruption of the volcano, catastrophic conditions, and the sudden interruption of administration, trade and supply routes.

1600 BCE was also the time when it is believed that people calling themselves Aryan first arrived in what is now the Punjab region of India/Pakistan, having migrated from the Caucasus region of Central Asia. The origins of these people were initially established through archeological and linguistic research (Witzel 2000); this has recently been confirmed through extensive genetic studies. These people spoke an ancestor of the Sanskrit language (hence the connections between the languages of northern India and Europe; the Indo-European family of languages); they had excellent horses and chariots, they loved cows, and they often engaged in battle.

These Aryan migrants, who did not number more than one or two thousand when they first arrived in South Asia, did not construct permanent buildings for many centuries. They brought with them the Central Asian cult of the sacred fire, some of their deities (such as Indra) and the cult of the consumption of a sacred potion, known as *soma* by South Asian Brahman priests and as *haoma* by Zoroastrians, the adherents of the main religion of pre-Islamic Persia. (The name for modern Zoroastrians is "Parsi".) The central elements of the religious lives of the bBahman priests of South Asia and of the Zoroastrians of Persia were (and are) the cults of the ritual potion (*soma/haoma*) and the sacred fire. In the ritual world of the Brahmans, the most esteemed of the many kinds of rites performed are the *soma* rituals and the making and drinking of *soma rasa* (juice), which have grand mythological connotations.

1600 BCE is also the time when it is believed that the mystery rites at Eleusis, near Athens, were first founded. The initiation at Eleusis was a completely secret affair, but it is known from various references in classical sources that at the climax of the ten-day ritual initiates drank a powerful, bitter potion known as *kykeōn* (meaning 'mixed potion' in Greek). It is suggested that this potion was, similarly to *soma/haoma*, an ayahuasca analogue.

THE PREPARATION OF SOMA/HAOMA

Sitting around sacred fireplaces, reciting long and complex sequences of mantras from their sacred texts, and offering substances such as *ghee* (clarified butter) into the fire, participants consume *soma* every two or three hours during rituals that may last one day or many days. The mantras and hymns that are recited during rituals are contained in the *Veda*s (composed between 1600 and 800 BCE), being the sacred texts of the Brahmans, and in the *Avesta* (the oldest parts of which date back to around 1200–1600 BCE), the sacred texts of Zoroastrians.

Soma/haoma is praised in the highest terms in these sacred texts. However, the term *soma/haoma* refers to a juice pressed out (from the root √*su* / √*hu*) from a plant (or plants); it does not refer to any plant in particular. It is prepared from stalks of plants, which in the Zoroastrian tradition are crushed in a mortar and pestle to extract the juice, and usually by pounding with stones on planks of wood in the tradition of the brahmans of South Asia. After the juice is extracted, it is mixed with water and a milk product (usually milk but sometimes with yogurt) and sometimes also with honey and barley groats. The fat in milk products would assist the absorption by the body of any psychoactive molecules in a plant.

These days brahman priests prepare *soma* from either non-psychoactive plants or, sometimes, up until around forty years ago in South India, from ephedra, a bush that contains the stimulant ephedrine, which has an effect similar to coffee or adrenaline. However, the brahmans know that they are nowadays using substitute plants, which they have been doing for probably more than a thousand years, and that they are not preparing the 'real' *soma*. In the Zoroastrian domain, *haoma* was prepared from ephedra until several decades ago.

The *Veda*s and the *Avesta* inform us Soma/*haoma* has a very sharp (*t vra*), bitter taste. It is usually described either as yellow, golden, reddish, brown or tawny in colour. It is said to provide health, truth, wisdom, power, poetic inspiration, and immortality. It could further the power of action and also inspire warriors in battle. The effect of it could be an ordeal. It was also a purgative; it caused vomiting. Importantly, one of the many names for *soma* in the *Veda*s is *am ta*, meaning 'non-death' or immortality.

INTERNAL SOMA/AMṚTA

In texts on (Hindu/Buddhist) Tantric yoga, the earliest of which date from around the fifth or sixth century CE, *am ta* becomes an internal nectar, which can be produced in the head through various yoga techniques, such as the *khecar mudr*, in which the tongue is curled back and the tip enters the gap above the palate (see, for example, Mallinson 2007). Although these techniques are said to lead to bliss and immortality, the internal *am ta* said to be activated or produced through yogic techniques has nothing to do with the extracted juice of plants. However, whether accessed through yogic practice, or, alternatively, engendered through the consumption of psychoactive plants, *am ta* has the same connotation: immortality.

THEORIES ABOUT THE BOTANICAL IDENTITY OF SOMA/HAOMA

Around 250 years ago scholars began speculating and theorizing about what the botanical *soma/haoma* could possibly be. Dozens of theories have been published (see O'Flaherty 1969; Houben 2003). Candidates for *soma/haoma* include various kinds of alcohol, datura, cannabis, the lotus plant, ginseng, mandrake, and various non-psychoactive plants, particularly *Sarcostemma brevistigma* and *Periploca aphyla*, as these latter plants are sometimes used in contemporary rituals as *soma*. Scholars have also proposed that *soma* is merely a concept, that it is rainwater, or that it was the product or ingredient of secret alchemical processes.

Looking at the sacred texts, however, it is apparent (and nearly all scholars agree on this point) that *soma* kept consumers awake: it was some kind of stimulant. As ephedra has been used by both Zoroastrians and brahmans as *haoma/soma*, probably the leading scholarly consensus on the botanical identity of *soma/haoma* is that it was (and still is) ephedra.

Further, in many local languages in South and Central Asia, ephedra is called *som/hum/hom* and the like. Scholars such as Madhihassan (1987), Falk (1989), Nyberg (1997) and Boyce (2012) have presented cogent arguments in favour of ephedra.

However, other scholars (see, for example, Thompson 2003) have argued that *soma* appears in a few passages in the *Veda*s and ancillary texts, and in the *Avesta*, to have been capable of producing visionary or psychedelic effects, though this is disputed by supporters of the ephedra thesis. Nevertheless, in the *Vedas* and *Avesta* there is occasional mention of how *soma* can transport one into the sky, into light, into Truth and the realm of immortality (see, for example, *gveda* 8.48.3–4; 9.64.4, 8; 9.107.20; 9.113.9; *H m Yašt*, Y9–11). In the *Veda*s, the term *soma* is frequently used in association with the term *mada* (or one of its variants), meaning strong, inspirational 'intoxication', which is not of the kind produced by drinking alcohol. The use of alcohol (*sur*), particularly by brahmans, was generally frowned upon in ancient India, so the idea that *soma* was some kind of alcoholic preparation can confidently be ruled out.

So, if *soma* was indeed originally some kind of psychedelic or visionary concoction, what could it have been? In 1968, the American banker-turned scholar, R. Gordon Wasson published *Soma: The Divine Mushroom of Immortality*. In this very influential book and in several subsequent articles, Wasson argued that *soma* was the red and white-spotted fly-agaric mushroom (*Amanita muscaria*). This mushroom is still consumed in parts of Afghanistan and in western and north-eastern Siberia. To date, the fly-agaric hypothesis is the only psychedelic candidate that has been proposed by scholars as *soma/haoma*.

However, opponents of this proposition have pointed out that fly-agaric mushrooms do not need crushing with stones or in a mortar and pestle; the caps are natively consumed either whole or peeled. Also, importantly, intoxication with fly-

agaric mushrooms is quite destabilizing: although capable of producing significant psychedelic effects, the mushrooms also usually cause dizziness, stomach cramps, tremors and blurred vision. Reports of ecstatic experiences are rare. Wasson himself tried fly-agaric mushrooms many times but never had an ecstatic experience; he only felt tired and nauseous (Wasson 1969:75). Wasson also proposed a 'third filter', whereby the pee of someone who had previously eaten the mushrooms is drunk. This happens in Siberia, as the toxins in the mushrooms can be partially eliminated in the pee of the consumer. However, Wasson's evidence of this practice supposedly alluded to in the *Vedas* relies on incorrect translations of various passages presented to support this idea (Brough 1971; 1973). Further, there are prohibitions on the consumption by brahmans of any kind of mushroom, which date back to the earliest brahmanical law codes (*dharma stra*), framed in the early centuries BCE. Nevertheless, despite these objections, a few scholars (for example, Stuhrman 1985; Levitt 2011) continue to argue for fly-agaric mushrooms as the 'original' *soma*.

In 1989, David Flattery and Martin Schwarz proposed, alternatively, in their learned publication *Haoma and Harmaline*, that *soma/haoma* was Syrian/mountain rue (*Peganum harmala*). This plant, which is widely dispersed, has a long history of medicinal use in Central Asia and elsewhere; it is also used as a red dye and as an aphrodisiac. Consumption of the angular reddish/brownish seeds produces a dreamy, and generally introverted condition. In a pioneering study conducted in 1964 of the effects of harmine and harmaline, which are the active ingredients in the seeds of rue, the researcher Claudio Naranjo (1973) described the effects as oneirophrenic (dream-inducing) and conducive to psychoanalytic investigation. However, Syrian rue is not a visionary or psychedelic plant. At doses sufficient to produce psychedelic effects, the experience usually becomes very unpleasant and destabilizing.

In summary, currently there are three theories about the botanical identity of *soma/haoma* that still have some scholarly support, namely ephedra, fly-agaric mushrooms and Syrian rue. It has been suggested that none of these three candidates seems to meet all the necessary requirements to be identified as *soma/haoma*. Other candidates that have been proposed appear to be either too weak, particularly when used regularly, or, on the other hand, too toxic. These considerations would make it improbable that *soma/haoma* was either the lotus plant or ginseng or any of the other dozens of identification with plants that are only mildly psychoactive, as they would be too weak; or mandrake or datura, which would be too toxic. Even though cannabis, another of the botanical candidates, can have a strong and occasionally psychedelic effect, only rarely does it have the effect on regular consumers similar to that of a stronger psychedelic drug, such as LSD, psilocybin or ayahuasca.

There is a possibility that *soma/haoma* was a plant that has become extinct, perhaps due to climate change or over-harvesting. However, if *soma/haoma* was a single psychedelic plant of some kind, it would seem highly improbable that we haven't yet found it.

SOMA/HAOMA AS AN ANALOGUE OF AYAHUASCA

Another suggestion, which I propose in my book on this topic (*The Tawny One: Soma, Haoma and Ayahuasca*), is that *soma* was never a single plant. It is now well known that in the Amazon region of South America there is a living tradition in several native communities of drinking ayahuasca. As noted in the Introduction, ayahuasca is usually made from two plants. The effects include visions, seeing light, inspiration, geometric patterns, sensations of flying and immortality, and of an encounter with the force of life. Ayahuasca is a purgative and it can be a terrifying ordeal. It is also occasionally used in the context of war by some South American tribes.

The proposition in my book [*The Tawny One*] is that *soma/haoma* was never a single plant, but was a combination of plants that had at its base both a plant containing DMT and another containing an MAOI. The plants used would have varied, depending on geographical location and availability. I believe I have gone some way in identifying some of the plants that may have been used. Also, as in the South American tradition, other plants would have been added to the basic formula, as boosters or enhancers. This would explain why, in the Indian *materia medica*, around twenty plants are called *soma* (Nadkarni 1954; Srivastava 1966): all of these plants, I suggest, would have been used at one time or another in the manufacture of *soma*, either as 'main' or additional plants. This also explains what continues to puzzle some scholars, that in both the *Vedas* and the *Avesta* there are quite a few references to many kinds of *soma* and 'many *hoamas*'.

MYSTERY RITES AT ELEUSIS IN ANCIENT GREECE

It was previously mentioned that migrants from Central Asia started extensive migrations around 1600 BCE, after the eruption of the Santorini volcano. Some migrants from Central Asia settled in Greece. It is believed that the temple of Eleusis, which is about twenty kilometres west of Athens, was founded around 1600 BCE. At this temple there was an annual, ten-day festival of initiation into the 'mysteries', which continued almost unbroken until it was outlawed by the Roman Catholic emperor Theodosius towards the end of the fourth century CE. Initiation into the mysteries was a rite of passage that was essential if one wanted to become a citizen of Athens and be entitled to vote. There were many mystery cults in the ancient Greco-Roman world, but all were based on the rites at Eleusis. The climax of the ten-day rites at Eleusis was the drinking of a bitter potion in the inner sanctum of the temple. It was absolutely forbidden to talk about the mysteries. However, it can be discerned from various scattered remarks and comments in classical sources that the experience at Eleusis was both terrifying and ecstatic. Initiates encountered death but also attained the highest beatific vision. The potion consumed was known as *kyke n*, which means 'mixed potion' in Greek. It was mixed with a milk product (sometimes cheese) and barley.

Similarly to the *soma/haoma* issue, scholars have proposed various theories about *kyke n*, some believing that no drug at all was involved in the mystery rites, that reports of ecstasies and the like were just the result of religious frenzy (Burkert 1987:108–109; Cosmopoulos 2015:21). Other scholars have proposed that *kyke n* was either psilocybin or fly-agaric mushrooms (Samorini 1998; 2000). However, probably the most widely believed hypothesis (Wasson *et al.* 1978) held currently is that *kyke n* was made from an ergot fungus, one of the psychoactive constituents of ergot being lysergic acid amide (LSA or ergine, the precursor used in the manufacture of LSD). However, adequately eliminating the other four or five, highly toxic molecules in the ergot fungus (which can cause gangrene and death), would, I believe, have been beyond the wit or technical capacity of the ancient Greeks, even though a few scholars have argued that it might have been possible (Webster *et al.* 2000). Further, even supposing that lysergic acid amide could have been safely extracted in ancient Greece, the 'high' produced by LSA is quite inferior to that produced by 'classic' tryptamines, such as DMT, LSD or psilocybin. I suggest, alternatively, and as mentioned before, that in the late Bronze Age there was sufficient botanical knowledge, through trial and error, to manufacture analogues of ayahuasca from a variety of plants, and that these analogues were the basis of not only the *soma* of the brahmans and the *haoma* of the Zoroastrians, but also the *kyke n* of the Greek mystery rites.

THE TERM AMṚTA AND HOW IT MAY HAVE ORIGINATED

It was noted that the Sanskrit term *am ta* means 'non-death' or immortality. Similarly, the originally Greek term ambrosia derives from *am brotos* ('non-death'), and nectar from *nek tar* ('keeping death afar'). I suggest that experience of non-ordinary states of consciousness permit access to a reality that appears (and is) timeless; and being timeless, there is no death: one knows that one's true Self is immortal.

Finally, on a note of speculation, could it have been the case that over many centuries of experimentation by the religious elite of the ancient world with non-ordinary states of consciousness, that some people devised yogic techniques of breath control and meditation to attain 'immortal' states, but without the use of psychoactive plants?

REFERENCES

Avesta: The Religious Books of the Parsees (from Professor Spiegel's German Translation of the Original Manuscripts, in three Volumes), trans. Arthur Henry Bleeck (2005) [1864]. Elibron/ [Hertford: Muncherjee Hormusjee Cama].

Boyce, Mary (2012) [1998]. 'Haoma ii. The Rituals'. In *Encyclopædia Iranica*, Vol. XI, pp. 662–667. http://www.iranicaonline.org/articles/haoma-ii (accessed 27/02/2015).

Brough, John (1971). 'Soma and *Amanita Muscaria*'. *Bulletin of the School of Oriental and African Studies*. vol. XXXIV, part II, pp. 331–362.

         (1973). 'Problems of the "Soma-Mushroom" Theory'. *Indologica Taurinensia*, vol. 1, part 1, pp. 21–32.

Burkert, Walter (1987). *Ancient Mystery Cults*. London/Cambridge, Massachusetts: Harvard University Press.

Clark, Matthew (2017). *The Tawny One: Soma, Haoma and Ayahuasca*. London/New York: Muswell Hill Press.

Cosmopoulos, Michael B. (ed.) (2003). *Greek Mysteries: The Archaeology and Ritual of Ancient Greek Secret Cults*. London/New York: Routledge.

Falk, Harry (1989). 'Soma I and II'. *Bulletin of the School of Oriental and African Studies*, Vol. LII, Part 1, pp.77–90.

Flattery, David Stophlet, and Martin Schwartz (1989). *Haoma and Harmaline: The Botanical Identity of the Indo-Iranian Hallucinogen "Soma" and its Legacy in Religion, Language and Middle Eastern Folklore* (Near Eastern Studies, vol. 21). Berkeley/Los Angeles/London: University of California Press.

Friedrich, Walter L. (trans. Alexander R. McBirney) (2009). *Santorini: Volcano, Natural History, Mythology*. Aarhus: Aarhus University Press.

Houben, Jan EM. (2003). 'The Soma-Haoma problem: Introductory overview and observations on the discussions'. *Electronic Journal of Vedic Studies [EJVS]*, vol. 9, Issue 1a (May 4).

Josephson, Judith (1997). *The Pahlavi Translation Technique as Illustrated by* Hom Yašt (Studia Iranica Upsaliensis 2). Uppsala, Sweden: Uppsala Universitetsbibliotek.

Labate, Beatriz Caiuby, and Henrik Jungaberle (eds) (2011). *The Internationalization of Ayahuasca* (Intercultural Studies on Ritual, Play and Theatre, vol. 16). Zürich/Berlin: LIT Verlag.

Levitt, Stephan Hillyer (2011). 'New considerations regarding the identity of Vedic *sóma* as the mushroom fly agaric. *Studia Orientalia*, vol. 111, pp. 105–118.

Madhihassan, S. (1987). *The History and Natural History of Ephedra as Soma.*Islamabad: Pakistan Science Foundation.

Mallinson, James (2007). *The Khecari vidya of A dina tha: A critical edition andannotated translation of an early text of* hathayoga. London/New York: Routledge.

Nadkarni, KM. (1954) [1908].*Indian Materia Medica*, vols 1–2, 3ʳᵈ edn. Bombay/Panvel: Popular Book Depot/Dhootapapeshwar Prakashan Ltd.

Naranjo, Claudio (1973). *The Healing Journey: New Approaches to Consciousness*. New York: Ballantine Books.

Nyberg, Harri (1997). 'The problem of the Aryans and the Soma'. In George Erdosy(ed.), *The Indo-Aryans of Ancient South Asia: Language, Material Culture and Ethnicity*, pp. 382–406. New Delhi: Munshiram Manoharlal.

O'Flaherty, Wendy Doniger (1969) [1968]. 'The Post-Vedic History of the Soma Plant'. In Wasson, pp. 95–147.

Ott, Jonathan (1996) [1993].*Pharmacotheon: Entheogenic Drugs, their Plant Sources and History*, 2nd edn.

(1997).'Pharmahuasca, Anahuasca and Vinho da Jurema: Human Pharmacology of Oral DMT Plus Harmine'. (Originally published in *Yearbook of Ethnomedicine 1997/98*.) http://ibogaine.mindvox.com/Articles/JO-Pharmahuasca.htm (accessed 3/06/2014).

(2001). 'Applied Psychonautics: Ayahuasca to Pharmahuasca to Anahuasca'. http://ibogaine.mindvox.com/Articles/JO-AppliedPsychonautics.htm (accessed 3/06/2014).

(2006).*Análogos de la Ayahuasca: Enteógenos Pangeicos*. Madrid: Ediciones Amargord.

(2011).'Psychonautic uses of "Ayahuasca" and its Analogues: Panacæa or *Outré* Entertainment'. In Labate and Jungaberle (eds), pp.105–122.

Possehl, Gregory L. (2002).'Indus-Mesopotamian Trade: The Record in the Indus'. *Iranica Antiqua*, vol. XXXXVII, pp. 325–342.

[Rgveda] Rig Veda Samhita, vols 1–12 (trans. and ed. R. L. Kashyap) (2007–2009). Bangalore: Sri Aurobindo Kapāli Sāstri Institute of Vedic Culture (SAKSHI).

Samorini, Giorgio (1998). 'The Pharsalus Bass-Relief and the Eleusian Mysteries'. *The Entheogen Review*, Vol. 7, no. 2, pp.60–63.

(2000). 'A Contribution to the Discussion of the of the Ethnobotany of the Eleusian Mysteries'. *Eleusis* (New Series), no. 4, pp.1–53.

Sarianidi, Victor (1999).'Near Eastern Aryans in Central Asia'. *The Journal of Indo-European Studies*, vol. 27, nos 3 & 4, Fall/Winter, pp. 295–326.

Srivastava, JG. (1966).'The Soma plant'. *Quarterly Journal of Crude Drug Research*, vol. 6, no. 1, pp. 811–818.

Stuhrman, Rainer (1985).'Worum handelt es sich beim Soma'. *Indo-Iranian Journal*, vol. 28, pp. 85–93.

Thompson, George (2003). 'Soma and Ecstasy in the Rgveda'. *Electronic Journal of Vedic Studies [EJVS]*, Vol. 9, Issue 1e (May 6).

Wasson, R. Gordon (1969) [1968]. *Soma: Divine Mushroom of Immortality*. New York: Harcourt Brace Jovanovich, Inc.

Wasson, R. Gordon, Albert Hofmann, and Carl A. P. Ruck. (1978).*The Road to Eleusis: Unveiling the Secret of the Mysteries* (Ethno-mycological Studies, no. 4). London/New York: First Harvest/HBJ edition/Harcourt Brace Jovanovich Inc.

Webster, Peter, Daniel M. Perrine, and Carl A. P. Ruck (2000).'Mixing the *Kykeon*'. *Eleusis* (New Series), vol. 1, no. 4, pp. 55–86.

Witzel, Michael (2000). 'The Home of the Aryans'. In Almut Hinze and Eva Tichy (eds), *Anusantatyai: Festschrifft für Johanna Narten* (Münchener Studien zur Sprachwissenschafft, Beiheft 19), pp. 283–338. Dettelbach: J. H. Röll Verlag.

(2003). 'Linguistic Evidence for Cultural Exchange in Prehistoric Western Central Asia'. *Sino-Platonic Papers*, no. 129, December, pp. 1–70

THE VAREITIES OF PSYCHEDELIC EPISTEMOLOGY

CHRIS LETHEBY

INTRODUCTION

Is it possible to gain knowledge[1] by taking psychedelic[2] drugs? One influential answer is 'yes': according to this conception, by inducing mystical states of consciousness, psychedelics afford direct knowledge of supernatural, transcendent dimensions of reality. This is an *entheogenic* conception of the drugs as agents that "generate the divine within". A second influential answer is 'no': since materialism or physicalism[3] is true, there are no transcendent realities, and psychedelics just cause compelling hallucinations or delusions. This is a *psychotomimetic* or *hallucinogenic* conception of the drugs as psychosis-mimicking or hallucination-generating agents whose essential effects are *anti-epistemic*[4]; far from facilitating knowledge gain, psychedelics actively hinder it.

A third, relatively unexplored view is that psychedelics can afford genuine epistemic benefits, even if materialism is true and there is no transcendent reality. From this perspective, the drugs' epistemic credentials do not depend on the existence of anything supernatural. Rather, psychedelics can afford genuine and sometimes transformative insights of a kind compatible with physicalism.

Several authors have recently made proposals along these lines. Here I offer a taxonomy and critical review of these proposals using standard categories from epistemology, the philosophical study of knowledge. This is intended as a contribution to the "progressive initiative to demystify the psychedelic experience" being pursued by Carhart-Harris and colleagues (Carhart-Harris et al. 2018).

While it is possible that psychedelics afford propositional knowledge gain, I suggest the most promising idea is that they offer *new knowledge of old facts* (Gertler 1999). Rather than helping us learn new factual information, psychedelics allow us to understand or appreciate already-known (or otherwise knowable) facts in deep, vivid, affectively and motivationally significant ways.

Some authors have tried to refute the very idea of psychedelic-assisted knowledge gain. Roche (2010) argues that psychedelics impair the operation of brain mechanisms whose function is to represent reality accurately. It is highly unlikely, he says, that such impairment would lead to epistemic benefits. But in this dialectical context, the claim that "impairment" is psychedelics' only or most important effect is question-begging. Certainly some of their paradigmatic perceptual effects are misrepresentational, as when they cause subjects to perceive stationary objects as moving (e.g. the phenomenon of 'walls breathing'). But the question at issue is whether *some* of their various effects on cognition and perception might be epistemically beneficial, even though others are detrimental or neutral. Looking through a telescope impairs one's ability to perceive near objects accurately, while improving one's ability to perceive distant objects accurately. Some practices and technologies that affect humans' epistemic capacities improve them in one domain despite impairing them in others (Bortolotti 2015).

Another sceptical argument is as follows: for any putative drug-induced (or altered-state-induced) knowledge gain, either we can verify it independently or we cannot. If we cannot, then we have no reason to trust it; and if we can, then the drug (or altered state) is redundant, since we could have obtained the knowledge anyway (cf. Windt 2011)

One possible response is to suggest that we might independently verify a *method of learning about a certain type of fact*, obviating the need to verify independently each specific fact learned by that method. For example, suppose that certain findings about psychedelics' neurocognitive effects, combined with independent evidence about the functional architecture of the brain, support the following claim: psychedelics promote accurate and unbiased introspection of hidden or repressed desires and motivations. In that case, we could adopt a general policy of trusting psychedelic-assisted introspection of this kind, without needing independent verification of each of its individual deliverances. A second possible response would be to concede the point regarding *factual* or *propositional* knowledge, but hold that psychedelics afford access to other kinds of knowledge, discussed further below.

In any case, I do not think that *a priori* master arguments can establish the existence or otherwise of psychedelic-assisted knowledge gain. Rather, we must consider specific proposals about psychedelic epistemology individually, on their own merits, in light of the best available evidence.

KNOWLEDGE THAT

When we think about gaining knowledge, we usually think of what philosophers call *factual* or *propositional* knowledge, otherwise known as "knowledge that". This is the kind of knowledge that one can gain (*inter alia*) through testimony, or through reading textbooks; it amounts to knowing that certain statements are true, that certain facts or states of affairs exist. Examples might be knowing that Paris is the capital of France, that next Thursday is aunt Judith's birthday, or that the boiling point of water at sea level is 100 Celsius. This is the kind of knowledge at issue in claims that psychedelics can promote genuine extra-sensory perception, such as telepathy or precognition—but such proposals are *prima facie* inconsistent with physicalism, and compelling evidence for them is lacking.

One less mysterious type of factual knowledge that psychedelics might afford is knowledge of one's previously hidden or unconscious mental states. Their putative ability to do this was the premise of the *psycholytic* form of therapy practised in Europe throughout the 1960s, in which patients were given low doses of psychedelics to facilitate psychoanalytic discoveries about their own repressed desires, motivations, and so forth

(McCabe et al. 1972). As Metzinger (2003, p. 249) points out, many patients given psychedelics report such apparent epiphanies, and seem to improve clinically; a simple explanation is that at least some of the insights are genuine (cf. Shanon 2010).

There is no doubt that people intoxicated by psychedelics have experiences of *apparent* insight into their own minds (Shanon 2002). There are two questions: first, do these insight-like experiences really cause clinical benefits? Second, are the apparent insights genuine? On the first count, there is little evidence as yet. Controlled and rigorous psychedelic research in the 21st century has tended rather to focus on correlations between mystical-type experiences and clinical benefits (Letheby 2015). It would be relatively straightforward, however, to see if subjective feelings of psychological insight predict clinical improvement, and Carhart-Harris (2018) has proposed doing this, using a scale developed to measure the feeling of emotional insight in dreams.

Whether or not it predicts clinical improvement, there is a separate question about whether the feeling of insight is veridical. On the face of it, confabulations that *feel* like insights could equally well have emotional and therapeutic benefits. As Windt puts it, "phenomenal certainty—the experience of persuasion or knowing—is not the same as epistemic justification" (2011, p. 246). So how can we know which it is? This is very difficult; as per the sceptical argument above, it would seem to require that we have some independent way of confirming or falsifying patients' psychedelic-induced claims about their own previously unconscious psychological states. This, of course, is the basic methodological problem of consciousness research: the unavoidability of heavy reliance on introspective verbal report.

As mentioned earlier, one solution might be if there were a theory of the cognitive functions of the brain regions affected by psychedelics that entailed psychedelic-induced changes should lead to veridical insights. Carhart-Harris and Friston (2010) offer a neo-Freudian, "neuropsychoanalytic" interpretation of the function of the brain's default mode network (DMN) and its interactions with limbic and other systems which suggests that psychedelic-induced downregulation of the DMN could facilitate genuine self-discovery. This is a possibility that deserves further theoretical analysis—which is beyond the scope of this chapter[5]. Another possibility is that subjects' putative insights could be tested against outcomes of behavioural measures—for instance, emotional and perceptual priming effects, obtained prior to the session. Ingenious methods have been used to probe the introspective accuracy of meditation practitioners (Fox et al. 2012) and some of these could perhaps be adapted to the psychedelic state, though the intense phenomenology of the latter may pose problems.

It has also been suggested that psychedelics can allow users to gain (non-telepathic) insights into *others'* minds. As Shanon (2010) points out, users of ayahuasca sometimes feel, when looking at another person, that they are grasping something fundamental about the other's character—perhaps as though the other's mental states, character traits, or aspects of their biography are 'written on their face'. Are these apparent insights genuine? They would be relatively straightforward to test, in principle—again, given some independent means of verification. Not all putative insights of this kind will be easy to operationalise. However, one possibility might be to have psychedelically-intoxicated subjects guess at others' approximate (relative) scores on the Big Five personality domains (Gosling et al. 2003) and see if their accuracy exceeds that of subjects under placebo, when relevant variables are controlled for.

One issue is that this kind of experiment would require multiple subjects taking the drug together in the same session, which does not typically happen in modern clinical research. (It happens in non-clinical contexts, of course, such as traditional ayahuasca rituals—but in such contexts other variables become harder to control.) It is also worth pointing out that there is some preliminary evidence that psilocybin *impairs* subjects' ability to recognise emotional facial expressions, although this is in relation to static, disembodied images of faces on screens; matters may be different when dealing with embodied, dynamic human beings (Schmidt et al. 2013).

Shanon (2010) also raises the interesting possibility that subjects can gain an abstract type of self-knowledge about patterns of thought and behaviour in their lives. He gives the example of a subject who saw visions of several episodes from her life juxtaposed *thematically*, rather than chronologically, leading her to see the abstract commonalities in superficially different events. It seems entirely plausible that psychedelics might afford this kind of knowledge, given their capacity to enhance pattern-recognition, and that such knowledge might be therapeutically beneficial. As always, however, it is difficult to know how to test this, and especially difficult to know how to distinguish cases of veridical pattern-recognition from cases of pareidolia, or pattern-imposition (which could equally well lead to clinical benefits.)

Finally, one famous pilot study raises the possibility that psychedelics might help subjects discover novel and creative solutions to problems in their fields of specialisation (Harman et al. 1966; cf. Shanon 2010). Although these results require more rigorous replication, this also seems plausible. One view is that psychedelics serve to enhance the *context of discovery*, as it is called in philosophy of science, allowing subjects to 'think outside the box' and come up with novel and creative ideas. The 'context of justification', however, in which ideas are scrutinised for adequacy and accuracy, would be another matter (Hoyningen-Huene 1987). So there are two possible claims here: (i) that psychedelics simply help people come up with interesting new ideas, and (ii) that they also help people reliably discern which of these ideas are correct. The latter would be much more controversial. This is an epistemological proposal on which more conceptual work is needed.

KNOWLEDGE HOW

A second type of knowledge is knowing *how* to do certain things, sometimes called 'ability knowledge' and roughly equivalent to the possession of skills. Examples include knowing how to ride a bicycle, how to dance, or how to program a computer. Is it possible that psychedelics facilitate the acquisition of new skills or abilities?

One proposal from Shanon is that psychedelic states allow subjects to learn *how to skilfully navigate psychedelic states*. As he says, "people may eventually become accomplished in the very art of drinking ayahuasca... drinking ayahuasca is an artful skill in its own right" (Shanon 2010). There is apparent experimental support for this claim: dysfunctions in executive processing under ayahuasca are considerably lessened in experienced drinkers, which could be interpreted as showing that these people have gained some skill in managing the intoxication (Bouso et al. 2013).

This may seem like a trivial form of knowledge gain, akin to claiming that psychedelic experience lets people learn what it is like to undergo psychedelic experience. But it depends on what kind of skill *navigating psychedelic states* actually is. One intriguing possibility is that it is similar or identical to the ability to let go, open, and accept inner experience— perhaps the same kind of skill in relating to one's mental contents that is deliberately cultivated in mindfulness meditation (Baer 2009).

There is a suggestive set of observations supporting this idea. The standard instructions given to subjects in psychedelic clinical trials emphasise the importance of an open, curious, non-reactive attitude toward whatever strange or frightening phenomena arise, and clinical wisdom suggests that following this instruction helps to ensure a beneficial experience. Some trials deliberately recruit subjects with experience of psychedelic states on the grounds that they are better able to navigate the experience calmly and (relatively) fearlessly. Psilocybin- and LSD-induced states have been found to increase the personality trait of Openness to Experience (MacLean et al. 2011, Lebedev et al. 2016).

Meanwhile, the posterior cingulate cortex (PCC), a key node of the DMN implicated in self-representation, is downregulated by psychedelics—correlating with ego dissolution (Carhart-Harris et al. 2012)—and exhibits thinning in long-term religious ayahuasca users, correlating with the extent of prior ayahuasca use and with psychometric scores for 'self-transcendence' (Bouso et al. 2015). Neurofeedback studies of experienced meditators find that PCC activity co-varies with the feeling of being 'caught up' in experience—in other words, becoming gripped by a train of thoughts or feelings such that one loses one's open, non-reactive stance (Brewer et al. 2013). Finally, the 'decentering' capacities cultivated by mindfulness practice are elevated in the days following an ayahuasca session, and these psychological changes correlate with neural changes centred on the PCC (Soler et al. 2016, 2018, Sampedro et al. 2017).

This suggests a straightforward experimental test, similar in spirit to recent studies exploring the effects of psilocybin sessions on novice meditators undergoing meditation training (Griffiths et al. 2017). It would be possible to explore prospectively any lasting effects of a series of psychedelic sessions on subjects' decentering capacities while sober, and the duration of any such increases. (Perhaps retention of executive function while intoxicated could also be used as a measure in this context.) Substantial positive results would support the claim that psychedelic experiences can help subjects gain knowledge of how to let go and accept inner experience.

Shanon (2010) lists a number of other putatively epistemic benefits of ayhauasca classified under 'knowledge how', such as increased well-being and stamina, and enhancements to artistic performance and creativity, while intoxicated. However, unless these enhancements lead to lasting improvements in the relevant domains while sober, it is not clear that they amount to *knowledge* of any sort. In my view they might better be described as transient performance enhancements.

KNOWLEDGE BY ACQUAINTANCE

A third category recognised in epistemology is *knowledge by acquaintance*, which is less conceptually straightforward than the others. The idea is simple enough on an intuitive level: consider the different ways in which you can know about Donald Trump. You can know all sorts of facts about the man indirectly, by watching TV, reading news articles, and the like. Or you can meet Trump and become acquainted with him directly. After this, you *know him* in a sense in which you did not before.

Thus, knowledge by acquaintance contrasts with indirect knowledge mediated by (mere) description or testimony.

One debate in philosophy of mind, relevant to psychedelic epistemology, concerns Frank Jackson's famous thought experiment 'Mary's Room'. This was originally given as an argument for mind-body dualism. Mary is a super neuroscientist living at a future time when neuroscientific and medical knowledge is complete. Everything about the functioning of the human brain and body is fully described and understood. Mary lives her whole life in a black-and-white room and never sees colours, but while in her room, she masters the entirety of neuroscience. (She is a super scientist, after all.) She learns everything there is to know about what goes on in the retina, the visual cortex, and so forth when a human sees something red. One day, Mary leaves her room for the first time and sees something red, such as a ripe tomato. Intuitively, she learns something new and important: she learns *what it is like to see red*. Since Mary supposedly already had all the *physical* information about seeing red, Jackson (1982, 1986) concludes that there is more information than this, and so physicalism is false.

Many philosophers share a strong intuition that Mary does learn something new, while remaining unconvinced that the argument refutes physicalism. Consequently, they have expended a lot of energy trying to say what sort of knowledge she gains, exactly, and how (despite first appearances) it is compatible with physicalism. The conceptual tools and distinctions developed in this literature could be useful for a sophisticated and precise characterisation of psychedelics' possible epistemic benefits. One prominent suggestion is that before leaving the room, Mary has only indirect knowledge by description about the experiential phenomenon of seeing red, but when she leaves the room, she gains knowledge by acquaintance with it (Conee 1994).

I have argued elsewhere that psychedelics afford knowledge by acquaintance of two important facts: the vast potential of the human mind, and the constructed nature of the normal sense of self (Letheby 2015, 2016). On the first count, psychedelics certainly demonstrate dramatically that the range of human experience is far bigger and stranger, for better and worse, than normal waking consciousness suggests. And even those intellectually aware of this fact can find the direct experience a very different matter. An obvious example is Aldous Huxley, the long-time student of mysticism, experiencing mystical consciousness for the first time under mescaline (Huxley 1954). Pahnke describes this insight based on his own clinical observations administering psychedelics to terminal patients:

> *At this point, unless the patient previously had experienced mystical consciousness spontaneously, he becomes intensely aware of completely new dimensions of experience which he might never before have imagined possible. From his own personal experience, he now knows that there is more to the potential range of human consciousness than we ordinarily realize. This profound and awe-inspiring insight sometimes is experienced as if a veil had been lifted and can transform attitudes and behavior. Once a person has had this vision, life and death can be looked at from a new perspective. Patients seem able to meet the unknown with a new sense of self-confidence and security. Logical arguments that human experience must be limited to the narrow range of ordinary human consciousness never can have the same force again.* (Pahnke 1969, p. 15).

On the second count, in ego dissolution experiences, psychedelic subjects come face-to-face with the fact that the ordinary sense of a separate and enduring self is a vulnerable, contingent, constructed feature of experience. They experience consciousness in the absence of the normal sense of self—perhaps of any sense of self at all (though this is controversial.) This does not entail that the self is an illusion, of course; psychedelic subjects also experience the dissolution of their bodies, which undeniably do exist. Some mystics and philosophers (myself[6] included) do hold the self to be ultimately illusory. But regardless, discovering the constructed nature of one's ordinary experiential *sense* of self is a big deal. Many psychedelic subjects, with or without prior belief in this constructed nature, experience it directly and intensely for the first time (cf. Albahari 2014).

There are other proposals in the same broad spirit as knowledge by acquaintance. Shanon suggests that a key epistemic benefit of ayahuasca may lie not in generating new factual knowledge, but in allowing a deeper apprehension of truths already known:

> *The information gained may be banal but its mode of appreciation might be experienced as special... looking at the leaves of plants observing how they were directed towards the rays of the sun, I felt I was actually seeing the nurturing sustenance of the solar light. Had I obtained any "information" I had not known beforehand? I doubt it. But I was open to see the world in a new light.*
> (Shanon 2010).

This is somewhat similar to Tupper's (2003) proposal that psychedelics facilitate access to evolutionary old but culturally neglected 'mythic' and 'somatic' forms of understanding. Not all of these proposals are captured by the idea of knowledge by acquaintance. Moreover, the notion of acquaintance is philosophically problematic. Russell (1910) originally defined knowledge by acquaintance as involving no mediation of any kind between the mind and the object of knowledge, but it is not clear that this ever happens. Finally, acquaintance is a relation, and anyone who thinks the self is illusory may wonder: *who* or *what* becomes acquainted with the constructed nature of the sense of self, or with the mind's potential?

One useful concept here may be that of *modes of presentation* (Alter and Walter 2007). Once again, the basic idea is intuitive enough[7]: consider the difference between viewing a painting, a photograph, and a CGI animation of the World Trade Centre falling on September 11th, 2001. To appreciate that the difference is not simply one of medium or representational format, consider too the difference between reading descriptions of the event by Al Qaeda, the US Government, and eyewitnesses. Even if the descriptions do not factually contradict one another, they will each paint a very different picture of the same event. They will each present it in different ways, or under different modes.

This may be the simplest unifying characterisation of the epistemic benefits afforded by psychedelics, other than factual or ability knowledge: they afford the apprehension of already-known (or otherwise-knowable) facts via new and different modes of presentation. This difference can be vast. Believing intellectually that *everything in the universe is deeply interconnected* is worlds apart from apprehending this profound interconnectedness as a visual, somatic, spatial, and affective sensation vividly pervading the entire conscious field. It is akin to the difference between a new recruit's belief that they will be shot at, and the experience of standing on a muddy battlefield with bullets whizzing past. We might even hold, with some cognitive scientists, that there is a crucial difference between mere (abstract propositional) knowledge and real *understanding*[8], which requires rich sensory, motor, and affective simulations (Zwaan 2004). Perhaps psychedelics, by increasing cross-talk between normally distinct brain networks (Tagliazucchi et al. 2016), connect memory and cognition more directly to affect and perception, allowing us to understand what we otherwise could merely know.

CONCLUSION

Even those sceptical about supernatural and transcendent realms should take seriously the possibility of psychedelic-assisted knowledge gain. I have suggested that psychedelics may afford the gaining of factual knowledge (of *one's own mind, others' minds, abstract patterns in one's life,* and *novel solutions to specialist problems*); of ability knowledge (especially *knowledge how to let go and accept inner experience*); and of greater *understanding* via new *modes of presentation*. I have also offered some suggestions about how to test these hypotheses. The epistemic claims of psychedelic subjects should not be accepted uncritically, but nor can they be refuted from the armchair. Specific proposals about psychedelic epistemology must be considered in their own right and subjected to rigorous interdisciplinary inquiry. Mounting evidence for the therapeutic efficacy of psychedelics behoves us urgently to understand the mechanisms of this strikingly novel treatment modality. One pressing question is whether it is a form of therapy based on genuine insight. I think it probably is—but only further research will tell. Most generally, we need to appreciate that there is a viable third way between traditional conceptions of psychedelics as *entheogens* disclosing transcendent supernatural realms, and as *hallucinogens* or *psychotomimetics* whose epistemic effects are solely detrimental.

ENDNOTES

1. [This term is examined closely later in the chapter. Ed.]

2. My sole focus in this paper is 'classic', serotonin-2a agonist psychedelics such as LSD, psilocybin, mescaline, and DMT/ayahuasca; I reserve the term psychedelic for substances of this class.

3. Despite philosophical complications, I will use the terms 'materialism', 'physicalism', and 'naturalism' interchangeably, to refer to views on which mind and consciousness always result from or depend on the complex activities of ultimately non-minded things (such as atoms): that is, views which hold that the mental is not fundamental to reality, but arises from or is constructed out of the non-mental. This excludes mind-body dualism, idealism and its variants (such as cosmopsychism), panpsychism and its variants (such as pan-experientialism and pan-protopsychism), and neutral monism (in Russellian and other versions.) It is also intended to exclude all metaphysically literal varieties of theism.

4. 'Epistemic' is a philosophical term meaning 'of or pertaining to knowledge'.

5. See Carhart-Harris and Friston (2019) for further discussion.

6. Irony unintended but noted.

7. I am riding roughshod over many important philosophical subtleties here.

8. I am indebted to Gavin Enck for raising this possibility.

REFERENCES

Albahari, M., 2014. Insight knowledge of no self in Buddhism: An epistemic analysis. *Philosophers' Imprint, 14*(21), pp. 1-30.

Baer, R.A., 2009. Self-focused attention and mechanisms of change in mindfulness-based treatment. *Cognitive Behaviour Therapy, 38(S1)*, pp.15-20.

Bortolotti, L., 2015. The epistemic innocence of motivated delusions. *Consciousness and cognition, 33*, pp.490-499.

Bouso, J.C., Fábregas, J.M., Antonijoan, R.M., Rodríguez-Fornells, A. and Riba, J., 2013. Acute effects of ayahuasca on neuropsychological performance: differences in executive function between experienced and occasional users. *Psychopharmacology, 230*(3), pp.415-424.

Bouso, J.C., Palhano-Fontes, F., Rodríguez-Fornells, A., Ribeiro, S., Sanches, R., Crippa, J.A.S., Hallak, J.E., de Araujo, D.B. and Riba, J., 2015. Long-term use of psychedelic drugs is associated with differences in brain structure and personality in humans. *European Neuropsychopharmacology, 25*(4), pp.483-492.

Brewer, J., Garrison, K. and Whitfield-Gabrieli, S., 2013. What about the "self" is processed in the posterior cingulate cortex?. *Frontiers in human neuroscience, 7*, p.647.

Carhart-Harris, R.L. and Friston, K.J., 2010. The default-mode, ego-functions and free-energy: a neurobiological account of Freudian ideas. *Brain, 133*(4), pp.1265-1283.

Carhart-Harris, R.L., Erritzoe, D., Williams, T., Stone, J.M., Reed, L.J., Colasanti, A., Tyacke, R.J., Leech, R., Malizia, A.L., Murphy, K. and Hobden, P., 2012. Neural correlates of the psychedelic state as determined by fMRI studies with psilocybin. *Proceedings of the National Academy of Sciences*, 109(6), pp.2138-2143.

Carhart-Harris, R. L. and Friston, K. J., 2019. REBUS and the anarchic brain: toward a unified model of the brain action of psychedelics. *Pharmacological Reviews, 71*, pp. 316-344.

Carhart-Harris, R.L., 2018. The entropic brain-Revisited. *Neuropharmacology.* DOI: 10.1016/j.neuropharm.2018.03.010.

Carhart-Harris, R.L., Erritzoe, D., Haijen, E., Kaelen, M. and Watts, R., 2018. Psychedelics and connectedness. *Psychopharmacology, 235*(2), pp.547-550.

Conee, E., 1994. Phenomenal knowledge. *Australasian Journal of Philosophy, 72*, pp. 136–150.

Fox, K.C., Zakarauskas, P., Dixon, M., Ellamil, M., Thompson, E. and Christoff, K., 2012. Meditation experience predicts introspective accuracy. *PloS one, 7*(9), p.e45370.

Gertler, B., 1999. A defense of the knowledge argument. *Philosophical Studies, 93*(3), pp.317-336.

Gosling, S.D., Rentfrow, P.J. and Swann Jr, W.B., 2003. A very brief measure of the Big-Five personality domains. *Journal of Research in personality, 37*(6), pp.504-528.

Griffiths, R.R., Johnson, M.W., Richards, W.A., Richards, B.D., Jesse, R., MacLean, K.A., Barrett, F.S., Cosimano, M.P. and Klinedinst, M.A., 2017. Psilocybin-occasioned mystical-type experience in combination with meditation and other spiritual practices produces enduring positive changes in psychological functioning and in trait measures of prosocial attitudes and behaviors. *Journal of Psychopharmacology*, p.0269881117731279. DOI: 10.1177/0269881117731279

Harman, W.W., McKim, R.H., Mogar, R.E., Fadiman, J. and Stolaroff, M.J., 1966. Psychedelic agents in creative problem-solving: A pilot study. *Psychological reports, 19*(1), pp.211-227.

Hoyningen-Huene, P., 1987. On the varieties of the distinction between the context of discovery and the context of justification. *Studies in History and philosophy of science, 18*, pp.501-515.

Huxley, A., 1954. *The Doors of Perception.* London: Chatto & Windus.

Jackson, F., 1982. Epiphenomenal qualia. *Philosophical quarterly, 32*(127), pp.127-136.

Jackson, F., 1986. What Mary didn't know. *The Journal of Philosophy, 83*(5), pp.291-295.

Lebedev, A.V., Kaelen, M., Lövdén, M., Nilsson, J., Feilding, A., Nutt, D.J. and Carhart☒Harris, R.L., 2016. LSD☒induced entropic brain activity predicts subsequent personality change. *Human brain mapping, 37*(9), pp.3203-3213.

Letheby, C., 2015. The philosophy of psychedelic transformation. *Journal of Consciousness Studies, 22*(9-10), pp.170-193.

Letheby, C., 2016. The epistemic innocence of psychedelic states. *Consciousness and cognition, 39*, pp.28-37.

MacLean, K.A., Johnson, M.W. and Griffiths, R.R., 2011. Mystical experiences occasioned by the hallucinogen psilocybin lead to increases in the personality domain of openness. *Journal of Psychopharmacology, 25*(11), pp.1453-1461.

McCabe, O. L., Savage, C., Kurland, A. and Unger, S., 1972. Psychedelic (LSD) therapy of neurotic disorders: Short-term effects. Journal of Psychedelic Drugs, 5(1), pp.18-28.

Metzinger, T., 2003. *Being no one: The self-model theory of subjectivity.* MIT Press.

Pahnke, W.N., 1969. The psychedelic mystical experience in the human encounter with death. *Harvard Theological Review, 62*(1), pp.1-21.

Roche, G.T., 2010. Seeing Snakes. In D. Jacquette (ed.) *Cannabis Philosophy for Everyone*, pp.35-49. Wiley-Blackwell.

Russell, B., 1910. Knowledge by acquaintance and knowledge by description. *Proceedings of the Aristotelian Society, 11*, pp. 108-128.

Sampedro, F., de la Fuente Revenga, M., Valle, M., Roberto, N., Domínguez-Clavé, E., Elices, M., Luna, L.E., Crippa, J.A.S., Hallak, J.E., de Araujo, D.B. and Friedlander, P., 2017. Assessing the psychedelic "after-glow" in ayahuasca users: post-acute neurometabolic and functional connectivity changes are associated with enhanced mindfulness capacities. *International Journal of Neuropsychopharmacology*, *20*(9), pp.698-711.

Schmidt, A., Kometer, M., Bachmann, R., Seifritz, E. and Vollenweider, F., 2013. The NMDA antagonist ketamine and the 5-HT agonist psilocybin produce dissociable effects on structural encoding of emotional face expressions. *Psychopharmacology*, *225*(1), pp.227-239.

Shanon, B., 2002. *The antipodes of the mind: Charting the phenomenology of the ayahuasca experience*. Oxford University Press.

Shanon, B., 2010. The epistemics of ayahuasca visions. *Phenomenology and the Cognitive Sciences*, *9*(2), pp.263-280.

Soler, J., Elices, M., Franquesa, A., Barker, S., Friedlander, P., Feilding, A., Pascual, J.C. and Riba, J., 2016. Exploring the therapeutic potential of Ayahuasca: acute intake increases mindfulness-related capacities. *Psychopharmacology*, *233*(5), pp.823-829.

Soler, J., Elices, M., Dominguez-Clavé, E., Pascual, J.C., Feilding, A., Navarro-Gil, M., García-Campayo, J. and Riba, J., 2018. Four Weekly Ayahuasca Sessions Lead to Increases in "Acceptance" Capacities: A Comparison Study With a Standard 8-Week Mindfulness Training Program. *Frontiers in pharmacology*, *9*, p.224.

Tupper, K.W., 2003. Entheogens & education: Exploring the potential of psychoactives as educational tools. *Journal of Drug Education and Awareness*, *1*(2), pp.145-161.

Windt, J.M., 2011. Altered consciousness in philosophy. In E. Cardeña and M. Winkelman (eds.) *Altering consciousness: multidisciplinary perspectives*, pp. 229-54. Santa-Barbara, CA: Praeger.

Zwaan, R.A., 2004. The immersed experiencer: Toward an embodied theory of language comprehension. *Psychology of learning and motivation*, *44*, pp. 35-62.

WHAT DOES IT MEAN TO CLAIM THAT A PSYCHEDELIC EXPERIENCE IS EDUCATIONAL?

LINDSAY JORDAN

Philosophy is concerned with making sense of ideas and arguments. Philosophy of education is concerned with making sense of ideas and arguments about education. When we debate what it means for all education to be self-education, or to argue for the autonomy of the learner, we are doing philosophy of education. The arguments by themselves are not philosophy; that in order to do the philosophical job properly we have to take things more slowly.

Our conceptions of education stem from our beliefs about what it means to be human, and therefore our beliefs about what constitutes human flourishing. If these fundamental ideas are taken for granted, we very easily end up with a system of education based on the beliefs of those in power. This is a perennial source of tension in educational systems across the world.

Take moral education in schools as an example. If we believe that human behaviour is governed by reasoning (rather than, say, by our emotions) we might support an education that assumes or teaches reasoning, rather than one that sets rules for behaviour, or inculcates certain habits.

In considering what we mean by 'educational', we might begin by looking at the etymology of the word. Education is thought to have emerged from the Latin *educare*, which means to lead or draw *out*, rather than towards something in particular. Many philosophers of education (e.g. Hogan 2012) have concluded that the purpose of education has to be intrinsic; that it must be an end in itself and not merely a means to an end. This is counter to the common assumption that education has specific extrinsic purposes—things that need achieving and problems that need addressing. It can be good to fix problems: it can also be good not to problematize everything.

If we apply this view of education as an end in itself to working with psychedelics, then to claim that psychedelic experience is educational is to claim that it can expose and lead us out of entrenched ideas and ways of thinking.

However, claims abound that psychedelics effect *particular kinds* of change in people. They have been claimed to make people happier, kinder, less violent, less authoritative, more liberal, and more connected to nature. Such claims are often sensationalized in the news media. For example, the finding of an article published in the *Journal of Psychopharmacology* that 'increased nature relatedness and decreased authoritarian political views after psilocybin for treatment-resistant depression' (Lyons & Carhart-Harris 2018) was reported in the online magazine *Alternet* as 'Magic Mushrooms Fight Authoritarianism'.

In Western scientific culture, to claim what 'psychedelics' do is different to claiming what a particular kind of 'psychedelic experience' does. Psilocybin mushrooms are not the same thing as psilocybin-assisted psychotherapy. In contrast, when we talk of SSRIs (classic antidepressant drugs) and SSRI therapy (merely prescription of the drug), the two are virtually synonymous. In making a claim about a certain kind of 'psychedelic experience', we specify the environmental setting (and to an extent the mindset) on which the claim is contingent, whereas a claim about the *substance* is independent of these factors (e.g. 'Psilocybin is broken down in the body to psilocin, which binds to several different serotonin receptors in the brain.')

Other cultures that are important to include in a discussion of psychedelics and education speak and think about their native psychedelic plant medicines in different ways. In the Andes, the name 'ayahuasca' is given not only to the *Banisteriopsis caapi* vine, it is also used to refer to the brew that contains the vine; *and* for the traditional drinking ceremony that controls the set and setting of the experience (to complicate matters, *B. caapi* does not provide the psychedelic ingredient in the brew, but the enzyme inhibitor that allows its absorption)

These examples are illuminating when considering what it means to argue that psychedelic *experience* is educational, and whether this argument is coherent. Western psilocybin therapy and the traditional ayahuasca ceremony are both specific psychedelic *experiences* where the environmental setting is under strict control. I will now consider the purpose of these environmental controls in terms of the direction they provide.

Psilocybin-assisted psychotherapy has been used to successfully treat a range of conditions. In trials for treatment resistant depression in the UK, subjects wear eye shades and listen to six hours of music specifically crafted to evoke memories and emotions, with frequent harmonious resolutions to bring forth feelings of joy or release. Participants undertake the therapy in a darkened room, with two facilitators sitting by their bedside to offer support as necessary. This particular kind of psychedelic experience aims to treat depression, and appears to be highly successful. Its mechanisms of action are partially understood and include the surfacing of suppressed memories and emotions and the facilitation of a sense of connectedness and openness in the subject, often for a considerable amount of time.

The environment of the ayahuasca ceremony is also controlled using music, and rituals are observed around the gathering of the plants and the preparation of the brew. From a Western perspective, the intended outcomes of the ayahuasca ceremony may not seem dissimilar to those of psilocybin therapy, given the body of ethnographic research with Western ayahuasca drinkers documenting successful outcomes in the treatment of similar conditions (e.g. depression, eating disorders). It has been suggested, however, that ayahuasca has been framed as an agent of healing for the benefit of tourists, and that locals attribute to them a more general capacity, e.g. as agents of neurological disorder (Narby

1999) or of generic power (Evans 2017). In any case, the indigenous peoples of the Amazon take a more holistic view of 'healing', and their animist explanations of the process have a different quality to the mechanisms recognised and validated by Western scientism. In the Amazon, it is the spirit of the *B. caapi* vine itself that one encounters during an ayahuasca ceremony as the *'planta maestra'* (plant teacher). Such cultural distinctions are by no means absolute. Many Western users of psilocybin also believe the mushroom is a conscious agent in the manifestation of the psychedelic experience, and discoveries in the relatively new field of plant neurobiology suggest that plants and fungi are far more intelligent than we previously assumed.

I have, above, outlined the ways in which the *environment* is controlled in these two types of 'experience'. Two decades before Humphry Osmond gave him 400 mg of mescaline, Aldous Huxley wrote that 'experience is not what happens to you. It's what you do with what happens to you.' (1932). On careful reading we see that Huxley is not simply pointing out that we can choose how we react or respond to an experience. He is saying that what we choose to attend to *in* and *during* the experience is *fundamental* to it. He is talking about *mindset*.

Ganeri (2017) presents an account of mind in which attention— rather than the 'self'—explains the scope and focus of our subjective experience. He points out that what we attend to corresponds with what we believe to be true, and expertise is what legitimates that belief. Our attention is determined by factors such as our memories/histories, our empathy for others; and the act of introspection, which makes us self-aware. Ganieri's account of attention corresponds with the 'ghost' conceptualised by Ryle (1949) and explained further by Koestler (1967) and Gellner (1974) as an agent of selection. The mechanistic explanations provided by science, and the situatedness of the ghost, offer two very different ways of conceptualising psychedelic experience.

Together, the ghost and the machine offer corroborating evidence that psychedelics disrupt the the normal order of the mind, and that this disordering is an important aspect of both the experience and the outcome. Beyond that, Ganieri's (2017) account of the mind allows us to see how the particular qualities of the experience are contingent on what is attended to during it, and how attention may be guided, e.g. through stimulus control, intention and various exercises, and/or the assistance of a guide or therapist.

Philosophy of education surfaces different conceptions of education and their implications for practice. I will now introduce three philosophers from across the ages who had something important to say about human flourishing—Aristotle, Kant and Nietzsche—and consider how their perspectives support and inform different approaches to learning with psychedelics.

Aristotle explicitly agrees with the premise outlined above that educational practice must stem from a clear philosophy of life that incorporates ethics and politics and defines human flourishing. His method is empirical; he describes what we *are*, rather than what he believes we *should* be.

Aristotle acknowledges our capacity for reason as a defining human feature, but highlights that we are, first and foremost, physical, emotional AND social beings, and our development in each of these aspects relies on those before it in the hierarchy. He concludes that what we all seek is *eudaimonia*, a word that literally translates as 'having good demons'. Demons are the forces that control us, and Aristotle is concerned with forces of habit. Our habitual thoughts and behaviours are our default responses to and actions in the world. They are a large part of who we are, but we can change them—and hence ourselves— through training, which is simply practising doing something until it becomes habitual.

Aristotle's quartet of human natures (physical > emotional > social > reasoning) is key to his view on education. It is similar, but not identical, to Maslow's hierarchy of needs: Aristotle is not saying that we need to have all the lower levels perfected before we can be said to be flourishing, he is saying that these are interconnected aspects of human flourishing that require attention throughout our lives. For Aristotle, a good education is an all-round, lifelong education that incorporates a balance of play, exercise, music, debate, science and philosophy.

If we take Aristotle's view, we know we need to work on our bodies, our emotions, our relationships and our intellect. This does not necessarily mean we all need personal trainers and therapists as well as teachers. Aristotle developed a theory of character traits that enable us to flourish across all four areas. He called these *virtues*, and the idea is very simple: all virtues lie at a sweet spot between deficiency and excess. For example, between addiction (always giving in to your physical desires) and ascetism (always denying them) lies the virtue of temperance; *calming* one's bodily passions and desires. Always acting on our desires won't lead to flourishing, but neither will always denying them, as we would be denying a component of our nature.

Education aims to teach us where that sweet spot is in each situation. We gain this *phronesis*—practical wisdom—through practice. 'We become just by doing just acts, temperate by doing temperate ones, brave by doing brave ones' (Rackman 1934, p. 1103). As children we are simply told and trained to share, be friendly, brave etc. As adults, we learn the reasoning behind the virtues and become responsible for our own characters.

The relevance of Aristotle's philosophy of education to working with psychedelics is clear in the therapeutic modes, which aim to dislodge vices and shift individuals towards the sweet spot. The clinical protocol for depression initiates the move from melancholy to spiritedness, while addiction therapy effects a shift to temperateness. What about other bad habits? Could we design a psychedelic protocol that would specifically move us from meanness to benevolence and from laziness to industriousness?

Microdosing has reportedly aided individuals along these particular lines. As an important aside, the microdosing debate presents a nice example of how our beliefs about human flourishing fundamentally change our beliefs about education. Some believe that the drive to industriousness—particularly in schooling—has either gone too far, or to the wrong ends, or was rotten to start with. They may deride microdosers for pandering to performativity and the capitalist beast. For Aristotle, however, industriousness is the sweet spot between laziness and single-mindedness, a virtue that—like all the virtues—enables us to flourish in *all* aspects of our humanity. Indeed, those who microdose do report exercising more, making healthier choices, and being kinder to their friends and family (Fadiman 2011). Aristotle would say they are developing better habits and good demons through habit. Whether the drug is actually working as claimed or if it is working as a placebo on those 'really good days' (Waldman 2017), it seems easier to practise being 'really good'.

There is plenty more to consider about the psychedelic experience with regard to Aristotle's model. We might explore how various virtue deficiencies and excesses are pathologized in Western society, e.g. rashness (impulse control disorder), boisterousness (ADHD), and single-mindedness (OCD), and how the temporary disordering of the brain observed in high-dose psychedelic therapy has been used to normalize thoughts and behaviour, *regardless of whether the virtue in question is in excess or deficient.*

In a recent interview with the *Evening Standard* (Jones 2018), neuroscientist Robin Carhart-Harris reports those who take psychedelics—both within and outside of the clinical trials—feeling reconnected 'within themselves to their emotions but also to other people...and even to some kind of higher cosmic order.' His theory is that psychedelics cause the parts of the brain dedicated to emotion and reason to connect in ways they normally would not. He suggests that a more harmonious interplay between the two systems restores neural functioning that is 'more akin to the rest of the natural world.'

In *Uber Pedagogik* (1803), Immanuel Kant also highlights the conflict between emotion and reason, and extrapolates from this that we are not moral beings by nature, but we have the capacity to *create our nature*—to overcome our basic impulses—and must do so. Modern moral psychologists like Haidt (2013) would say that we *believe* we act according to reason, but in most cases we simply use it to justify the actions that follow our physical, emotional, and social drives. The two views aren't in conflict; Haidt—like Aristotle—is observing what we do and what we are, while Kant is proposing an ideal; what we *should* be doing.

Kant observed that human beings find it impossible to relinquish our freedom once we have a taste for it. He proposed that the main point of early schooling is to get us accustomed to the subjugation of our basic instincts, so we don't grow up impulsively acting on our every whim. His view of discipline corresponds with what we know now about children's inability to empathise; he advises teaching children that behaving badly will result in other people not liking them, and if they tell lies they won't be believed in future. This is one aspect of Kant's philosophy of education that merges with Aristotle's: to develop good habits by any means.

Kant was optimistic about education; he believed that it was the path to perfecting human nature. He thought it was ultimately possible for us to agree on universal principles, develop our natural gifts and fulfil our destiny, like animals seemingly do unselfconsciously. Crucially, Kant concluded that we can't do this as individuals: in order to imagine and create such a perfect state of affairs we need to work together. In *The Conflict of the Faculties* (1798) he presents the Prussian university as an institution organised for peaceful conflict, and, indeed, as a model for world peace.

Kant was a wholehearted supporter of the study of education in order that progress could be achieved from one generation to the next. One generation may have to pull down what another had built up, and education must be adapted to a future idea of humanity. The problem is that parents often harbour ambitions for their children that are based on their own conception of individual success in the world as it is now, while governments look upon their subjects as tools for their own purposes. Universal good and the perfection of man are nobody's priorities. Kant believes it is our duty to become not only clever, but good, and to bring the future nearer to a state of perfection than earlier generations managed to achieve.

For Kant, the four pillars of education are: *discipline*—restraining our unruly animal nature; *culture*—developing knowledge and abilities that may be adapted to various ends; *discretion*—learning manners that allow us to be liked and to gain social influence, and *moral training*— enabling us to *choose good ends that are universally approved.*

Kant observed that moral training was the aspect most lacking in education. He had mixed feelings about religion; he regretted that moral training was left to the church and hence gave the impression that vices are bad only because God says so, rather than genuinely bad for individuals and humanity.

We can see how Kant's way of organising or categorising human development is different to Aristotle's virtues. Kant pushes us beyond what we currently are, rather than steering us within a happy medium. He strives for a perfection that does not yet exist, recognises that we are so very far away from agreeing on universal ends, and proposes that we need to get far more experimental with our education, to break away from what parents want for their offspring and what governments want from their young people. Kant believed an education should achieve the following:

- Cheerfulness and good humour. Cheerfulness arises from the fact of having nothing to reproach oneself with (i.e. vices).
- A regard for matters of duty. Actions are worthy because in performing them we fulfil our duty (e.g. it is our duty to become a cheerful companion in society).
- A love for others. We should take an interest in ourselves and our families, and rejoice in the progress of the world.
- A certain detachment from the enjoyment of life's goods, so that we don't worry too much about death.
- A strengthening of the attention. Distraction is the enemy of all education.

The entheogenic modes of psychedelic practice—particularly those that privilege ritual and ceremony, but also the Western therapeutic modes—resonate with Kant's philosophy of education. We may gain a better sense of our duty by feeling more connected with others and the natural world. Experiencing something larger than the self has helped people to reduce their attachment to material things and address their fear of death. The therapeutic aspect of the experience may aid in the elimination of vices and the maintenance of a cheerful disposition. Underground guides and facilitators of group psychedelic retreats encourage the setting of intentions that may include gratitude, forgiveness, kindness, and the courage to be honest. Integration counselling may be focused on introducing new routines and rituals (such as journaling and meditation) that can facilitate attention and detachment.

Nietzsche's approach is very different from the prevailing moralities. He takes issue with various moral theories (particularly Kant's) primarily on the basis that they favour the interests of the 'lowest men' over the 'highest', but also because they take for granted three things that cannot be assumed, which he outlined in 1881 in *Daybreak: Thoughts on the Prejudice of Morality*:

- *Free will:* We may desire to have a belief in our own free will, and such a belief may indeed be good for us. This does not mean it is true.
- *The transparency of the self:* We don't really know why we do the things we do: 'nothing…can be more incomplete than [one's] image of the totality of drives which constitute [a man's] being' (1997, p. 119).
- *The similarity of all people:* We all have different psycho-physical constitutions. What we think are reasoned judgements are 'only images and fantasies based on a physiological process unknown to us' (1997, p. 119). If this is true, there cannot be a universal morality that is good for everyone.

Nietzsche's project is to understand the type of person who would bear particular thoughts and values. As an educationalist I am interested in what it means to become a *different* type of person, with different thoughts and values, but Nietzsche would say that one's desire or willingness to change in a particular way is already a type-fact of their constitution and that there are no conscious mental causes. The desire for change might accompany personal development, or equally it may accompany frustration or resentment.

Nietzsche's philosophy is fatalistic. It may appear that there is no point in trying to change anything or anyone. Then, if we take that attitude we risk corrupting or impeding a 'natural' drive for change, and so on. It is fascinating to consider how our beliefs around free will and motivation influence our actions; there has been a wealth of classroom-based research on 'growth mindsets' and self-efficacy that demonstrates the power of these forms of priming. Priming plays a significant role in working with psychedelics. One of the criticisms of microdosing (if it *is* a criticism) is that the mere *expectation* of having a 'really good day' could be a sufficient condition for better decision-making and a more positive outlook. Psychedelic therapists often prime their patients and clients for a spiritual experience because research shows that the more an experience is rated as spiritual, the better the therapeutic outcomes.

Nietzsche took a much more individualistic view of human perfectibility than Kant. He was particularly interested in the flourishing of the creative genius, and his primary objection to moral theories was the threat they posed to the 'higher man'. His concern was that the realization of human excellence requires self-interest, suffering, and a sense of hierarchy, all of which are undermined by the normative component of conventional moral theories that value compassion, happiness, and equality.

In this sense, Nietzsche's philosophy provides us with a different view of education again; one that promotes flourishing by allowing the exceptionally talented to be self-interested, and not devaluing or pathologizing the suffering that Nietzsche claims is essential to their achievements. There are some interesting links with psychedelic experience here; one is the tradition of the solo psychonaut, the individual who pushes themselves with high doses and aims for cosmic, intellectual insights rather than the cultivation of moral virtues. Another obvious link is the disregard for the law exhibited by many psychonauts, and the ample evidence that more psychedelic experience does not necessarily lead to more humility, more compassion, or more happiness. It should be noted that much of the music used in the Imperial College depression trials (Kaelen 2014) that has engendered peak experiences of spiritual and personal significance for so many, enabling human flourishing of a more Aristotelian or Kantian type—was composed and/ or performed by single-minded, antisocial geniuses.

I have begun here to assess the coherence of the claim 'psychedelic experience is educational' through an analysis of what is meant by 'educational' and a brief consideration of selected modes of psychedelic experience. There is a good deal of scope for further work in this area, particularly in the imagination of new modes of experience that correspond with other conceptions of the educational endeavour. In the meantime, and in the absence of a universal morality, we should continue to interrogate claims about psychedelic experience and its effects on moral attitudes and behaviour.

REFERENCES

Evans, J. 2017. Can psychedelics make you a better person? [Online]. *Philosophy for Life.* Accessed 15 December. http://www.philosophyforlife.org/can-psychedelics-make-you-a-better-person/

Fadiman, J. 2011. *The Psychedelic Explorer's Guide.* Inner Traditions Bear & Company.

Ganieri, J. 2017. *Attention, Not Self.* Oxford University Press.

Gellner, E. 1974. *Legitimation of Belief.* Cambridge University Press.

Haidt, J. 2013. *The Righteous Mind: Why Good People are Divided by Politics and Religion.* Penguin.

Hogan, P. 2010. *The new significance of learning.* London: Routledge.

Huxley, A. 1932. *Texts and Pretexts.* Chatto & Windus.

Jones, A. 2018. 'London's new drugs parties: hallucinogens are making an unlikely comeback with otherwise clean-living Londoners.' *Evening Standard,* 15 June.

https://www.standard.co.uk/lifestyle/esmagazine/londons-new-drugs-parties-hallucinogens-are-making-an-unlikely-comeback-with-otherwise-cleanliving-a3861171.html

Kaelen, M. 2014. *Playlist (Psilocybin for depression, Imperial College London, version 1.3).* Mixcloud. Available from: https://www.mixcloud.com/MendelKa/playlists/psilocybin-v13/

Kant, I. 1798. 'The Conflict of the Faculties. In Wood', A. & Di Giovanni, G. (Eds.). 1996. *The Works of Immanuel Kant.* Cambridge University Press. pp. 233–328.

Kant, I. 1803. *Über Pädagogik.* Königsberg: Friedrich Nicolovius.

Koestler, A. 1967. *The Ghost in the Machine.* Hutchinson & Co.

Lyons, T., and Carhart-Harris, R. 2018. 'Increased nature relatedness and decreased authoritarian political views after psilocybin for treatment-resistant depression.' *Journal of Psychopharmacology.* https://doi.org/10.1177/0269881117748902

MacLean, K. A., Johnson, M. W. and Griffiths, R. R. 2011. 'Mystical experiences occasioned by the hallucinogen psilocybin lead to increases in the personality domain of openness.' *Journal of Psychopharmacology,* 22 (11), pp.1453–1461.

Narby, J. 1999. *The Cosmic Serpent: DNA and the origins of knowledge.* Orion Books.

Nietzsche. F. 1997. Daybreak: 'Thoughts on the Prejudices of Morality.' Cambridge University Press.

Rackman, H. 1934. *Aristotle in 23 Volumes* (19). London: Heinemann.

Ryle, G. 1949. *The Concept of Mind.* University of Chicago Press.

Waldman, A. 2017. *A Really Good Day: How Microdosing Made a Mega Difference in My Mood, My Marriage, and My Life.* Knopf Publishing Group.

PSYCHEDELIC KYRIARCHY: SUBHUMANIZATION, FEMINIST REFLEXIVITY & TRANSFORMATION IN PARADOX

NADIA VE

The best mind-altering drug is truth
– Lily Tomlin

UTILITY OF FEMINIST THEORY

What we will examine throughout this piece is how humanness is allocated. feminism is about everyone. So what does feminist analysis actually do? It allows for what is hidden to be seen. It allows for an anti-normalisation approach and one that sees power dynamics that are usually invisible—that are in the shadows. This is why it has been often seen as a threatening form of understanding. To give an example of what that awareness means, at the very least: it can help us to see discriminatory assumptions in our own prejudices. More broadly, it allows us to critique historically discriminatory beliefs, explore the intersections between identities and categories, and to pinpoint globalised configurations of "the human".

The matter that must be addressed constantly and forcefully is the differential allocation of humanness: the perpetually shifting and variably positioned boundary between those who are rendered properly human and those who are not (Butler & Athanasiou, 2013, 31).

Of course, feminism also has a disturbing side. Like many other fields, it has a history of racism, classism, colonialism, transphobia and other harms. These harms and its situatedness must be regularly acknowledged, and redressed wherever possible, also known as reflexive practice. Quite rightly, due to this history, some cultures who do similar work prefer to refer to feminism using different names (Horáková, 2018). This paradoxical reality is a consistent theme not only within feminism itself but throughout what feminism reveals to us, shown throughout this article.

Third wave and intersectional feminisms have begun to thoroughly address these issues. Through analyses of the oppression of women, Third wave feminism has expanded critical responses to race, sexuality, disability amongst other—indeed every—typology of human. However, this reality still has not yet "resulted in any general awareness of sexual harms as a link connecting many oppressed groups" (Wilkerson, 2011, 200). Intersectional feminism has been used to help highlight this link. It's a form of feminism which recognises that "forms of oppression and prejudice are interconnected and feed into one another" (Devenot, 2016, 361).

FEMINISM AND PSYCHEDELICS

Feminism is relevant to the psychedelic experience and community in many significant ways. At the Diversity panel at Breaking Convention in 2017, one question (which is thematically very common) was: "Don't you think that diversity is a side issue [in the psychedelic community]?". My response was that not only should intersectional diversity issues be a central concern in the community, but that such concern is a central component of the very *purpose* of the community, as will become clear. Let's start with some important crossovers between psychedelics and feminism:

1. They both have deconditioning potential and the ability to dramatically change consciousness. Through showing us invisible dynamics that are usually ignored or not seen, for example. they allow us to transform and go beyond what is accepted in the mainstream.
2. They help to show the limitations of dichotomy and the reality of paradox.
3. They both show the fluidity of categories, conditioned assumptions and the prevalence of identity destabilisation.
4. They (therefore) allow us to see new relationships and dynamics and the ability to critique these dynamics. If they are not seen, then how can we address them?
5. They show the complexity of the world and allow an awareness of this (illustrating, for example, the possibility of intersectional experience and oppression).
6. They are both shunned for the same reason: because they challenge and destabilise the status quo (they are threatening to how things are).
7. They are also primarily accessed by the most privileged in society (ironic and problematic considering their potential to help those most marginalised).
8. The last point adds a critical duty of responsibility to those who have access to them. Having psychedelic and academic communities that do not (beyond formally) reflect feminist teachings is profoundly ironic, when so much of psychedelic experience and thought echoes feminist teachings.

HISTORICAL LOCATION

Feminist theory thinks about our historical location. As an example let's take politicians and scientists from contemporary Anglo-American culture, who often claim to embody neutrality. Under feminist analysis, it can be seen that theirs are not such neutral locations. Politicians and scientists come from very loaded historical backgrounds, undercurrents of which dramatically affect their perception and reality. Instead of being neutral, these are contexts which are tied to "militarism, capitalism, colonialism, and male supremacy" (Haraway, 1988, 581). Indeed, we exist within a "kyriarchy". A kyriarchy was defined by Elisabeth Schussler Fiorenza (2001) to recognise the limited scope of the term "patriarchy" in its ability to address oppression. Patriarchy is primarily concerned with gender oppression when all forms of oppression are linked and important to challenge. Kyriarchy is:

> *a neologism...derived from the Greek words for "lord" or "master" (kyrios) and "to rule or dominate" (archein) which seeks to redefine the analytic category of patriarchy in terms of multiplicative intersecting structures of domination...kyriarchy is best theorized as a complex pyramidal system of intersecting multiplicative social structures of superordination and subordination, of ruling and oppression.* (Fiorenza, 2001, Glossary)

It is from these histories that our discourse of "normalness", of "humanness", comes from. Culturally (on a macro and micro level), the hegemonic views that this historical background "become internalised as norms and accepted without question...they are notoriously difficult to recognise and challenge" (Devenot, 2016, 370). It structures how people relate to the world and this discourse keeps reproducing itself (these mainstream historical, cultural and categorical assumptions). One way of looking at this complex makeup is by using the ecofeminist theorist Plumwood's Master Model (1993). This helps to illustrate the power dynamics that exist around marginalised people and categories and helps us to understand why both nature and other oppressed groups (people of colour, queer people, people with disabilities) have been devalued (dehumanised) in Anglo-American history.

Below (Figure 1) are two columns. These two columns are things we often dichotomise, by that I mean separate into two. Those in the left-hand column are often masculinised and therefore valued in Anglo-

American culture (white, human, colonisers, man, straight, cis, able-bodied, neurotypical). The right column illustrates categories that are feminised and therefore de-valued (black, nature, colonised, women, queer, trans, neurodivergent). Figure 2 is an extension I have created according to this "logic". They distinguish who and what constitutes "the human" (left column) and who and what is ontologically nullified and dehumanised or "the human-less" (Lugones, 2010). Through models such as this, you can clearly see how the oppression of people of colour, women, nature, and other "Others" are all closely linked in their domination and exploitation. This is so prevalent that, in ecofeminist theory, it is called the "logic of domination".

PLUMWOOD'S MASTER MODEL

Masculinised (Valued)	feminised (Devalued)
Human	Nature
Colonisers	Colonised
Men	Women
Civilised	Uncivilised

Figure 1

MY EXTENSION OF PLUMWOOD'S MASTER MODEL

Masculinised (Valued)	feminised (Devalued)
Straight	Queer
Cis	Trans
Able-bodied	Disabled
Neuro-typical	Neurodivergent

Figure 2

This not only shows the gendered nature of inequality but also how creating oppositional binaries privileges those at the "intersection of privilege in terms of race/ class/ gender/ species/ sexuality" (Gaard, 2001, 158) (this is why white straight men are often referred to as a benchmark for discussions around oppression, because they are the most privileged of peoples). Mies & Shiva (1993, 266) believe that this method of devaluing the "Other" exercises tremendous influence over, and is a central and *integral* part of, globalised capitalism and colonialism. The theory argues that it is *through* dichotomisation—in this case gendered binary thinking and perceiving—that allows the process of valuing one over the other.

Gloria Anzaldúa (1987), another ecofeminist (and someone who is also known to have used magic mushrooms—clearly influencing her theories and poetry), believed that realising the whole out of dualism is a pivotal part of the healing process in individuals, society and the larger Earth. This place of in-betweenness allows healing to happen: In her theorising and poetry, 'Anzaldúa eloquently describes this living between the cracks, this inhabitation of paradox (Anzaldúa, 1987). This is the borderlands, a place beyond oppositional binary. The beauty of feminist theories such as ecofeminism is that they can fundamentally re-value (re-humanise) these spaces, ones that have been devalued.

Feminist praxis works towards re-valuing (re-humanising) knowledges that are often ignored, and mental landscapes that are considered negligible, for example, re-valuing indigenous knowledge is an important part of ecofeminism (as it is in other facets of feminism and critical approaches). My MSc thesis "Cognitive Dispossession: Entheogens, Ecofeminism and Neuroqueering Drug Policy" which I presented at Breaking Convention 2017, shows that when applied to cultural artefacts (such as, in this case, policy), these theoretical lenses can reveal significant assumptions embedded in them. Nutt et al. (2007) found that in the Misuse of Drugs Act (MDA 1971) the penalties for psychedelics were strikingly high compared to other drugs and described this process as "arbitrary", meaning "random" (Nutt et al 2007, 1052). However, I challenged this view and reviewed whether it is merely coincidental, or are a result of specific moral codes and systemic discriminatory influences on policy.

Using the above methods, I found that the prejudices which led up to the Misuse of Drugs Act 1971 were informed by a history of racism, colonialism, and a (related) prejudice against neurodivergent landscapes. By neurodivergence, I mean mental landscapes that are considered outside the prescribed "norm" in our culture (such as psychosis, disassociation, autism, being high). This includes innate neurodiversity and neurodivergence that is caused by outside influences (trauma, psychedelics) (Walker et al, 2014).

It clearly shows that the primary reason *why* legislation against psychedelics (and divergent mental landscapes) has been so harsh is *because* of this racialized association and colonised history (Montagne, 1988; Tupper 2012; Blackman 2010). One must only compare the legal responses to Native American use of peyote, West African usage of khat or ibogaine, Rastafarian usage of cannabis and Christian ceremonial use of alcohol to see there is a racialized trajectory (Bone, 2014).

Applied to psychedelic research, this can also help to explain some of the breakthroughs in therapy. For example, psychedelic researchers have found that often long term healing happens *because* of the ability of psychedelics to invoke intense seemingly psychotic and/or dissociative experiences (Shorthall, 2014, 195). This wouldn't be so surprising if we were aware of and valued indigenous approaches towards mental health or neurodivergence across the globe. For example, the Dagaara tribe in West Africa considers psychosis as a fairly normal mental landscape, a form of liaising with the spirit world and a place of potential great healing and power if managed correctly (Some, 1995). So here it is clear how re-investing in devalued knowledges is essential in psychedelic work.

Indeed, Longden (2013), someone who is a voice-hearer herself, notes some of the features of neurodivergence and transpersonal states which create strong similarities with psychedelic experiences, such as "ego-fragmentation, dissolution of self-experience" (Longden, 2013, 23:09:00). When we start to re-value these spaces, we start to recognise that our whole mental health, medical and classification system is out of date and therefore inadequate. Mad Studies and the anti-psychiatry movement, emerging fields of activism and academia, highlight the damages of this system and work against the idea that neurotypical experiences are the only ones that are valuable (Beresford, 2016; Sweeney, 2016).

Applying a feminist approach, we can see how ideas are often drawn from a history steeped in racism and colonialism and other harmful systemic patterns. Analysing things without this acknowledgement would lead to missing key information and would continue to diminish the quality of debate and understanding. It would contribute to continuing related prejudices and harms.

PSYCHEDELIC KYRIARCHY

Above I have made clear the importance of critical perspectives and feminism in psychedelia. Troubling power dynamics are these things that many people, institutions and communities deal with, as these are global problems that are systemic and have micro and macro consequences. These are areas that the psychedelic community is also known to struggle with and it is this to which I will now turn.

To give an idea of the scale of the issues, Corbin (2006) notes a lack of analysis and discussion of power relationships in various psychedelic projects. Gelfer's (2012) study affirms this, and reports very low levels of gender equality in these communities, and the feminist psychedelic activist Zoe Helene (2015), mostly known for her work with "psychedelic feminism", a term she coined and popularized to describe a sub-genre of feminism, describes her deep concern with the lack of gender equality and feminist discourse in the community. Research shows a lack of awareness of power relationships also leads to little accountability for excess and abuse of power. There have been growing accounts of sexual abuse in psychedelic settings (MacLean; 2018; Monroe, 2017; Ross, 2019). This has been so prolific that groups such as the Psychedelic Sisters in Arms have been created so that brave women have a space where they can share their experiences and raise awareness on sexual abuse in psychedelic communities (Psymposia, 2019).

Gelfer's (2012) research reveals men in these communities ignoring gendered inequality whilst enjoying their gendered privileges (if you don't know about gendered privileges, do have a read of articles such as "160+ Examples of male privilege" at *Everyday Feminism*). Girl (2007) notes the omission of women in the history of psychedelic discovery; Corbin finds that much psychedelic literature is, "unaccountable to colonialism and the politics of location in a global capitalist system" (Corbin, 2006, 245) and 90% of all of the board members and directors of the top funding agencies for psychedelic research are all white men (MacLean, 2018, 15.13:00). All the above shows that oppressive dynamics in the psychedelic community is a significant issue and deserves considerable attention.

Even though these issues have been around for a number of years, there is also a culture of silence around these issues. There are many reasons for this, some of which I outline below. The way power structures work means that addressing damaging dynamics difficult. Many people correctly feel that they are not safe or supported enough to express their truths. Due to the ways that power relationships operate, this means that there are great risks (their wellbeing, social and professional risks) if they were to expose the violence, and oppression that they have experienced (Maclean, 2018). This cautiousness is well-founded; some people who have spoken out, myself included, have experienced further violence including victim-blaming and being frozen out of their communities (Ross, 2019; Devenot 2019). The community has, for many, proved to be a dangerous place to tell their truths.

I would also argue that it is not the responsibility of survivors to share their most troubling experiences in the unlikely hope of changing the wider structure of things, although that is what is happening out of necessity. What would be much better is that we make a safer and more aware community in the first instance which would deter these things from happening in the first place.

COMMUNITY RESPONSE

What scares me about the so-called 'conscious community' is the lack of consciousness, the lack of an analysis and deep willingness of going inside to look. (MacLean, 2018, 42.11:00)

Victim-blaming and gaslighting is very prevalent in New Age culture (as it is in mainstream culture), and many people who experience violence subsequently experience even more from the very community that they need help from. It can be so appalling that it has been cited as an even more traumatic experience than the initial instance of violence (Anonymous, 2018; MacLean 2018). The lack of support, both structural and emotional, from communities explains the difficulty of raising any issue of oppressive power dynamics. These kinds of responses de-prioritise the survivors. They imply that the "safety of community and its inclusivity is not more important than the optics of the community" (Anonymous, 2018, 1). It gives the impression that keeping people safe and being inclusive is not as important as keeping up the false impression that the psychedelic community is perfectly progressive (even though you can't be progressive without being actively inclusive and keeping people safe).

Sometimes there is no action because people are invested in the very power dynamics that are perpetuating abusive harms. Once when I was talking about abusive power dynamics I had seen with someone in the community, the response was that they didn't care as those responsible "throw good parties". There are various themes that keep appearing including: "this will ruin the good/party vibe". When there was public outcry against white organisers hosting an "Edgy Slave Market" at the Borderlands festival, organizers "defended the event by telling those who were offended to lighten up" (The Race Card, 2017, 1). There has also been the co-option of experiences. This is when marginalised narratives and even vocabulary are absorbed by the dominant group only to work *against* the interest of the marginalised group concerned (Penny & Prescott, 2016) like when I heard at a psychedelic conference white people complaining about People of Colour (POC) "appropriating" their culture. I was privileged enough to be able to correct this gross instance of co-option.

There is also, across culture, a common narrative whereby people are discounted as being "unreliable" because of the very fact that they are survivors of violence. Convenient for those perpetuating the oppression, as Survivors understand the reality of violence the most (Sweeney, 2016). We, unfortunately, are the experts. In such unsupportive environments, marginalised groups can easily be at risk of becoming re-traumatised. This is a space where they thought they could be vulnerable, let their guard down, and be protected and healed. Instead, many end up traumatised, ostracised and forgotten.

An overarching theme that emerges is that the community "doesn't care" about the oppression happening. One of the worst trajectories I've heard when people have come forward about their experiences of danger, harassment and/or abuse is "you will destroy decades of work on psychedelics". Awful. Decades of work which is being used to excuse and silence instances of oppression, violence, and sexual violence? The very opposite is true.

The truth is that silence on this matter is what has the most risk of destroying decades of psychedelic work. Abuse is not only unacceptable on its own, it also completely opposes the main tenet of psychedelic work, which is that psychedelics are a profoundly effective healing agent.

Healing is a central component of psychedelic research, its community and its validity and is why many vulnerable people come to search for healing (ex-drug addicts, drug addicts, traumatised individuals, neurodivergent people, POC, trans people, people with disabilities). The psychedelic renaissance has been built largely on this premise, its utility in treating anxiety, depression and post-traumatic stress disorder (PTSD) (Carhart-Harris et al., 2015; Carhart-Harris et al., 2012). Psychedelics can even have anti-colonial influences, develop a mind-set of critical awareness and help improve things such as gender dysphoria (Anonyomous, 2014; Kaufman 2018). Addressing trauma and abuse is of *central* importance to psychedelic research and, more importantly, to individuals, our species and our biosphere. Continuing to address these issues diligently continues this work.

What is the movement? A movement that we are afraid will be derailed because of coercion or rape? If that's the movement then I want no part of it. (MacLean, 2018, 1:04:50)

For inequalities to permeate counter-cultural communities is not at all uncommon (Conway, 2011) and that only adds to the absolute necessity of putting feminist prevention methods into practice. It is important that we create the structures which prioritise marginalised experiences so we can support people properly. Some excellent examples of anti-oppression work include the Breaking Convention Safer Spaces Policy, their 2017 Diversity Panel, Cosmic Sister, and Psychedelic Sisters in Arms.

Psychedelic research is predicated on the potential of psychedelics to heal trauma. However, if they are used in ways that perpetuate toxic harms, if they aren't being used to help the most marginalised groups (communities that actually need these substances); if they are actually re-traumatising the very people that need it most, then we have inadvertently nullified the very basis of psychedelic work. These are the shadows at the crossroads. We need to face this, just like every other community and every other field. It is essential that oppression is addressed and that this is taken seriously. This would then help better protect, prioritise and heal vulnerable people and groups.

TRANSFORMATIVE POTENTIAL

More women, more Indigenous [voices], more voices from the South, more anthropology, more plants. Less molecules, less clinical trials— more healing in context. – Zoe Helene
(Richardson, 2017, 1).

A reason why taking psychedelics does not automatically make someone a better person is because these substances are being taken in this reality— the Kyriarchic environment that I detail above (militaristic, colonial, patriarchal), and which has an ever-present, thick, toxic presence in our everyday lives. Indeed, we are all "in a structure that promotes and feeds on this" (MacLean, 2018, 01:03:09). We have to acknowledge the society that we are in, become self-aware, work on ourselves and recognise our privileges in order to effectively move past these histories. That way we can see that we are a part of this larger system, we are not exempt from it. We are proponents of it and that is why people must thoroughly invest in critical approaches of our culture and ourselves (Badham, 2018). This is not possible without critical awareness. This is lifetime work, and without it we run the risk in partaking in circular harms and ultimately our downfall.

The psychedelic community is extremely unique in its position to help *heal* trauma. This privilege means that we have a great duty to do this work thoroughly. No, it is not a "side project" or of "secondary importance" that I've heard so many times. It is T H E work. Otherwise, somebody tell me, what is the point in all this work we're doing? Who are we doing it for? If we are just complicit in the exacerbation of harms and if we don't prioritise vulnerable people? We have been given the tools to do the work, the "destroying, dismantling, naming this killing that's happening amongst us all...patriarchy, racism, homophobia transphobia...capitalism" (MacLean, 2018, 41.26:00). It is time to do the work.

What can be done to help address these issues? There are many things that can be done. One good way is considering how different communities have tried to address issues. One method is consulting the survivors, diversity experts and centralising and celebrating the people who occupy marginalised experience. You can centralise those experiences by finding podcasts, articles and books written by them and investing—time and/or money—in their projects which address these issues. For example, in 2017 Breaking Convention hosted their first Diversity and Psychedelics panel to which I and a superb panel contributed; myself and a Breaking Convention organiser worked together and produced a Safer Spaces Policy which is included in the back of the 2017 booklet. I was so pleased to hear people independently say how happy (and relieved) they were to see it in their booklet. This policy addresses these themes, recognises intersectional experience and Breaking Convention's commitment to creating safe spaces for everyone.

I hope I have shown from many angles why intersectional feminism needs to be a major feature of psychedelic communities and in related analysis. feminism is engaged in the application of theory to structures of power and can enable us to dig deeper into the forms inequalities take. It helps us to map out power relationships and consider what produces them in order for them to be challenged and changed. Without this, we run the risk of continuing a culture of silence around oppression, undoing the very healing that psychedelics provoke. Judging by the current political and environmental climate, we might miss a unique and one-time opportunity to provide real healing to people, and the world as a whole.

REFERENCES

Anonymous (2014). Just Say Yes: Legalize Psychedelics. *Fuck the Cistem* [Online] [Available at: https://fuckthecistem.wordpress.com] [Accessed 20.06.2018]

Anonymous (2018). Caleb Shaw Raped me; Bristol's Story Slam community including Kitty Aston Stern and Sophie Dig are rape apologists. *My Words Are Powerful.* [Online] Available at: https://mywordsarepowerful205547109.wordpress.com [Accessed 19.06.2018]

Anzaldúa, G. (1987). *Borderlands/La Frontera, The New Mestiza.* San Francisco: Aunt Lute Books

Badham, 2018. That's patriarchy: how female sexual liberation led to male sexual entitlement. The Guardian. [Online] Available at: https://www.theguardian.com/commentisfree/2018/feb/02/thats–patriarchy–how–female–sexual–liberation–led–to–male–sexual–entitlement [Accessed 29.06.2018]

Blackman, S. (2010). Youth subcultures, normalisation and drug prohibition: The politics of contemporary crisis and change? *British Politics,* 5(3): 337 – 366

Beresford, P. (2016) The role of survivor knowledge in creating alternatives to psychiatry. In Russo, R., & Sweeney, A. (Eds). *Rose Garden, Challenging Psychiatry, Fostering Mad Studies.* Edited by Jasna Russo and Angela Sweeney. Ross–on–Wye: PCCS Books

Butler, J., & Athanasiou, A. (2013). *Dispossession: The Performative in the Political.* Cambridge: Polity Press

Bone, M. (2014). From the Sacrilegious to the Sacramental: A Global Review of Rastafari Cannabis Case Law. (2014). In Labate, C, B., Cavnar, C. (Eds.). *Prohibition, Religious Freedom, and Human Rights: Regulating Traditional Drug Use.* London: Springer

Carhart–Harris, L, R., et al. (2012). Implications for psychedelic–assisted psychotherapy: functional magnetic resonance imaging study with psilocybin. *The British Journal of Psychiatry,* 200(3): 238—244

Carhart–Harris, L, R., et al. (2015). LSD enhances the emotional response to music. Psychopharmacology. [Online] Available at: link.springer.com/article/10.1007%2Fs00213–015–4014–y [Accessed: 15.08.2015]

Corbin, M. (2006). Facing Our Dragons: Spiritual Activism, Psychedelic Mysticism and the Pursuit of Opposition. *Human Architecture: Journal of the Sociology of Self–Knowledge,* 4(3): 239 – 247

Devenot, N. (2016). Psychedelic Drugs. *Gender: Nature.* 7(1): 361—377

Devenot, N. (2019). Time's Up For "Silencing" Tactics [Online] https://www.psymposia.com/magazine/times–up–for–silencing–tactics/ [Accessed 14/04/2019]

Fiorenza, S, E. (2001). Wisdom Ways: Introducing feminist Bibilical Interpretation

Gaard, G. (2001). Women, Water and Energy: An ecofeminist Approach. *Organization and Environment,* 14(2): 157 – 172

Gelfer, A. (2012). Entheogenic Spirituality and Gender in Australia. *Paranthropology: Journal of Anthropological Approaches to the Paranormal,* 3(3): 22—33

Girl, N. (2007). Remembering Miss Ramstein: feminism and LSD. *DoseNation.* [Online] Available at: www.dosenation.com/listing.php?id=3196 [Accessed: 06.08.2015]

Haraway, D. (1988). Situated Knowledges: The Science Question in feminism and the Privilege of Partial Perspective. *feminist Studies,* 14(3): 575—599

Helene, Z. (2015). Cosmic SIster [Online] Available at: http://zoehelene.com/ [Accessed: 27 / 08 / 2015]

Horáková, M. (2018). Talking back, talkin' up: Voicing indigenous feminism. In Horáková, M. *Inscribing difference and resistance: indigenous women's personal non-fiction and life writing in Australia and North America.* Brno: Filozofická fakulta, Masarykova univerzita

Kaufman, R. (2016). *Ayagogy: Ayahuasca as a social change agent and learning model.* Inner Dimensional Media

Longden, E. (2013). The voices in my head. [Online] Available at: https://www.ted.com/talks/eleanor_longden_the_voices_in_my_head/transcript?language=en [Accessed: 28/08/2015]

Lugones, M. (2010) Toward a Decolonial feminism. *Hypatia,* 25 (4):742–759

MacLean, K. (2018). Psychedelic Patriarchy ~ February 7, 2018 ~ NYC [Online video] Available at: https://youtu.be/nmzDUK–EZqQ [Accessed: 28.06.2018]

Maisha Z. Johnson. '160+ Examples of Male Privilege in All Areas of Life', Everyday feminism,

 February 25, 2016. Available at: https://everydayfeminism.com/2016/02/160–examples–of–male–privilege/

Montagne, M. (1988). The Metaphorical Nature of Drugs and Drug Taking. *Soc. Sci. Med,* 16(4): 417 – 424

Misuse of Drugs Act (1971). Misuse of Drugs Act 1971 [Online] available at: http://www.legislation.gov.uk/ukpga/1971/38/pdfs/ukpga_19710038_en.pdf [Accessed: 28.07.2015]

Nutt, D., et al. (2007). Development of a Rational Scale to Assess the Harm of Drugs of Potential Misuse. *The Lancet,* 369: 1047–1053

Monroe, R. (2017). Sexual Assault in the Amazon As the ayahuasca tourism industry grows, so do account of abuse. https://www.thecut.com/2017/01/sexual–assault–ayahuasca–tourism.html [Accessed 14.06.2018]

Plumwood, V. (1993). feminism and the mastery of nature. New York: Routledge.

Plumwood, V. (1996). Nature, self and gender: feminism, environmental philosophy, and the critique of rationalism. In Warrem, K. (Ed.). Ecological feminist Philosophies. Bloomington: Indiana University Press.

Psymposia (2019) Psychedelic Sisters in Arms [Online] https://www.psymposia.com/psychedelic–sisters–in–arms/ [Accessed 14/04/2019]

Richardson, K. (2017). These Women Are Fighting Sexism in Psychedelic Research. *Vice.* [Online] Available at: http://www.zoehelene.com/these–women–are–fighting–sexism–psychedelic–research–vice [Accessed 10.06.2018]

Ross, L, K. (2019) I Survived Sexual Abuse In The Amazon And Victim Blame At Home [Online] [Available at: https://www.psymposia.com/magazine/i–survived–sexual–abuse–in–the–amazon–and–victim–blame–at–home/ [Accessed 14/04/2019]

Russel, D (2015). How a West African shaman helped my schizophrenia son in a way Western medicine couldn't. *The Washington Post*. Available at: https://www.washingtonpost.com/posteverything/wp/2015/03/24/how–a–west–african–shaman–helped–my–schizophrenic–son–in–a–way–western–medicine–couldnt/?noredirect=on&utm_term=.46a0d0fd5f82. [Accessed 29.06.2018]

Shorthall, S. (2014). Psychedelic Drugs and the Problem of Experience. *Past & Present*. 9(1). 187–206

Some, M. (1995). *Of Water and the Spirit: Ritual, Magic, and Initiation in the Life of an African Shaman*. Penguin, London

Sweeney (2016). The transformative potential of survivor research. In Russo, R., & Sweeney, A. (Eds). *Rose Garden, Challenging Psychiatry, Fostering Mad Studies*. Edited by Jasna Russo and Angela Sweeney. Ross–on–Wye: PCCS Books

The Race Card (2017). White people throw 'Edgy Slave Market' event in Denmark, because slavery is So Fun! *Afropunk*. Available at: afropunk.com/2017/07/white–people–throw–edgy–slave–market–event–denmark–slavery–fun/ [Accessed 21.06.2018]

Tupper, K, W. (2008). Ayahuasca healing beyond the Amazon: the globalization of a traditional indigenous entheogenic practice. *Global Networks*, 9(1): 117 – 136

Tupper, K.W. (2012). Psychoactive substances and the English language: "Drugs," discourses, and public policy. Contemporary Drug Problems, 39(3), 461–492

Walker, S. et al (2014). Neurodiversity: Some Basic Terms & Definitions. Neurocosmopolitanism

Wilkerson, A. (2011). Disability, Sex Radicalism, and Political Agency. In Hall, Q, K. (Ed.). *feminist Disability Studies*. Bloomington: Indiana University Press

PSYCHOTHERAPIES AND PSYCHOACTIVES OF SUBMISSION AND ENGAGEMENT

NIKLAS SERNING

INTRODUCTION

One of the lectures I give at the University of the West of England is on the therapeutic use of psychedelics. A central speculation in this lecture is whether certain types of psychoactives—controlled or otherwise—can serve a similar purpose as certain kinds of therapy, indeed certain types of spirituality and religion. Is there a class of escapist drugs such as heroin or tranquilisers that, like therapist-led psychotherapies and monotheisms, tend to move people towards submission? By contrast, is there another class of drugs such as LSD and psilocybin that, like client-led psychotherapies and shamanism, might move them towards engagement?

The picture is complex of course, and it is important to note the ever competing modalities of psychotherapy (psychodynamic, CBT, cognitive analytic, existential, every day new flavours are added to the list) populate both strands. There are for example disempowering psychodynamic practices encouraging submission (Kernberg, 2004) just as there are mystical psychodynamic practices promoting engagement (Eigen, 1998). In a similar way, ketamine or cannabis can be seen to have both dulling and engaging aspects.

The aim of this paper is to illuminate the two aspects using Nietzsche's *On the Genealogy of Morality* (1887/1994), and then look at the implications for both psychotherapies and psychoactives.

NIETZSCHE

Before we attend to psychotherapy or psychoactives specifically, we must zoom out and look at more overarching patterns of human existence. One such pattern is the slave–master–priest phenomenon identified by Nietzsche (1887/1994). One way to look at this triune phenomenon is to see mastery as the part of an individual who engages with their life proactively, using the tools available to them in order to achieve the goals they freely imagine. This does not have to be in the style of some Aryan master race or bully, it can equally be the sense of calmness in a Zen monk truly taking in their situation and being in it. This is the path of loving one's fate, no matter how un-lovely it may be. Of course, life is difficult, many of us lack the strength to bear it all, and Nietzsche's concept of the slave is useful here. This is the side of us that folds, that gives up, that does as it is told. There is a certain relief in not fighting, not striving, and simply accepting. Nietzsche has no problem with these two aspects of being human, nor do I. I may be tapping into my mastery side in writing this paper, whilst I'm most certainly tapping into my slavish side by accepting to do it in Microsoft Word on a PC. Looking at it from a genetic viewpoint, we can allow ourselves to be enslaved to the propensities our genes give us, or we can choose to be masters in what we do with these propensities.

The problem is the priests. The priests rally the slaves to oppose the masters, not in a masterly way but rather in a resentful way. They tell us not to become strong like the masters, for we cannot, we are but slaves—instead we should glorify our weakness and be disgusted by the master's strength. Inactive in our weakness, we shall seek solace through the priest, for only they have the wisdom and divine access. This sense of impotence is then weaponised into active resentment and scorn of anything that grates or offends. In my impotence, I become precious, wary of any infringement or micro aggression, to the point at which my moral story begins to oppress the flow and life of others. The priestly engendered slavish impotence and preciousness has become an oppressive morality—perhaps we could call it oppreciousness?

Thus the world proceeds—parts of us embrace our situations, parts give in to it, and parts are encouraged to be resentful and impotently passive-aggressive about it. How does this pertain to psychotherapy and psychoactives?

PSYCHOTHERAPY AND PSYCHOACTIVES OF SUBMISSION

I have spent years in therapy hanging on to my therapists' every word, trying to learn from their wisdom. I am not alone in this; indeed the profession and its professionals often actively promote such dependency and power imbalance. The psychotherapist is taught to remain anonymous and boundaried, untouchable and neutral (Simon, 1989, Smith, 1991, BACP, 2015). If information is power, the power imbalance is considerable, with the client baring their soul to the silent and analysing psychotherapist. The client's account is then interpreted through the modality and worldview of the psychotherapist, a new story is created according to the psychotherapeutic modality the therapist favours. What the client thought was genuine sadness over the loss of a loved one is largely fuelled by the eternal repercussions of the occasional absence of the maternal breast (Klein, 1946). What the client thought was fury against a system that does not allow them to be who they are is actually mostly unskilful thinking and feeling loops (Padesky, 2015). The slave is kept dependent on the priest, rarely mastering their world or their experience of it. It would be easy to blame the priestly psychotherapist here, but they are only following the rules of the profession, indeed actively holding themselves back, actively trying to retain fidelity to the model (Cucciare, 2016).

The oppressive tendencies of some versions of psychotherapy grew further with the development of psychiatry, a science aiming to identify diseases of the mind that, unlike diseases of the brain observed within the field of neurology, had no clear biological base. There are of course genetic predispositions to our traits and personalities, but taxonomising some of these traits as pathological allows the psychiatrist to pathologise entire swathes of human experience, some from genuinely distressed patients seeking help, and some phenomena that simply characterise what it is to be alive, from excessive joy to misery to social eccentricities (Plomin, 2018). As psychiatry became embedded into Western medicine, it also acquired power from the state to enforce treatment and even incarceration without the consent of its patients.

As the range of medications that could be sold to 'cure' mental distress and eccentricities grew, so did the categories of things they were supposed to be curing. Each year saw new areas of human affect and cognition adopted into the category of disease. Traits of personality, ways of relating and ways of behaving entered an odd grey zone in which they were supposedly pathological in character, and thus became diseases seen to be a real and observable thing in the same way that illnesses of the body are a real and observable thing. However, as we look over time and across cultures at these traits, we find that there is scant evidence for them being persistently seen as problematic. Being aggressive is seen as an illness in Stockholm, whilst it was seen as imperative in Sparta; being unassuming and sad in a difficult environment makes sense, whilst it looks depressive in other environments.

The effect of this medicalisation of the mind is that an element of your experience is taken away from you and made into an object apart from you. Your sadness is not an intrinsic part of you and your journey and your choices and Life—you have simply caught a bit of depression. The effects of the social isolation you experience, living alone without family or friends, and those feelings of fear and mistrust that beset your perception of the outside world, are generalised anxiety disorder (GAD) or social phobia. If certain versions of psychotherapy promote submission, traditional psychiatry risks doing the same thing but in a harsher and sometimes state-sanctioned manner.

People living in difficult situations, whether socioeconomic deprivation or high-conflict environments, are more likely to experience distress. In a world where many people have few options other than to struggle on in these suboptimal environments, the prospect of being given a magic tool (a psychiatric diagnosis or perhaps a psychodynamic theory that pins it all on mum and sorts it all out through the care of the therapist) to fix all this is highly appealing to both client and practitioner.

Psychiatrists and psychotherapists genuinely want to help. The need to provide help feels important, even urgent. But both are encouraged to deploy simplistic taxonomical tags in order to somehow fix the endlessly complex enigmas of human individuality and social complexity. Power is never without its complications, and being empowered to identify what is wrong or who is to blame runs the risk of creating a class of priests colluding in the disempowerment of their clients.

This then brings us to the question of self-medication. Suppose your taxonomical system leads to an assumption that there is little hope of the client mastering their difficulty; suppose it leads to even less hope of a social revolution that would reshape the environmental sources that tend, at the very least, to contribute; suppose furthermore, that pressures of time and funding are thrown into the mix. The priest despondently seeks to dull the pain, to divert the slave's gaze from the here and now, knowing that the here and now is something that the slave cannot bear. Mild agents (SSRIs) to blunt mild suffering, heavy-duty sedatives (so-called antipsychotics) for severely unorthodox thoughts, feelings and behaviours. These medicines don't engage with so-called depression or so-called psychosis as a cure, or a means to changing it— their job is to dull and divert (Moncrieff, Cohen and Mason, 2009). Like religion, they are the opiates of the mind that soothe the pain of the world, but they also hamper the revolution that would change it (Marx, 1844). The analogy has become reality.

The new wave of genetic insights into psychological traits will offer a depth of understanding into endogenous causes of mental distress, but getting stuck into a deterministic rubber-stamping of the old psychiatric taxonomies creates a God-ordained truth for its priesthood. Even within a biological paradigm, environmental factors and individual autonomy are at play. Reducing complex stories and experiences to pathological dysfunction is no more sophisticated than reducing them to God's will.

PSYCHOTHERAPY AND PSYCHOACTIVES OF ENGAGEMENT

There is, however, hope. There is a strand of psychotherapy and psychiatry refreshingly devoid of priests, and it is unsurprisingly the strand that promotes joy and relieves distress most effectively.

There a solid body of research into the efficiency of differing psychotherapeutic modalities, with the majority of this research establishing support for the preferred modality versus the others. All modalities are the best, just pick one, and make sure that you only read the research that supports it. This counterintuitive research situation is explained by the minute levels of difference between the results from the different modalities, and the scientifically problematic ways in which the experiments were set up in order to 'prove' the preferred theory. CBT can be shown to be more effective than other therapies if you pick the right clients, compare trained CBT psychotherapists with untrained therapists, and then choose to interpret a miniscule improvement rate as significant (Cromby, Harper and Reavey, 2013).

What the research *does* show conclusively and consistently is that modalities do not matter. What matters is the quality of the engagement (Cooper, 2008) and the level to which the client's own strengths are recruited and empowered (Duncan, Miller and Sparks, 2004). This fits well with the description of mastery and slavishness above, where masterful engagement empowers the client to find masterly qualities within themselves, and also finds solace in accepting the slave aspects. By truly engaging with the client based on the client's experience and interpretation of the world, actively bracketing out the psychotherapist's world view, there is a creative space within which the client can flex their wings, gradually strengthen both muscles and courage, and eventually take flight themselves, leaving the psychotherapist smiling below. For example, whereas traditional psychiatry tries to sedate away the experience it calls psychosis, and psychotherapies of submission fit the client into their systems, the psychotherapist of engagement actively engages with the individual's experience. As traditional ego boundaries dissolve and sub-personalities take more solid forms, there is an opening to enter a form of engagement with the multiplicities of ourselves (Nietzsche, 1878/1984) and the world that can be deeply healing and enlightening. Indeed, there is a growing body of therapeutic work that engages with the 'illness' of psychosis, seeing the emergence of this experience as something potentially organic and beneficial (Marohn, 2003).

The psychotherapist supports but crucially couples this support with faith in the client's own ability. The psychotherapist relates to the client on the client's terms, bringing in their whole being without unnecessarily rigid boundaries. This is demanding work—the psychotherapist cannot simply rely on or rest in established theory. Indeed, a new theory has to be built up for each client. I as the psychotherapist need to be extremely flexible and need to have experienced a world as wide as possible myself in order to challenge all that I 'know'. Be it through art or my own life's journey, be it through following many religions or querying all, be it through deep engagement with self or other, preferably all these things, I need to be able to be as open as possible to all that the client can be.

If the epitome of the psychotherapy of submission is the traditional psychiatrist, the epitome of the psychotherapy of engagement that emerges in the sketch above is the shaman. I am certain that there have been priestly shamans promoting adherence to vacuous rules and hierarchies, but the ones I am talking about here are the brave ones who accompany their clients deep into their lifeworlds and beyond. The shaman is part of the community and engages with individuals as well as groups, without insisting on artificial divisions. I noticed above how priestly Truth corralls our complex individual realities into one dominating story of religion or biological psychiatry—the shaman goes in the opposite direction. Starting out from the complex story of the client's lifeworld, the shaman *adds* even more stories. Call them analogies or alternate realities, the effect is a broadening and deepening rather than reduction and confinement.

Correspondingly, if sedatives are the drug of choice for the psychotherapy of submission, psychedelics like LSD, psilocybin, ayahuasca and peyote are the psychoactives resonating with the therapy of engagement. Considering the importance of flexibility, a wide range of experience and openness to the unfamiliar identified above, the psychedelic journey strengthens the qualities the psychotherapist relies on. This is the territory of the shaman, the archetypal psychonaut, and I believe that a psychotherapist or psychiatrist becomes better at their calling should they choose to enter it. Equally, given a safe and useful set and setting, allowing a suitably robust and prepared adult client to psychedelically trip whilst supported by the practitioner, and for them both to subsequently integrate the experience into the client's everyday life, could well be the most powerful, transformative and healing way of psychotherapy. Perhaps this is why shamans have done it for millennia, and perhaps this is why psychiatrists, psychologists and psychotherapists are showing renewed interest in these ancient medicines. Indeed, defying my wish for neat delineations, one free-thinking psychiatrist is even labelling MDMA as 'psychiatry's antibiotics', praising its ability to simultaneously strengthen the client's confidence in self and therapist, elevate mood, and promote new ways of thinking (Sessa, 2017).

CONCLUSION: PSYCHOTHERAPY ENGAGING WITH SHAMANS AND PSYCHEDELICS

Imagine two settings, one for each strand I have described above. In one, the broken client pours their heart out to the blank faced therapist, as they have done once a week for years. In the other, we see a circle, a community of people. There is a therapist (be they shaman, psychotherapist or psychiatrist) guiding the proceedings and perhaps ayahuasca is involved, but the community is holding a space together. Everyone in the circle brings their distress, their joy and their beauty to share. There is a complex and textured dynamic of the many drives and challenges we face in our worlds. Maybe some people in the circle will struggle with parts of this process. The role of the therapist, if this happens, is to follow them on their journey and intervene in their world, within their paradigm, to positive effect. Not to simply reflect stuff back at them, or offer an interpretation the therapist finds useful, but to lend them energy and assistance in dealing with their demons, literal or otherwise.

The world out there and our worlds within us have suffered priests too long. It is time to throw off their yoke. In the world of psychotherapy and psychiatry, the way to do this is to engage beyond modalities, engage directly with the experience of the client and their strengths and weaknesses. This is the way of the shaman, and as such can be deeply supported by psychedelics. Through the psychedelic encounter with the unfamiliar and the innermost, the therapist learns to be intimately in difference as opposed to indifferent. Furthermore, there is conclusive and current international research on the safety (Winstock, Barratt, Ferris and Maier, 2017) and benefits of clients using psychedelics and integrating their experiences with psychedelically experienced therapists, much of it even done in this country at for example Imperial College London (Nutt, 2012), Cardiff and Bristol (Sessa, 2017). An unprejudiced and open society is duty bound to honour such research and cease the prohibition of substances so useful for human experience and joy.

BIBLIOGRAPHY

BACP, (2015). *Ethical Framework for the Counselling Professions.* Lutterworth: British Association for Counselling and Psychotherapy.

Cooper, M. (2008). *Essential Research Findings in Counselling and Psychotherapy: The Facts are Friendly.* London: Sage Publications.

Cromby, J., Harper, D., Reavey, P. (2013). *Psychology, Mental Health and Distress.* Basingstoke: Palgrave Macmillan.

Cucciare, M.A. et al. (2016). *Assessing fidelity of cognitive behavioral therapy in rural VA clinics: design of a randomized implementation effectiveness (hybrid type III) trial.* In Implementation Science, Volume 11, Issue 65. Available at https://doi.org/10.1186/s13012-016-0432-4

Duncan, B., Miller, S., Sparks, J. (2004). *The Heroic Client: A Revolutionary Way to Improve Effectiveness Through Client Directed, Outcome Informed Therapy.* Hoboken: John Wiley & Sons.

Eigen, M. (1998). *The Psychoanalytic Mystic.* London: Free Association Books.

Kernberg, O. (2004). *Discussion: "Problems of Power in Psychoanalytic Institutions".* In Psychoanalytic Inquiry, pp 106–121, Volume 24, Issue 1.

Klein, M. (1946). 'Notes on some schizoid mechanisms'. *Envy and gratitude and other works.* London: Hogarth Press.

Marx, K. (1844). 'A Contribution to the Critique of Hegel's Philosophy of Right'. In *Deutsch-Französische Jahrbücher, 7 & 10.* Paris: Jahrbücher.

Moncrieff, J. (2014). *The Nature of Mental Disorder: Disease, Distress, or Personal Tendency?* In Philosophy, Psychiatry, & Psychology, pp 257–260, Volume 21, Number 3.

Moncrieff, J., Cohen's, D. and Mason, J. P. (2009). *The subjective experience of taking anti-psychotic medication: a content analysis of Internet data.* Acta Psychiatrica Scandinavica. 120(2): 102–111. Available online: http://www.ncbi.nlm.nih.gov/pubmed/19222405. Accessed 11/05/17.

Marohn, S. (2003). *The Natural Medicine Guide to Schizophrenia.* Newburyport: Hampton Roads Publishing Company.

Newnes, C., (2015). *Inscription, Diagnosis, Deception and the Mental Health Industry: How Psy Governs Us All.* Basingstoke: Palgrave Macmillan.

Nietzsche, F. (1878/1984). *Human, All Too Human: A Book for Free Spirits.* Lincoln: University of Nebraska Press.

Nietzsche, F. (1887/1994). *On the Genealogy of Morality.* (trans. Carol Diethe, ed. Keith Ansell-Pearson). Cambridge: Cambridge University Press.

Nutt, D. (2012). *Drugs—without the hot air: Minimising the harms of legal and illegal drugs.* Cambridge: UIT.

Padesky, C. (2015). *Mind Over Mood, Second Edition: Change How You Feel by Changing the Way You Think.* New York: Guilford Press.

Plomin, R. (2018). *Blueprint—How DNA makes us who we are.* London: Allen Lane.

Sessa, B. (2017). *The Psychedelic Renaissance, 2nd edition.* London: Muswell Hill Press.

Simon, R. (1989). *Sexual exploitation of patients: how it begins before it happens.* Psychiatric Annals. 1989; 19:104–122.

Smith, D. (1991). *Hidden conversations: introduction to communicative psychoanalysis.* London: Routledge.

Winstock, A., Barratt, M., Ferris, J., Maier, L. (2017). *Global Drug Survey.* Available online: https://www.globaldrugsurvey.com/wp-content/themes/ globaldrugsurvey/results/GDS2017_key-findings-report_final.pdf. Accessed 24/05/2017.

ARE YOU HAVING A LAUGH? HUMOUR AND THE PSYCHEDELIC EXPERIENCE

OLI GENN-BASH

Within the field of psychedelic research, and arguably people's own experiences, it seems as though the topics surrounding humour and comedy (terms which I will use interchangeably) have been somewhat overlooked. This could be down to humour only being seen as a by-product of the psychedelic experience, manifesting as moments of joy which give us a release from what may be viewed as the more important or serious aspects of this kind of experience, such as the potential for healing or spiritual development. Humour or comedy may even be viewed as being at odds with the more stern intention for such experiences to, for example, extract something tangible or move us past unresolved issues. Here I will make the argument that humour is in fact the most important focus of the psychedelic experience, and if you've never laughed during a trip then you've been doing it all wrong! Many of us choose friends to have experiences with based on who we'll mutually feel comfortable and safe with, which are of course very important things, as the majority of those embarking on such an adventure understand the need for correct set and setting—however, it is equally important to find those who you can mutually express joy and laughter with. The novel instances and possible strangeness within a psychedelic experience, I believe, bring everything into this rather funny space where things aren't necessarily straightforward, and as such may require the adoption of a corresponding mindset.

When talking about humour in this instance, it's important to understand how this is experienced or expressed, and largely that seems to be in the form of laughter. Laughter is clearly a visible expression of one's finding something funny, and possibly expressing joy. This is why it is so fascinating, as more often than not, it is impossible to hide. We may be offended by something but manage to hide our disgust, or put on a brave face and smile through hard times. Laughter however seems to grip us in the moment and is almost inescapable. The twentieth-century French philosopher Henri Bergson explored the concept of laughter, particularly laughter which was caused by the comic. Paramount to Bergson's understanding of laughter was that it could not exist outside the human realm. We may find our natural environment to be beautiful or inspiring, but we never laugh at it. If we have ever laughed at animals within our environment it is only because we have attached some form of human characteristic to them. Laughter is inherently human and relates to our feelings towards something or a situation. For Bergson, laughter is that which is devoid of emotion and cannot be produced if one is too weighed down by problems. If we are to laugh *at* someone then in this moment we are suspending our pity, becoming a disinterested observer with a lack of sympathy. We may ultimately view the dramatic moments in a new comedic manner through this detached position. Bergson offers the analogy of entering a room full of people dancing to music that one is unable to hear—the people dancing would obviously look quite ridiculous. In this sense, laughter appeals to intelligence rather than to sentiment. The intelligence that laughter appeals to exists in relation to other intelligences. There is always a sense of complicity with others when laughing, as an appreciation of humour would be extremely difficult in isolation from a group. Laughter does not just serve to satisfy the intellect, but instead has an important social and moral function.[1]

The social function of laughter is of some interest when looking at the relationship between humour and the psychedelic experience. To illustrate this point further we can look to Bergson's notion that the absent-minded individual is made fun of in order to reveal their various indulgences or dispositions. Laughter in this sense can serve the purposes of making the absent-minded individual aware of the aspects of their nature that may seem ridiculous to others, potentially allowing for some sense of improvement. Laughter therefore can provide the basis for someone to undergo a moral transformation through making them aware of themselves.[2]

This notion, coupled with the intensity of the psychedelic experience may allow for healing processes to take place, through providing the potential to move past certain issues in a way that allows us to see them for what they are, and maybe not as things which require so much serious energy to be invested. This is not to diminish the perceived difficulties or issues that we may experience in life, but rather to help re-jig the effects of these issues to lessen the impact on our mental state, and in fact provide a moment of resistance or liberation in light of these difficulties. Humour in this sense goes further than providing any sort of healing. It can be used as a tool to dispel fixed thoughts or concepts, which can serve as the basis for spiritual awakening or enlightenment. When looking at this notion of humour as a tool, we may be drawn towards the philosophy contained within Zen Buddhism, particularly the concept of the *koan*.

The Zen koan is a riddle which seeks to shake one's mind out of its ordinary thought patterns, creating non-rational connections between the descriptive aspects of the riddle and that to which the linguistic expression refers. It is an attempt to produce a different state of mind and 'baffle the intellect', rather than to propose a logical problem which must be solved through an employment of one's own understanding or intelligence. There is the story of a Zen master addressing a monk on the topic of a bamboo stick: 'The Zen master asks, "If you call this a stick, you affirm; if you call it not a stick, you negate. Beyond affirmation and negation what would you call it?"'[3] The *koan* can be viewed as that which causes one to become comfortable with and internalise paradoxes, whilst dispelling the presupposition that there is something to be figured out or truth to be found in what has been proposed. Much like the Zen master who simply laughs when asked what Zen Buddhism is, these *koans* can potentially help to keep the individual grounded once they come to the conclusion that not everything is meant to be figured out. We may find that during psychedelic experiences we come to similar points where we are unable to figure things out, or we feel like there's a point we need to reach and can't get to, and then we potentially become frustrated. The concept of the *koan* however may provide respite in allowing us to accept the paradoxes we encounter and even get to the point of embracing them!

This embrace of the paradoxes we may encounter leads us to the notion within certain spiritual practices known as 'crazy wisdom' or 'divine madness'. In Buddhist practice this refers to the Tibetan philosophy of *drubnyon* which traditionally combines exceptional insight and magical power with a brazen disregard for conventional behaviour. The process of crazy wisdom involves letting go of the need to find an answer, as once the subject goes deeper and deeper into self-exploration, they may reach a point where there is no answer.[4]

There is a lot of comfort to be found in not needing an answer and safely revelling in the crazy paradoxes. Certain psychedelic substances may produce experiences which appeal to this sentiment of stepping outside of the normal confines of conventional thought, particularly from a comedic perspective, or more specifically in the instance of laughter. My own personal experiences with magic mushrooms have brought about some of the greatest incidences of laughter, so much so that I have wondered whether or not this laughter would end, or if I would spend the rest of my days cackling away to myself. In the moment, there is a real connection to something magical, special, wondrous and even divine through laughter. The chance to step outside of yourself and enter into a universal and ecstatic moment provides an opportunity for growth and acceptance of the perceived strangeness of life and the situation you find yourself in. Psychedelic experiences are not everyday experiences (at least for the majority of people), so we can see how they might be perceived as weird or just funny in general. The novel moments within a trip can provide not just a great source of entertainment for us and our friends, but also a moment to really shift our perspective. A number of years ago I had an experience with a fairly strong dose of dried liberty cap mushrooms (roughly 3.5–4 g, so certainly not a beginner experience, but certainly neither an inter-dimensional adventure where I had to battle against any giant insectoid beings with my chakra rays) and for the most part I had no difficulties, until I sat down in my garden to smoke some cannabis (as I often enjoy when tripping) which seemed to expand the flow of thought to thinking about the nature of the universe.

Now this isn't something which is untypical to think about during a psychedelic experience, and it is not necessarily my thoughts surrounding this which are important, but rather how I was able to free myself from what I perceived to be a philosophical rut. I'd reached the point where I understood the universe to be infinite and everywhere—but this concept threw me. How can something be everywhere? Surely 'some-thing' had to exist within something, but if it's infinite and everywhere then it is everything. My mind couldn't settle on this point and I was becoming slightly worried that due to the strength of my experience, I could become stuck on a frustrating thought loop which wouldn't go anywhere. I perceived it as a cruel trick being played on humanity by the universe that we couldn't wrap our heads around, and this knowledge felt like some kind of burden that I would have to carry—that is until, for some reason (probably due to the strong visionary power of the mushrooms), in my mind I saw my friend (some of you might know the University of Kent lecturer William Rowlandson) as a water vole looking up at me from the bank of a river, reassuring me that everything was alright. He was very joyous in letting me know that this is the beautiful cosmic joke, where things weren't made to make sense, and that we should celebrate this. The universe is sticking its tongue out at us when we try to make sense of it all, and I began to laugh and laugh—then I laughed some more. I went from feeling philosophically stuck to feeling thankful to the universe for providing existence with such humour! This cosmic joke provides us with the capacity to ponder these ideas, without ever letting us get to the bottom of everything.

I am reminded of a moment in the 'Reincarnation' episode of the sci-fi cartoon *Futurama* where the character Professor Farnsworth discovers the Grand Unified Theory which reduces all the laws of nature to a single equation, claiming that 'this is the greatest moment in scientific history! At last, there are no more questions left to answer!' The professor then is stuck by the notion that there are in fact no more questions left to answer, and is dismayed at his decision to spend his life answering the most crucial questions in science, only to have spent that time mostly in solitude. He realises that he was not living for the answers, but more so for the questions themselves. The character Fry then responds comically, 'Too bad the universe made it turn out that way and not some other way. I wonder why it did that'[5]. This last bit seems to reiterate the big cosmic joke whilst the previous lines remind us that life could be potentially very dull if we were to suddenly figure everything out.

The psychedelic experiences which bring us face-to-face with cosmic paradoxes can too be met with this ecstatic delight which manifests as laughter, instead of being stuck on the idea of needing to know everything. Humour as an adjunct to the psychedelic experience has both the power to ground us within difficult or dark periods, and also bring more joy into the fun moments we share with our friends during these experiences. There does seem to be a kind of mutual energy being shared, where humour can help the psychedelic experience along but also the experience itself amplifies comical moments, or allows us to view things in a way that we've never done before.

The impact of the psychedelic substances on humour itself, particularly within stand-up comedy, is of great interest. There are certain comedians who have been somewhat influenced by their use of substances, such as George Carlin, Doug Stanhope, Joe Rogan, Shane Mauss, and in particular the late American comedian Bill Hicks who was rather explicit about the psychedelic experience within his work.

Despite possessing the necessary attributes of a popular student at high school—good looks, athleticism, and humour—Hicks didn't yearn for the somewhat stereotypical American high school experience of cheerleaders, football players, or beer-keg parties. Instead he preferred to read. *Huckleberry Finn, The Hardy Boys,* and *The Hobbit*—books such as these were of particular interest, stories that owed more to mystery and adventure rather than everyday routine. Hicks however was not what one might call a 'loser' at school, but neither was he part of the 'cool' clique of students. He stayed somewhat in the middle, having good friends around but desperately needing his privacy at other times. After meeting his comedic partner Dwight Slade at school, Hicks no longer felt completely isolated in his ideas. He finally formed a great affinity with someone who, like him, desired to be creative and think outside of the norm. When feeling lost, Hicks was able to find solace in someone who he believed to be as crazy as he was. Through this friendship, both began to discover their own spirituality as they perceived themselves to be outsiders to the traditional Baptist upbringing which provided a large source of discomfort. Slade lent Hicks a book by Ruth Montgomery called *A World Beyond*, causing him to think about life and death differently than in a manner driven by destiny or fate. This book focused on different concepts within the spiritual realm, such as whether or not there is life after death or the possibility of one having out-of-body experiences. This sparked Hicks'ss and Slade's interest in Eastern philosophy and spirituality such as Buddhism, which allowed them to bond over shared ideas and help them find comfort in the greater mysteries of life whilst remaining as outsiders within their traditional community.[6]

Hicks's comedy began to take shape in the early 1980s, however he felt that despite this development there was an inability to move on to a different level. During this time drug use—particularly cocaine—amongst comedians had increased significantly. Individuals such as Richard Pryor, John Belushi, and Robin Williams had become very fond of cocaine, talking about it often in their material. Despite his own personal spiritual discovery during his teenage years, Hicks had not encountered any drugs or mind-expanding substances until 1982 when he first took a dose of LSD. The impact of this experience on Hicks's comedy was extremely significant with regards to his creativity. For Hicks, such experiences made room for comedy which he perceived to be free from previous barriers and helped bring in new ideas within a different level of awareness. An experience such as this allowed Hicks to explore the smaller details of life and existence through various avenues of thought which undoubtedly aided the surreal nature of his work. This experience was so influential that it caused Hicks to commence with a six-year-long indulgence in many different drugs. The use of alcohol and drugs created a somewhat 'new' Bill Hicks who was now fearless and angry. Whilst there were times where this anger became rather nonsensical within his work, the important points that Hicks sought to bring to his comedy still could be seen even in moments of nondescript rambling, allowing the audience to think whilst laughing at the absurd nature of things. His controversial demeanour brought lots of attention to his act, mostly positive but also negative (there is an unconfirmed story of Hicks having his leg broken by Vietnam war veterans who didn't take so kindly to one of his routines). Some people didn't want to think about certain issues, but this merely added to his view of a country filled with subservient individuals.[7]

Hicks's use of drugs was no secret, and he was clearly a strong believer in the creative potential that this indulgence could produce. In his 1993 show *Revelations* Hicks states that;

> *drugs have done good things for us. If you don't believe they have, do me a favour—take all your albums, tapes, and CDs and burn 'em, cause you know what? The musicians who made that great music that has enhanced your lives throughout the years? Rrrrreal fucking high, ha ha ha. OK And these other musicians today who don't do drugs, and in fact speak out against them? Boy, do they suck! What a coincidence!*[8]

It was not just that the use of drugs could enhance one's creativity. For Hicks it seemed to be avenue which formed a division between those who enriched the world and those who made it less desirable.

He had an interest in the work of the contemporary psychedelic philosopher Terence McKenna who put forward certain theories to suggest that psychedelic substances had facilitated human evolution.

Hicks makes a reference to McKenna's 'stoned ape' theory (the idea that the apes evolved through eating hallucinogenic plants once they moved into the grasslands) by acting out an ape eating a mushroom, then eventually having the idea of going to the moon. Hicks entertained McKenna's view that mushrooms were left behind by an alien race in order to further our own knowledge.[9]

Hicks's use of certain substances, particularly psychedelic drugs, did not just influence the way in which he performed or bring new ideas to his material. Nor were the new ideas which were taken from such experiences used just to make people think. These experiences allowed Hicks to pierce through what he saw as a covering up of the truth. It was not just about creative or surreal comedy, but a dismantling of societal conditioning and the taking down of that which was seemingly worshipped in a heavily commercialised world.

In the early 1990s, Hicks formed a relationship with the progressive metal band *Tool* who had also been heavily influenced by psychedelic substances, and seemed to resonate heavily with Hicks's ideas surrounding consciousness. The band were so fond of his work that they dedicated their 1996 album *Aenima* to Hicks, with a particular reference to a sketch about him wishing the undesirable Los Angeles would just fall off into the Pacific Ocean.[10]

Bill Hicks's use of psychoactive substances in his personal life opened him up to experiences which ultimately shaped the underlying current in his performances. These experiences are not just a background aspect to his comedy or philosophy. These moments of being pulled out of ordinary thought patterns, and awakening to the notion that the nature of reality may not be fixed, allowing one to view reality in a paradigmatic manner. This may ultimately provide an incredibly useful adjunct to stand-up comedy performances, particularly of the surreal type. It also allowed Hicks to cement his political viewpoints, seemingly drawing from the interconnectedness felt through his various experiences. Hicks was particularly fond of certain substances, including LSD, cannabis, cocaine, and ecstasy. But more importantly his experience with magic mushrooms provided a means for him to explore different avenues of thought within a wider context, exploring the seemingly interconnected nature of everything in reality. For Hicks, such experiences peeled back the false materialistic veneer placed on reality in order to distract the masses.

Hicks was particularly fond of magic mushrooms, often speaking about them in his act:

> *I'm glad they're against the law, 'cause you know what happened when I took 'em? I laid in a field of green grass for four hours, going "My God, I love everything." The heavens parted, God looked down and rained gifts of forgiveness onto my being, healing me on every level, psychically, physically, emotionally. And I realized our true nature is spirit, not body, that we are eternal beings, and God's love is unconditional 'n' there's nothing we can ever do to change that. It is only our illusion that we are separate from God, or that we are alone. In fact the reality is we are one with God and He loves us. Now, if that isn't a hazard to this country...Do you see my point? How are we gonna keep building nuclear weapons, you know what I mean? What's gonna happen to the arms industry when we realize we're all one. Ha ha ha ha ha! It's gonna fuck up the economy! The economy that's fake anyway! Ha ha ha! Which would be a real bummer. You know. You can see why the government's cracking down on the idea of feeling unconditional love.[11]*

There is an intrinsically creative aspect to comedy and humour which is rather powerful. If creative enough, it has the ability to take control of the situation, despite the actual outcomes or turn of events. It is more than just poking fun at those in control. It is an attempt to reclaim some essence of sanity amongst the absurdity. For Hicks, the absurdity concerns the greed and dominance of a commercialised society which seeks to induce control and order, and without the influence of psychedelic experiences on his work this window of sanity could potentially have become lost amongst the chaos. Humour and the psychedelic experience seem to share a mutually beneficial and supportive bond which both breeds creativity and provides a grounding mechanism within the perplexities of life. This mindset can allow for greater learning and increase confidence as we enter into the depths of the unknown.

In the words of the late, great, Hunter S. Thompson, 'when the going gets weird, the weird turn pro'.[12]

ENDNOTES

1. Bergson, H. (2008) *Laughter: An Essay on the Meaning of Comic* – Wildside Press LCC: pp. 5–7

2. Bersong, H. (2008): pp. 8–10

3. Zug III, C.G. (1967) The Nonrational Riddle: The Zen Koan – *The Journal of American Folklore*, Vol.80, No.315 – American Folklore Society: pp. 81–88

4. Trungpa, T.T (2001) *Crazy Wisdom* – Shambhala Publincations Inc; New Edition – pp. 9–10

5. https://theinfosphere.org/Transcript:Reincarnation – Futurama, Season 6; episode 26

6. Booth, K., and Bertin, M. (2005): pp. 13-15

7. Outhwaite, P. (2003) *One Consciousness: An Analysis of Bill Hicks's Comedy* – DM Productions: pp. 84–85

8. Outhwaite, P. (2003): pp. 89

9. Outhwaite, P. (2003): pp. 87

10. http://toolshed.down.net/articles/index.php?action=view-article&id=May_1997--The_Austin_Chronicle.html

11. Outhwaite, P. (2003): pp. 90

12. http://www.gonzo.org/articles/lit/jgoley.html - 1998

HOW ACID CAUSED POSTMODERNISM* *OR DIDN'T

ELI LEE & NINA LYON

1967 was the year of the Summer of Love. On one side of the Atlantic, a bunch of hippies throbbed their ecstatic way out of the old social and political strictures of postwar American culture. On the other side, the French philosopher Gilles Deleuze was working on his radical magnum opus *Difference and Repetition*.

Difference and Repetition was published in 1968. That year, the photographer Gerard Uféras took an iconic picture of the philosopher leaning nonchalantly beside a large mirror, itself reflected in another, unseen mirror. It was an appropriate framing for a thinker whose next book would take a Carrollian tumble into sense and self-reference, and, like *Through the Looking-Glass* (1876), it had a psychedelic quality. The hall of mirrors besets the common-sense notion that a photograph depicts an object. Which was Deleuze and which is his reflection? How can we know exactly what it is that we are looking at? In the psychedelic experience, all the frames we have for holding the world stop working normally. They break down, fall to pieces, melt away. We want to look at the synchronicity between the psychedelic revolution of the late 1960s and its postmodern context. In this paper, we hope to explore what the Californian Summers of Love and the emergence of post-structuralism in Paris might have in common, timing aside, and to look at the some of the philosophical themes that underpin what we sometimes lazily call postmodernism.

★ ★ ★

The 1960s were a time when old ideas were collapsing, and with them old ways of organising society and the human experience. As new ways of thinking began to proliferate, there was a rejection of straightforward stories about the world—the accounts of culture, society and history that were established and agreed-upon and true described by the philosopher Jean-Francois Lyotard in *The Postmodern Condition* (1979) as the 'totalizing metanarratives' of history.

Post-structuralism tends to concern itself primarily with the collapse of orders and systems of thinking. However, alongside the collapse hastened by psychedelics came a utopian sense of the limitless possibilities beyond it, as well as its flipside, a nihilistic vision of an undifferentiated void.

'How Acid Caused Postmodernism' is a flippant title in a lot of ways. It is hard to use the term 'postmodernism' without wincing. It has an impossibly broad spectrum of meanings: it pins nothing down well; it also has one set of meanings specifically about its inability or refusal to pin things down. We could get lost in a psychedelic rabbit-hole in which the word 'cause' imposes teleological conditions that may not exist, but we will try to desist from that. We will use 'postmodernism' as a shortcut for describing some of these phenomena and meanings as they arise from the 1960s onwards.

When we were writing this paper, it occurred to us that postmodernism might best be described as a very strange trip. It shares all the characteristic tropes of a psychedelic experience. Postmodern thinkers all sound quite Erowid. Here, therefore, is an account of postmodernism in the form of a trip report, because it makes more sense that way.

POSTMODERNISM: A TRIP REPORT

Phase One: FUCKING WITH REALITY
Phase Two: THE VERTIGO OF UNLIMITED POTENTIAL
Phase Three: THE VOID
Phase Four: RECOURSE TO THE ONE

1. FUCKING WITH REALITY

In 1967, Derrida published *Of Grammatology*. Two years later, Deleuze published *The Logic of Sense*. Both of these books are about what happens when we come up against the limits of language.

We tend to think of language as something that refers to stuff out there in the world. It is a system of denotation: a desk is a desk, a room is a room. The signifier—the word 'desk'—refers to the signified real-life desk out there in the world.

For Derrida, the endeavour of creating a workable distinction between the two falls apart, and with it the notion that there is a *logos*, an entity beyond language to which the linguistic tag refers:

'Not that the word 'writing' has ceased to designate the signifier of the signifier, but it appears, strange as it may seem, that 'signifier of the signifier' no longer defines accidental doubling and fallen secondarity. 'Signifier of the signifier' describes on the contrary the movement of language: in its origin, to be sure, but one can already suspect that an origin whose structure can be expressed as 'signifier of the signifier' conceals and erases itself in its own production. There the signified always already functions as a signifier. The secondarity that it seemed possible to ascribe to writing alone affects all signifieds in general, affects them always already, the moment they enter the game. There is not a single signified that escapes, even if recaptured, the play of signifying references that constitute language.' (Derrida, 1967, p.7)

The unpacking and undermining of the idea of language denoting reality that we see in Derrida isn't unique to him. It wasn't even new. F.H. Bradley, a today-near-forgotten British Idealist philosopher who was working in the late nineteenth century, did something notably similar in his book *Appearance and Reality* (1893). In *The Logic of Sense (1969)*, turns to more Victorian thought in the form of Lewis Carroll's obsession with paradox to set out some of the problems language falls into when it tries to denote the outside world, citing the example of the White Knight's song in *Through the Looking-Glass* (Deleuze, 1969).

The name of the song is called 'Haddocks' Eyes.'" "Oh, that's the name of the song, is it?" Alice said, trying to feel interested. "No, you don't understand," the Knight said, looking a little vexed. "That's what the name is called. The name really is 'The Aged Aged Man.'" "Then I ought to have said 'That's what the song is called'?" Alice corrected herself. "No, you oughtn't: that's quite another thing! The song is called 'Ways And Means': but that's only what it's called, you know!" "Well, what is the song, then?" said Alice, who was by this time completely bewildered. "I was coming to that," the Knight said. "The song really is 'A-sitting On A Gate': and the tune's my own invention." (Carroll, 1874, p. 306)

Deleuze's commentary on the White Knight's Song unpacks the notion that naming something can straightforwardly denote its reality:

There are indeed in Carroll's classification four names: there is the name of what the song really is; the name denoting this reality, which denotes the song or represents what the song is called; the sense of the name, which forms a new name or reality; and the name which denotes this reality, which thus denotes the sense of the name of the song, or represents what the name of the song is called...but it goes without saying that the series, taken in its regressive sense, may be extended to infinity in the alternation of a real name and a name which designates this reality.'(Deleuze, 1969, pp. 36–37)

In *The Logic of Sense*'s opening chapter, Deleuze sums the process up more succinctly, and in doing so extends it into something that shifts the breakdown of language into a more metaphysical realm:

But when substantives and adjectives begin to dissolve, when the names of pause and rest are carried away by the verbs of pure becoming and slide into the language of events, all identity disappears from the self, the world, and God. (Deleuze, 1969, p.5)

Deleuze and Derrida were at war with the notion that anything in the world can be pinned down as it is, or sufficiently described as a fixed and discrete entity.

While this philosophical revelation was being forged out of language in Paris, a bunch of tripped-out kids were rolling around in Californian sunshine coming to a similar set of realisations. The part of the psychedelic experience where objects cede to flux so that they turn out to be not what you thought they were at all can do much the same thing to your preconceptions of how to understand the world.

In 1968, in between Derrida's *Of Grammatology* and Deleuze's *The Logic of Sense*, a novelist called Ursula Le Guin who grew up in Berkeley, California, published *A Wizard of Earthsea,* the first novel in a fantasy series called *The Earthsea Quartet.* Fantasy and science fiction can also be considered analogues to the psychedelic experience—they take reality and render it expansive and limitless. One way they do this is through magic—about which Le Guin, in *A Wizard of Earthsea,* says: 'Magic consists in this, the true naming of a thing.' (Le Guin, 1968, p. 54)

At first glance, this suggests we can attribute a fixed signifier to a thing—its true name. The magic in *Earthsea* therefore at first appears to be structuralist: it depends on the apprehension of this idea of the 'true name' of things. That said, what happens when we try to pin down true names?

Le Guin tells us: 'Many a mage of great power has spent his whole life to find out the name of one single thing—one single lost or hidden name—and still the lists are not finished. Nor will they be, till world's end.' (Le Guin, 1968, p. 36)

What might it mean if you spend your whole life trying to find out the name of one single thing, but that thing keeps running away from you? There's a sense here that we're back in the same hall of mirrors Deleuze stood in, surrounded by uncertainty and slippage. In *The Farthest Shore*, the third book of the *Quartet*, we find out what has happened to the magicians who have spent their lives chasing the 'true names' of things. Postmodernism is setting in in the world around them: language no longer denotes reality. One friend they meet, who is on a drug called 'hazia' that gives him visions, says:

> 'Names don't matter there—that's the point, that's the point! You have to forget all that, to let it go. That's where eating hazia helps, you forget the names, you let the forms of things go, you go straight to the reality." Names do not matter anymore; they do not inherently equate to magic—magic has untethered itself from the straitjacket of names. Magic can lie elsewhere, anywhere, and everywhere. All that's required to see it is the unshackling of names from the thing they're meant to represent.' (Le Guin, 1972, p. 286)

2. VERTIGO OF UNLIMITED POTENTIAL

Michel Foucault, in his 1970 essay *Theatrum Philosophicum* finds a swarming magical vitalism in LSD, which is odd, because, at least on the surface of it, Foucault hadn't actually taken acid yet at this point, an experience that would follow in a Californian desert in 1975. Perhaps he was merely fascinated by what he had heard about it, or was not yet out as a psychonaut; perhaps it was a psychedelic spacetime distortion.

> We can easily see how LSD inverts the relationships of ill humor, stupidity, and thought: it no sooner eliminates the supremacy

of categories than it tears away the ground of its indifference and disintegrates the gloomy dumbshow of stupidity; and it presents this univocal and acategorical mass not only as variegated, mobile, asymmetrical, decentered, spiraloid, and reverberating but causes it to rise, at each instant, as a swarming of phantasm-events. As it slides on this surface at once regular and intensely vibratory, as it is freed from its catatonic chrysalis, thought invariably contemplates this indefinite equivalence transformed into an acute event and a sumptuous, appareled repetition. (Foucault, 1970, p. 190)

This comment on acid is an aside in an essay mostly concerned with *The Logic of Sense.* Phase Two of the trip report: we have undermined consensus reality. It is built on shifting sands. It has fallen down. Now a lot of things are happening, all at once, all changing, and we haven't yet made sense of them.

Foucault identifies a set of similar experiences in the LSD trip and *The Logic of Sense. The Logic of Sense* has to be the trippiest book about language out there; there is no evidence to suggest that Deleuze was tripping his nut off when he wrote it, but there is a sly little nod to LSD in it, very selectively quoted from a little-known satirical skit by Lewis Carroll involving an algorithm for reaching enlightenment. 'Differentiating once,' Carroll writes, 'we get L.S.D., a function of great value.' (Carroll, 1865, p.18)

Taken alone, it is of little significance, but Deleuze plays on allusions constantly in *The Logic of Sense,* using them to imply particular senses and meanings. Foucault didn't seem to have written off Deleuze's mention of LSD, picking up on its trippy disorientation throughout his *Theatrum Philosophicum* discussion of *The Logic of Sense* and *Difference and Repetition.* And that was fair enough, because *The Logic of Sense* sometimes reads like a particularly out-there Erowid experience:

Becoming unlimited comes to be the ideational and incorporeal event with all of its characteristic reversals between future and past, active and passive, cause and effect, more and less, too much and not enough, already and not yet. The infinitely divisible event is always both at once. (Deleuze, 1969, p. 10)

Foucault and Deleuze's insight that reality is built on shifting sands, and is all too easily undermined, is matched again by the writers of this period, and by none so perfectly as by Philip K. Dick.

Within this same short era, Dick wrote some of the most vertiginous novels ever produced: *Ubik, Do Androids Dream of Electric Sheep, The Man in the High Castle, The Three Stigmata of Palmer Eldritch* and *A Scanner Darkly*, to name a few. Central to Dick is the idea that we can never really know what is real. Any time you think you're in a stable reality, it is swiftly undermined.

Dick is believed to be a psychedelic writer primarily because his novels are trippy and visionary. Yet what makes him a truly psychedelic—and postmodern—writer, is his refusal to reify. He will never confirm what is—or isn't—real. Everything, in Dick's scheme, can liquify at any second; everything is subject to ontological collapse. An example of this is his novel *The Man in the High Castle*, in which reality appears to be in part constructed by the *I Ching*. Another example is the famous story from Dick's life, wherein he had a series of visions that revolved around his feeling that he was simultaneously experiencing the life of a first century Christian called Thomas (Sutin, 2006, p. 216). Deleuze's account of 'becoming unlimited', 'reversals between future and past' and 'already and not yet' (Deleuze, 1969, p. 10) also serves as an uncanny description of Dick's liquifying chronology.

Dick's panoply of simulations and alternatives, his refusal to accept totalizing answers to the question of what reality is, and his endless slipping between plural worlds, are exemplary of the vertigo of unlimited potentials. They also tell the tale of peering over the precipice of sanity.

3. THE VOID

Ontological vertigo is not generally a comfortable experience. It can feel, at least for a time, like a trip gone bad. If the structures of belief collapse, what is left can look dangerously like a void, or, in Deleuze's words, 'a formless, fathomless nonsense':

Nothing is more fragile than the surface. Is not this secondary organization threatened by a monster even more awesome than the Jabberwocky—by a formless, fathomless nonsense…? At first, the threat is imperceptible, but a few steps suffice to make us aware of an enlarged crevice; the whole organization of the surface has already disappeared, overturned in a terrible primordial order. (Deleuze, 1969, p. 95)

Deleuze later frames this 'terrible primordial order' through the lens of Antonin Artaud's writings on madness. This reference to Artaud, whose understanding of psychology, language and metaphysics was profoundly influenced by his experiences with peyote with the Tarahumara in the 1930s, might be Deleuze throwing in a further psychedelic allusion. 'In this collapse of the surface,' Deleuze writes, 'the entire world loses its meaning.' (Deleuze, 1969, p. 100) A world without order and meaning can feel monstrous, too:

'Nonsense has ceased to give sense to the surface; it absorbs and engulfs all sense, both on the side of the signifier and the signified. Artaud says that Being, which is nonsense, has teeth.' (Deleuze, 1969, p. 103)

The accurate naming of reality has been discredited, reality itself has been discredited, and now we face annihilation.

In June of this year the patient experienced an attack of vertigo, nausea, and a feeling that she was going to pass out…The Rorschach record is interpreted as describing a personality in process of deterioration with abundant signs of failing defenses and an increasing inability of the ego to mediate the world of reality and to cope with normal stress. Emotionally, the patient has alienated herself almost entirely from the world of other human beings… (Didion, 1979, p. 14)

This is a psychiatric report for Joan Didion, taken in the summer of 1968, from her essay 'The White Album'. In 'The White Album',

Didion puts the end of the Summer of Love into context—within the space of two years, the West had seen its psychedelic idylls flip over into nihilism, violence, riots and war. The Vietnam war, the assassination of Martin Luther King, the Manson murders and the Hells' Angels at Altamont, and Timothy Leary sentenced to ten years in prison—this all accumulates towards a paranoid heart of darkness, a world that makes no sense. As Didion says, 'a demented and seductive vortical tension had built in the community' (Didion, 1979, pp. 41–42). It is a moment beyond chaos; the void at its centre.

4. RECOURSE TO THE ONE

Let us return to Deleuze for deliverance from this primordial terror because, far from seeing the void as a threat, Deleuze finds it underpinned by univocity. This is the point where the bad trip transitions into a mystical experience. Things are getting cosmic.

What is univocity? In *Difference and Repetition*, it is a 'single voice of Being'—the One entity in which the All can be held, or, in Deleuze's phrase, the 'One–All' (Deleuze, 1968, pp. 44–45). We might find that the discrete thingness of individual objects falls apart upon examination, but it's okay, because it isn't that all those many things don't exist at all; more that, at root, they are all one sort of thing.

Deleuze writes that 'A single voice raises the clamour of being'— all that limitless flux and noise and the possibility and terror that exist within it comes from a single source (Deleuze, 1968, p. 44). It might sound theistic, and it definitely sounds monistic—it brought Deleuze an accusation of being a Philosopher of the 'One' from his arch-realist arch-enemy Badiou; it certainly finds common ground with the end of the psychedelic trip report, as we will see momentarily.

Univocity means that it is the same thing which occurs and is said:
the attributable to all bodies or states of affairs and the expressible of
every proposition...Univocity raises and extracts Being, in order to

distinguish it better than that from which it occurs and from that of which it is said. It wrests Being from beings in order to bring it to all of them at once, and to make it fall upon them for all times...In short, the univocity of Being has three determinations: one single event for all events; one and the same aliquid for that which happens and that which is said; and one and the same Being for the impossible, the possible and the real. (Deleuze, 1969, p. 206)

The nothingness can therefore be resolved. It was really an everythingness all along, for we are all spiritually connected—Deleuze's One-All. It is a sentiment expressed extensively by writers of that era too.

Aldous Huxley documented the novelties and fractures of twentieth century modernity and died in 1963, just as many of the cultural implications of that time were about to explode into the sixties. A bleak view of the forces of modernity characterizes the end of his utopian 1962 novel, *Island*, but a sense of utopia—of a psychic utopia at the very least—remains, holding deep beneath impending doom, made possible via *Island*'s famous psychedelic scene where *moksha medicine* is taken. This invention was Huxley's great unifier:

"Luminous bliss." From the shallows of his mind the words rose like bubbles, came to the surface and vanished into the infinite space of living light that now pulsed and breathed behind his closed eyelids. "Luminous bliss." That was as near as one could come to it. But it—this timeless and yet ever-changing Event—was something that words could only caricature and diminish, never convey. It was not only bliss, it was also understanding. Understanding of everything, but without knowledge of anything... (Huxley, 1962, pp. 308–309)

Huxley's description of the univocity underpinning the void is rapturous. It is a much-needed deliverance:

Luminous bliss was only a knowledge and understanding, only union with unity in a limitless, undifferentiated awareness. This, self-evidently, was the mind's natural state...From a preternaturally wretched and delinquent self he had been unmade into pure mind, mind in its natural state, limitless, undifferentiated, luminously blissful, knowledgelessly understanding. (Huxley, 1962, pp.308–309)

★ ★ ★

Sometimes trippy revelations aren't quite so straightforward in the cold light of day. Perhaps acid and other psychedelics didn't cause the anarchic reshaping of worldviews we call postmodernism, but they did seem to facilitate its uptake, melting philosophical and cultural frames ready for some novel and mindbending new ideas to take hold. Perhaps the psychedelic experience also found a way to hold the fragmentation and brokenness of the postmodern world. Once we could experience what it was like to see the things we knew melting away, it was easier to understand it back in consensus reality.

It's important to note, too, that the writers and thinkers we talk about here are not the first to engage with these sorts of ideas, radical as they might feel. We can see the same characteristics of the 'postmodern' in the two-thousand-year-old *Satyricon*, the four-hundred-year-old *A Tale of a Tub*, the one-hundred-and-fifty year-old work of Lewis Carroll, the 100-year-old work of Joyce and Woolf. Those are all products of their times, and what their times have in common are technological and philosophical paradigm shifts in how people understood the world.

If Lyotard describes the postmodern condition as the collapse of the 'totalising metanarrative' (1979), by that standard all those times were postmodern times, and the psychedelic experience is forever postmodern. Perhaps the shared psychedelic experience of the 1960s created enough of a metanarrative collapse that its shockwaves disseminated out into the straight world on the brink of one anyway.

At the same time, the psychedelic experience also implied a new, far more profound, story—that of underlying univocity, of 'union with unity in a limitless, undifferentiated awareness' (Huxley, 1962, p. 273) as the ultimate state. The totalizing metanarrative of organized Christianity might have taken a body blow, but a new way of apprehending spiritual experience was available to take its place.

There are often many paths to this outcome. You don't need to take 'moksha medicine' to have the *moksha* experience; the same phenomenal experience can arise from breathwork, meditation, or digging away at the oddities of language or mathematics until they fall apart. And bigger stories about our place in the world can sometimes blow our minds.

It was an era of adventures beyond our physical consensus reality too; the era of the moon landing. In December 1972, the crew of the Apollo 17 spacecraft took an image of the Earth, 18,000 miles from the surface. Only in this era could this image have been possible; only in this era could everyone on earth see themselves as unified—as together, all-one—on just one of billions of perfect circles in the universe.

BIBLIOGRAPHY

Bradley, Francis Herbert (1893) *Appearance and Reality*. London: Allen and Unwin.

Carroll, Lewis (1939), *Complete Works*. London: Nonesuch.

Carroll, Lewis (1876) *Through the Looking-Glass, and What Alice Found There*. London: Macmillan.

Deleuze, Gilles (1968), trans. Patton (1994). *Difference and Repetition*. New York: Columbia University Press.

Deleuze, Gilles (1969), trans. Lester (1990) *The Logic of Sense*. New York: Columbia University Press.

Derrida, Jaques (1967), trans. Spivak (1976). *Of Grammatology*. Baltimore: Johns Hopkins University Press.

Dick, Philip K. (1962) *The Man in the High Castle*. New York: Putnam.

Dick, Philip K. (1968) *Do Androids Dream of Electric Sheep*. New York: Doubleday.

Dick, Philip K. (1969) *Ubik*. New York: Doubleday.

Dick, Philip K. (1977) *A Scanner Darkly*. New York: Doubleday.

Didion, Joan. (1979) 'The White Album', in *The White Album*. New York: Simon and Schuster.

Foucault, Michel (1970) 'Theatrum Philosophicum', *Critique*, no 282. November 1970, pp. 885–908.

Huxley, Aldous (1962) *Island*. New York: Harper.

Le Guin, Ursula (1968) *A Wizard of Earthsea*. Berkeley: Parnassus Press.

Le Guin, Ursula (1972) *The Farthest Shore*. New York: Atheneum.

Lyotard, Jean-François (1979), trans. Bennington and Massumi (1984). *The Postmodern Condition: A Report on Knowledge*. Minneapolis: Minnesota University Press.

Sutin, Lawrence (2006) *Divine Invasions: A life of Philip K. Dick*. London: Gollancz SF.

MUSIC AT NIGHT: THE POLITICS OF TEMPORALITY IN J.B. PRIESTLEY AND ALDOUS HUXLEY

LUKE GOAMAN-DODSON

This paper examines the themes of temporality in the work of Aldous Huxley and his friend and associate, the writer J.B. Priestley. I argue that Huxley and Priestley were engaged in a mission to reformulate the cultural conception of time in Western society, and that this mission had a socio-political dimension as well as a metaphysical one. In attempting to regenerate what Jesse Matz has called the 'temporal environment', the two writers sought to resolve the crisis of modernity that had led to spiritual malaise, ecological destruction, and the threat of nuclear war. Priestley, who has been undergoing a serious theatrical revival since Steven Daldry's production of *An Inspector Calls* in the 1990s, is still a rather misunderstood and occasionally maligned writer, whose interests in radical politics (as a founder-member of the Campaign for Nuclear Disarmament), esoteric philosophy, and psychology make him a strong candidate for a critical reassessment as an important figure in British countercultural history alongside Huxley.

While partial to tobacco and the odd whiskey, Priestley appears not to have experimented with the classical psychedelics as Huxley did. However, much like William James and the Russian thinker PD Ouspensky, to whom we will return shortly, he did have a mystical experience when he was given nitrous oxide, during a visit to his dentist:

Then I saw, felt, apperceived that the problem of self-consciousness and with it the whole problem of the universe. My vision penetrated to the very heart of all things, and I cried out in ecstasy, Eureka! (1941: 308)

Priestley's interpretation of his experience is similar to Huxley's notion, adapted from the ideas of philosopher Henri Bergson, that psychedelics bypass the brain's 'reducing valve' that filters out information irrelevant to our physical survival, and allows greater access to a more unitive awareness that Huxley terms 'Mind at Large'; elsewhere, Priestley calls this consciousness 'The *Overmind*' (Peake 2018: 22). Priestley suggests that in 'blocking all access to ordinary reality', nitrous oxide releases some faculty of the mind able to 'see further and fare better':

There is no metaphysical ecstasy in nitrous oxide gas, the ecstasy is somewhere in me, buried deep, buried so damnably deep that I had to lose seven teeth finding it. (1941: 309)

His description of a 'world of shapes' from no 'geometry that I knew' that 'gave the impression somehow of being alive', with colours travelling over their surfaces and '*through* them towards me' (ibid, emphasis original), is reminiscent of Huxley's account of 'sumptuous red surfaces swelling and expanding from bright nodes of energy that vibrated with a continuously changing, patterned life' seen while on mescaline (1994: 6). Perhaps a more interesting parallel between the two men's experiences is the sense of transcendence that they both report; both men were of an introspective, philosophical temperament, and had been exposed to various mystical traditions including Advaita Vedanta, so their pre-trip 'set' would have prepared them for such an experience. As Priestley it, the ecstasy was already present within, 'buried deep', but unearthed by a chemical intervention and an intellectually curious mind.

This curiosity led both men to the doctrines of Vedanta. Priestley had first read of Vedanta in the years just prior to the First World War, in his late teens:

*Although it was over 50 years ago, I have not forgotten the moment when,
after exploring the maze of Indian metaphysics, I reached its central
thought. I read that if we go deeper and deeper into the self we can arrive
at last at the recognition of Atman, the essential self; and that if we go
deeper into the not-self, the world that seems so solid and real, pulling
aside veil after veil of illusion, we shall find Brahman, the ultimate
reality; and that Atman and Brahman are identical.* (1962: 171)

As Anthony Peake has exhaustively shown in his biography *Time and
the Rose Garden*, Priestley's interest in these ideas crops up throughout
his body of work. Peake suggests that Inspector Goole's powerful
statement that 'we are members of one body', during his sermon to the
Birling family in *An Inspector Calls*, may be an echo of this doctrine;
that the phrase is also reminiscent of Corinthians 12:12–31, in which
Paul speaks of the emerging Christian Church as 'one body' formed
of 'many parts', only lends weight to a essentially religious or mystical
interpretation of this curious phrase, and it is difficult to believe that
Priestley did not have Advaita Vedanta somewhere in the back of his
mind when writing it. His 1938 play *Music at Night*, the title of which
was borrowed from a 1931 collection of essays by Huxley,[1] depicts a
private concert held in the living room of widow Mrs Amesbury; as
the concert progresses, each character is given an internal monologue,
during which they descend from a personal consciousness, consisting of
memory and identity, to a unitive consciousness; this blending of Asian
spirituality and Jungian psychology is somewhat typical of Priestley's
approach, as can be seen from his play *Johnson Over Jordan*, inspired by
Jung's 'Psychological Commentary on The *Tibetan Book of the Dead*' and
depicting one man's journey through a series of *bardo*-states. Huxleyans
may note the similarity to Huxley's *Time Must Have a Stop*, which also
depicts a post-mortem consciousness.

Huxley developed an interest in Vedanta through his friend
Gerald Heard, whom he met in 1929, and the two became 'nearly
inseparable', in the words of biographer Dana Sawyer, after 1934 (2002:
88). Heard advised Huxley, who had previously been cynical about
Eastern mysticism, to adopt meditation and yoga; Huxley took his

advice, and eventually the two joined the Vedanta Society and began learning meditation from Swami Prabhavananda after having moved to California in the late 1930s. Heard was also an associate of Priestley, who felt that, with Heard's *The Third Morality*, Huxley's *Ends and Means*, and his own *Midnight on the Desert*, all published in 1937, the three men were 'moving in the same direction' (Priestley 1941: 96), with regards to the problem of time, and the spiritual crisis of modernity. In a general sense, all three were responding to the breakdown of two distinct, although closely related, faiths: traditional Christianity, having been severely disrupted by the scientific and philosophical upheavals of the Enlightenment; and the mechanistic rationalism that itself emerged from those same upheavals, now called into question by seemingly 'irrational' discoveries about the nature of time and space in the physical sciences, and—even more controversially—by the emerging discipline of parapsychology. For none of them was this breakdown confined to the ivory towers of intellectual discourse: theirs was a political mission as well as a metaphysical one. As Huxley put it, he was trying 'to relate the problems of domestic and international politics, of war and economics, of education, religion and ethics, to a theory of the ultimate nature of reality' (2002: 100). This functions as a good description of what Priestley and Heard were also attempting. Priestley, Heard, and Huxley sought to bring the political sphere in harmony with a higher cosmic order; not an uncommon desire in the history of radical politics, as historians such as James Webb and Gary Lachman have shown.[2]

That Time was of foundational importance to the development of a 'theory of the ultimate nature of reality' scarcely needs to be said. Huxley, writing in his 1936 essay 'Time and the Machine' that 'industrialized man has to a great extent lost the old awareness of time in its larger divisions' (2010), is perfectly complemented by Priestley in *Man and Time*: 'with increasingly accurate time instruments at our command or commanding us, we have been compelled to become more and more aware of smaller and smaller divisions of time' (1964: 168). The views of Time that Priestley and Huxley found in certain strands of Eastern religion, in which temporality is seen as an aspect of *Maya*, or illusion, were complemented by the ideas of two thinkers: the Anglo-Irish aeronautical engineer John William Dunne, and the Russian esotericist Pyotr Demianovich Ouspensky.

After having revolutionised early aircraft design by stressing the importance of inherent aerodynamic stability, as well as coming up with an innovative method of dry fly fishing, Dunne became increasingly preoccupied with the problem of time. Of his many precognitive experiences, perhaps the most striking is a dream of 1902 in which a volcano in the French Caribbean was about to erupt and claim the lives of 4,000 people; a short time later, the news arrived that a volcano on Martinique had erupted, killing 40,000 people, a figure that Dunne initially misread as 4,000. His book *An Experiment with Time*, published in 1927, was immensely successful, and argued for a very peculiar hypothesis that became known as Serialism (not to be confused with the musical movement of the same name). "Serial Time" proposed a higher dimension of time, t_2, from which the passage of one's life through the time of our everyday experience, t_1, is perceivable as a solid four-dimensional block of spacetime. In t_2 there is also a second observer, seeing past, present, and future simultaneously, who may be able to interact with t_1 through dreams, déjà vu, and the like; in turn, the second observer's passage in t_2 would itself be observed by a third observer, and so on, leading to an infinite regress. Dunne's ideas were enormously influential, inspiring Priestley, Huxley, Heard, T.S. Eliot, Virginia Woolf, Jorge Luis Borges, J.R.R. Tolkien, and numerous others.

Similar literary types, including Huxley, Heard, and Eliot, could be found in the audience of lectures given by Ouspensky after his arrival in London in 1921. Ouspensky is usually mentioned in conjunction with Greek-Armenian mystic George Gurdjieff, a complex, enigmatic figure, whom Ouspensky befriended in Moscow in 1915. However, Ouspensky's career as a writer and lecturer had already begun, having already written *Tertium Organum* in 1911; the title alone is sufficient to indicate the breadth of Ouspensky's brazen ambition, as it positions his work as the third and final part of a trilogy beginning with Aristotle's *Organon* and continued with Francis Bacon's *Novum Organum*. As

Lachman puts it, '[a] précis of the book is nearly impossible, as the ground covered includes Kantian epistemology, Hinton's cubes, animal perception, sex, Theosophy, cosmic consciousness, the superman, and Ouspensky's own experiences of mystical states' (2006: 55). Ouspensky, who experimented with hashish and nitrous oxide in his quest for revelatory experience, came up with a theory of time strongly influenced by Charles Hinton, author of 'What is the Fourth Dimension?' and coiner of the word *tesseract* (a four-dimensional cube). Like Dunne, Ouspensky rejected the notion of time as linear and the future as unknowable. However, instead of proposing an infinitely regressing sequence of observers, Ouspensky believed that one's life could be lived over and over again, with subtle differences that could turn the circle into a spiral (reminiscent of Emmanuel Swedenborg's description of the path of a soul as a spiral).

Huxley managed, along with Heard, to meet Ouspensky at his residence in Lyne Place, Surrey, through the mutual contact of Robert de Ropp, a biochemist and author of *Drugs and the Mind* and *The Master Game*. Priestley attempted the same, but unfortunately was unsuccessful; Ouspensky had started to become reclusive, and suspicious of people 'stealing' his ideas (2006: 235). Those people included Huxley, whose 1939 novel *After Many a Summer* features a character called Mr Propter who voices some of Ouspensky's notions of personality, and Priestley, whose 1937 play *I Have Been Here Before* is essentially a dramatic illustration of Ouspensky's ideas of eternal recurrence: a mysterious Dr Görtler, based on Ouspensky himself, arrives at a northern English guesthouse in search of Oliver Farrant and Janet and Walter Ormund. With the aid of 'certain narcotics', Görtler has recalled meeting Janet and Oliver in a previous incarnation; their affair had caused the suicide of Walter and numerous other catastrophes. Through his intervention, Görtler is able to prevent Walter's suicide and allow him to accept his wife's feelings without reproach.

The ideas of Ouspensky, Dunne, and Indian metaphysics provided Huxley and Priestley with methods of, as Jesse Matz has put it, restoring the 'temporal environment' that had become polluted by modernity and the oppression of clock-time. The emergent field of parapsychology provided further support for this 'ecological' regeneration; Huxley joined the Society for Psychical Research in 1956, while Priestley famously broadcasted a request for experiences related to precognition and other temporal anomalies to viewers of the BBC's *Monitor* programme in 1963, which led to the publication of one of Priestley's non-fiction masterpieces, *Man and Time*. The analytical psychology of Carl Jung was another development that fed into this concern; in taking psychoanalysis away from Freud's reductionism, Jung brought it into contact with the atemporal, in the timeless world of archetypes and the theory of synchronicity, that Roderick Main has called a 'rupture of time' through which the modern world could be resacralised. Both Huxley and Priestley were social reformers, and saw their metaphysical mission as having practical social value. However, with so much in common, the points of departure become all the more striking. Huxley had been involved with the Fabian Society and had espoused the Society's eugenic and hierarchical ideals even while he was satirising them in *Brave New World*; Priestley, while he had numerous Fabian associates, was never a member, preferring his own brand of quasi-anarchistic 'Liberal Socialism' to the Fabians' top-down approach. Huxley did soften his views as he became further involved in mysticism, and turned to the co-operative libertarian socialism of Peter Kropotkin and Mahatma Gandhi, an ideal that took narrative shape in his 1962 utopian novel *Island*.

The novel depicts the society of Pala, a utopian analogue to *Brave New World's* dystopia; instead of using sedatives to control the population, the Palanese use psilocybin mushrooms to heighten awareness and gain higher meditative states. This brings us to another important difference between Huxley and Priestley; where both of them agreed about the emancipatory potential of drugs to open up the filters of the brain, they did not occupy the central position in Priestley's thinking that they did in Huxley's. Priestley's 1954 novel *The Magicians*, published in the same year as *The Doors of Perception*, depicts a similar dichotomy as represented by Huxley's *Brave New World/Island* duality; the forces of authoritarian control through the use of powerful anxiolytics, as represented by Lord Melvill and the experimental drug Sepman-18, are contrasted with the three 'magicians' Wayland, Marot, and Perperek, who represent a combination of Gurdjieffian/Ouspenskyite esotericism, Jungian depth psychology, and Dunne-esque views of block-time. However, the trio only achieve their ends through hypnotic regression, with no recourse to chemical shortcuts. This mild wariness towards the use of psychedelics is amplified in Priestley's *Over the Long High Wall,* in which he expresses qualified sympathy for the hippy movement, but still refers in sardonic terms to 'Hippies bumming around...the half-doped types making for Khatmandu to be thoroughly doped' (1972: 25).

Perhaps this hesitation is part of what prevented Priestley from being adopted by the 1960s counterculture in the way that Huxley was. Priestley certainly felt that older radicals such as himself were being marginalised by the younger hippies: 'Certain gimcrack values accepted by our society may have been rejected by the Hippy movement, but then many of us, now considered to be too old to be worth a hearing, have been challenging such values for years and years, long before the first hippy arrived on the scene' (11). Perhaps Huxley would have felt the same, had he lived long enough to see the movement he helped to create achieve fruition; in any case, it might be reasonable to say that his cautious approach to psychedelics did not find favour within the hedonistic drug-culture that followed. This generation gap is a simply a by-product of the cultural instability that rapid societal shifts can create; if the present-day psychedelic movement is to withstand the ever-more-turbulent shifts generated by technological and social upheavals, a sense of temporal perspective could prove invaluable. Even post-2012, the dream of a secular utopia at the end of history is still one that energises some psychedelic discourse to this day, but this dream was thoroughly rejected by Huxley and Priestley, and has more recently come under fire by philosophers such as John Gray. Perhaps, in so insistently pointing to a dimension beyond the veil of time, this is one of the strongest lessons that Huxley and Priestley have to give us today.

ENDNOTES

1. A 1938 letter from Huxley to Priestley addresses Priestley's asking for consent to use the title; he had evidently forgotten that it had already been used by Huxley when he wrote the play.

2. See Webb's *The Occult Establishment* (alternately entitled *The Flight from Reason*) and *The Harmonious Circle*; Lachman's *Turn Off Your Mind: The Mystic Sixties and the Dark Side of the Age of Aquarius, Politics and the Occult: The Left, the Right, and the Radically Unseen,* and *Dark Star Rising: Magick and Power in the Age of Trump.*

BIBLIOGRAPHY

Dunne, JW. 1927. *An Experiment with Time.* London: Faber & Faber.

Huxley, Aldous. 1938. *Ends and Means: An Enquiry into the Nature of Ideals and into the Methods employed for their Realization.* London: Chatto & Windus.

Huxley, Aldous. 1986. *Island.* London: Grafton.

Huxley, Aldous. 1994. *Brave New World.* London: Flamingo.

Huxley, Aldous. 1994. *The Doors of Perception and Heaven and Hell.* London: Flamingo.

Lachman, Gary. 2006. *In Search of P.D. Ouspensky: The Genius in the Shadow of Gurdjieff.* Wheaton, IL: Quest Books.

Main, Roderick. 2004. *The Rupture of Time: Synchronicity and Jung's Critique of Modern Western Culture.* London: Routledge.

Matz, Jesse. 2012. 'J.B. Priestley in the Theater of Time'. *Modernism / modernity,* vol. 19, no. 2: 321–342.

Ouspensky, PD. (trans. Bragdon, Claude). 1922. *Tertium Organum: The Third Canon of Thought.* New York: Alfred A Knopf.

Peake, Anthony. 2012. *The Labyrinth of Time: the illusion of past, present, and future.* London: Arcturus.

Peake, Anthony. 2018. *Time and the Rose Garden.* Winchester: O Books.

Poller, Jake. 2015. 'Beyond the Subliminal Mind: Psychical Research in the Work of Aldous Huxley'. *Aries—Journal for the Study of Western Esotericism,* 15.

Priestley, J.B.. 1941. *Rain Upon Godshill.* London: Readers Union & William Heinemann.

Priestley, J.B.. 1948. *Works: Plays I.* London: Heron.

Priestley, J.B.. 1950. *The Plays of J.B. Priestley,* volume III. London: Heinemann.

Priestley, J.B.. 1954. *The Magicians.* London: Heinemann.

Priestley, J.B.. 1964. *Man and Time*. London: Aldus.

Priestley, J.B.. 1972. *Over the Long High Wall: Some Reflections & Speculations on Life, Death & Time*. London: Heinemann.

Priestley, J.B.. 1974. *Time and the Conways and Other Plays*. London: Penguin.

Sawyer, Dana. 2014. *Aldous Huxley: a Biography*. Maine: Trillium.

THE JOINT SHOW: WHEN PSYCHEDELIC ART WAS EXPERIENCED

MICHAEL MONTAGUE

San Francisco, 1967. The Summer of Love. Young people descended upon the city looking for peace, love, drugs; something new, radical, anti-establishment. Along with the growing psychedelic scene, this influx of energy and hope, commercialized and promoted by everyone looking to make a buck, created a perfect storm of radical ideas, psychedelic visions, and artistic creativity.[1]

By 1967, the San Francisco psychedelic scene was about a year old, but the concert posters, a retinal explosion of clashing, bright, neon colors, designed for shows at the Avalon Ballroom and the Fillmore Auditorium, were already popular collectors' items among the counterculture youth of the Bay Area. Five young graphic artists, Rick Griffin, Wes Wilson, Victor Moscoso, Stanley "Mouse" Miller, and Alton Kelley, had established themselves as the masters of the psychedelic poster. The popularity of psychedelic posters was noted in the *Newsweek* magazine issue of March 6' of that year.

First, let us back up to the previous year to understand better how we got to this special summer fifty years ago. The Trips Festival kicked-off 1966 on January 21 at Longshoremen's Hall. It was the link between Ken Kesey's acid tests of 1965 and what became the dance hall concert scene in 1966. The Beat generation mingled with the younger LSD generation to protest the war and preach utopianism. The Psychedelic Shop opened earlier that month on Haight St. A month later, the first music concert was held at the Fillmore Auditorium followed by the first concert at the Avalon Ballroom in late April.

Mass media went moral panic and produced lurid stories of drug-sex orgies, mind-expansion never to return, and the influence of psychedelic drugs on art, music, and culture. The state of California made LSD possession and use a crime on October 6, and the Love Pageant Rally was held to mark this ominous prohibition. On Halloween weekend, Kesey held his last acid test which included a graduation ceremony.

One year after the psychedelic movement began, the Gathering of the Tribes at the Human Be-In opened on January 14 1967 in Golden Gate Park with Leary spouting his "Tune In, Turn On, Drop Out" mantra, Alpert, Ginsberg, and others speaking against the establishment and war, asking for a new age of peace. Media response that spring to this movement and accompanying lifestyle was negative and of course shocking, so it may be surprising that a summer devoted to love would soon be at hand. On April 5, Gray Line Tours began busing tourists into the Haight Ashbury neighborhood to see the "Hippieville" action, advertising it as "the only foreign tour within the continental limits of the US."

In May, the song *San Francisco (Be Sure to Wear Flowers in Your Hair)*, written by John Phillips of the Mamas and the Papas, was released and immediately went to #3 on the US charts. The prelude to that summer was the famous Monterey Pop festival, with Jimi Hendrix's incendiary performance, followed by the official opening of the Summer of Love with the Solstice party at Golden Gate Park.

At the peak of this psychedelic movement, an art exhibit glorified psychedelic poster art to fine art status: the *Joint Show*, held on July 17, 1967. Before we remember the *Show*, a quick review of both music concert poster art and the past artistic influences on the five poster artists represented at the *Show*.

Pre-psychedelic poster art was simple and straightforward, designed to quickly convey the most important information about the event. Black and white or with simple colors, block, bold-faced lettering and perhaps photos of the performers were the norm. It was easy and quick to read, a bit colorful, and cheap to produce. The transition to the psychedelic poster design was abrupt with radically different principles.

These principles were sstretched-out, lettering, difficult to read from a distance; color contrasts, and graphic illustration that reversed the traditional approach. The viewer had to take time looking at the poster to absorb it all. Drug themes became popular illustrations as is shown in the Mouse/Kelley poster of the famous *Zig-Zag* cigarette papers container for the Avalon on June 24, 1966 (FD-14). Wilson's *Red Flames* poster for the Fillmore on July 22, 1966 (BG-18) is considered by many to be the first psychedelic poster.

There were a number of artistic influences on the psychedelic poster artists. Mouse and Kelley copied a famous 1896 Mucha poster for their Avalon poster of October 7, 1966 (FD-29). They would go to the library and search through Art Nouveau and Art Deco art books for images and ideas. Wilson also copied many of Mucha's stylistic elements for his Fillmore poster of May 5, 1967 (BG-62). Mouse and Kelley followed the lead of another famous French Art Nouveau artist, Jules Cheret (known for his *Vin Mariani* coca wine poster of the late nineteeth century) for their January 13, 1967 poster (FD-43).

Wilson's greatest influence came from another Art Nouveau movement, the Vienna Secessionists, notably artist Alfred Roller. He also was influenced by contemporary artists in the Op Art and Pop Art movements, such as Victor Vasarely's *Banya* from 1964, as shown in his poster for the Fillmore on May 20, 1966 (BG-7). Moscoso was greatly influenced by his Yale Art School teacher, Josef Albers, as can be seen in his poster of June 29, 1967 (FD-68), and by another of Albers' students, Rich Anuszkiewicz, and his *Intrinsic Harmony* (1965). Moscoso also drew on earlier influences, such as the artist Francis Picabia's *Optophone* (1921–22), for his posters. He designed some posters so that images would shift or disappear under black light. The artists even hit on the same theme, as seen in Moscoso's and Wilson's peacock posters from March 10 and 31, 1967 (FD-51 and BG-57), based on many such images from the late nineteenth century, such as the one by Albert Turbayne, in his illustration circa 1895.

The Big Five psychedelic poster artists are shown together in Figure 1 (this image was used on the mustard-colored and fold-out invitations for the *Joint Show*, and it is reproduced in most books on psychedelic poster art and the Haight Ashbury scene of the late 1960s). Rick Griffin was the California surfer-dude who started his career in illustration art by creating the famous surfer character after Murph the Surf. He used drug themes and Native American, Old West, and other cultural imagery in most of his posters. Stan Mouse began his artistic career creating wildly crazy pinstriping and detailed imagery on hot rods and motorcycles, and airbrushing t-shirts in Detroit before moving to San Francisco in 1965. Alton Kelley lacked drafting abilities and was a collagist who also pinstriped hot rods and created early posters based on the traditional style, while incorporating collages, until he teamed up with Mouse. They started together to create colorful, exotic posters that contributed many elements to the psychedelic style. Wes Wilson's first work, beyond his wedding invitation, was an anti-war poster from 1965. His major contribution was in changing the lettering style, stretching, elongating, dragging the letters all over the poster filling every available space, and he moved the lettering into a fluid female form in many of his posters. Moscoso took Albers' color contrast theory and applied it to his posters especially the Neon Rose series for the Matrix that began in early 1967. Like many graphic artists, however, the five poster designers sought to be taken seriously as artists and thought about an exhibition at an upscale art gallery.

(Right Facing Page, Top) *Figure 1: The Big Five Poster Artists (credit: Bob Seidemann; courtesy of the Edwina Albright collection [1974] at the Smithsonian Archives of American Art)*

KELLY   VIC MOSCOSO   RICK GRIFFIN   WES WILSON   MOUSE

Their wish was granted when they were approached by the Charles Moore Gallery to organize a traditional gallery exhibition of original art. This group exhibition of the Big Five poster artists opened on July 17, 1967 at the Moore Gallery on Sutter Street in San Francisco. The exhibition was titled "*Joint Show*". The *Joint Show* was a pioneering event in the evolution of psychedelic poster art. This was the first time an artistic spotlight focused on these talented illustrators at a high profile gallery exhibition. Up to this point they were generally regarded as just the "poster guys".

A press conference for the *Joint Show* was held at the Moore Gallery on Tuesday, July 11. ABC, NBC and the Bay Area press were present along with the *Berkeley BARB*. Moore said these artists soon would be doing oil paintings rather than posters. The artists were noncommittal when responding to the media's questions at the press conference. The following comes from the *Berkeley BARB* review of the press conference (July 14, 1967, p. 6):

The TV newsmen and press began to ask questions. 'Are you in danger of being ostracized by your associates for going commercial?' No answer but Kelly's noiseless laugh as he bent over double in his chair. 'Is your motivation money or are you serious about all of this?' 'Yes, we're serious, we're all serious,' Wilson said. 'Will you be taking a year or so off for serious work now?' 'Yes, we're going to be serious,' said Kelly. 'Off from what?' asked BARB. 'I don't know yet,' Kelly smiled. 'Do you think this show will help us to understand your art?' asked the big media. Quiet shrugs. 'Do you think psychedelic art is the next step?' No answer. 'Well do you want us to understand you or not?' No answer. An uptight newsman said, 'You called this press conference. What's it for? Is there a point?' 'We get to meet you and you get to meet us – in the flesh,' said Moscoso. He went on; 'You ask us these funny questions. There's a gap. "Is it the next step?" I don't know what you're talking about.' Wilson asked the press a question—'Are your ties comfortable?' The press hurried to appease him except for one who muttered, 'Yeah, but would you want your daughter to marry one?'

To promote the *Show*, the artists created an invitation portfolio, a facsimile slipcase of an over-sized replica of a pack of *Zig-Zag* cigarette rolling papers, containing 19 printed enclosures (some experts claim only about 150 copies of the portfolio were produced). This was a signal to the popular Mouse/Kelley *Zig-Zag* poster of June, 1966. There were two announcements for the *Show*: a mustard-colored large postcard featuring a group photo of the Big Five (Figure 1, see Figure 3); and a fold-out one elaborately lithographed in psychedelic red and yellow colors designed by Wilson (shown below the container in Figure 2). The reverse side of the fold-out invitation also had the classic picture of the Big Five (Figure 1, and see bottom of Fig 3).

(Right Facing Page, Top) *Figure 2: Joint Show promotional materials: Zig-Zag portfolio container and fold-out exhibit invitation (signed by Wilson) (credit: author).*

Of the nineteen enclosures in the *Zig-Zag* portfolio, in addition to the two exhibition announcements/invitations, there were nine postcard or handbill size examples of rock posters, lithographed in color by the artists for concerts with musical groups such as the Grateful Dead and Quicksilver Messenger Service (see Figure 3). Some dealers claim that surviving examples of these promotional packets contain only five or six postcards, but I have discovered, and some ephemera dealers confirm, that the original version had nine postcards. The eight mustard-colored biographies are as follows: a folded Rick Griffin bio featuring his famous image of a Native American smoker on the outside and an illustration for Allen Ginsberg's *Renaissance or Die* on the inside; a folded Wes Wilson bio featuring a drawing and self-photo on the outside and an oration on the inside; a folded Stanley Mouse bio featuring a natal chart and self-photo on the outside, artwork on the inside; a folded Alton Kelley bio featuring a Kelly on Kelly statement and self-photo on the outside, artwork on the inside; and a folded Victor Moscoso bio featuring two self-portraits on the outside and a motorcycle trip on the inside. In addition, there were unfolded single sheets that have a photograph on the front and a bio on the back for three lesser-known Bay Area artists who also participated in the *Show*: Gerhard Nicholson, a creator of light shows; Richard William Leonard, a mobile sculpture artist; and Ralph Cheese, a painter. Music was provided by Country Joe and the Fish and other bands.

The five artists each were invited to design a unique poster for this exhibition. The dimensions of their posters were 22" x 28", except for Wilson's which was 37 ½" x 25". While the five posters reflected the artist's own style, it was Griffin's image of a pack of marijuana cigarettes, with a *Joint Show* label, borrowing the image of the Orientalist man that became one of the iconic images of the Psychedelic Era. Wilson chose a larger size for his poster with a design featuring an image of a nude woman whose voluptuous form comprised the text regarding the artists and the *Show*. In her hand she holds a yin and yang symbol that reads "*Joint Show*." This is now one of the most famous images in many museums' poster collections.

Moscoso chose an image of a reclining nude and juxtaposed her with a slice of cherry pie. This poster has a blue and pink striped border with the title, *Joint Show*, in a continuous psychedelic strip at the top. In the center is a double-exposed image of a man in white and green holding a bar above his head, with a flying goose on either side. Kelley's design included industrial gears and machinery with mountains in the background and black gloved hands in the foreground. The human figure behind the gloved hands is Ron *Pig Pen* McKernan, a founding band member of the Grateful Dead. Mouse's poster featured an image of a Star Child type figure.

(Above) *Figure 3: Joint Show promotional materials: contents of Zig-Zag portfolio (top right) with reverse side of fold-out invitation (bottom), mustard-colored biographies on the artists (left), and concert postcards (right) (credit: author).*

All *Joint Show* posters were printed on two different paper stocks. The first was a white, glossy-coated, index stock, and the second was a silver or gold foil stock, by far the rarest. The pre-*Show* printed posters on glossy stock carried the "First Edition 1200" credit in the lower margin; the foil posters did not have this credit. Norman Moore had some additional posters printed on glossy stock one month after the *Show*. They are indistinguishable from pre-concert posters except they do not have the edition credit. No original *Joint Show* posters were printed after August, 1967. Each artist also signed and numbered 50 of these for the *Show*.

The *Show* was advertised in the *Berkeley BARB* on Friday, July 14 (p. 6). The preview party opened late Monday afternoon and by evening the buzz had generated huge crowds and massive publicity (Figure 4), including a review in the *San Francisco Chronicle*. Griffin said at the time that the *Show* was a great success. "Holy shit. I had no idea, none of us did," Moscoso remembers of the *Show*. "We did posters to get people to go to the dance hall. Sure, it got smart, we did it to entertain them, and the information became entertaining. Here I am doing what I want to and getting paid. Goodbye, Van Gogh syndrome" (Urquhart, 2010). The psychedelic poster art wave culminated with this *Show*.

The posters from the event are well known and hold a place in every concert poster collection. Only eleven days after the *Show's* opening, *Joint Show* posters were offered in a massive sale, $2.50 each, $10 for all five of them (ad in the *Berkeley BARB*, July 28, 1967, p. 14). The Griffin and Wilson images are unquestionably the most popular of the five, each a classic 1960s image. Posters were pulled from walls, street corner lampposts, and handbill boards and hung up in the rooms of the young people who had descended on Haight Ashbury. By the 1970s, original posters were selling on the secondary market for $25, today for hundreds of dollars.[2]

The *Joint Show* was unfortunately short-lived and not hugely popular after the opening day. It is unclear when the final day of the *Show* occurred, but it was advertised in the *Berkeley BARB* through September 7th. The five psychedelic artists were innovative poster designers who had pioneered an art form, but they were not sophisticated artists whose work fit easily into a fine art gallery setting. Young people who enjoyed the artists' work typically could not afford to collect fine art and make the *Joint Show* artists successful. The *Joint Show* was the only attempt at a serious exhibition of psychedelia held in the 1960s.

(Right Facing Page, Top) *Figure 4: Preview party for the opening of the Joint Show on the evening of July 17, 1967 (credit: Stan Creighton, San Francisco Chronicle; courtesy of the Edwina Albright collection [1974] at the Smithsonian Archives of American Art).*

While a milestone event of the Summer of Love, the *Show* is rarely remembered or discussed today, and much of what is written about it is erroneous. On September 1, 1967, Griffin and the other artists, except Mouse, were featured in a *Life* magazine cover story called "The Great Poster Wave", but the *Show* and subsequent publicity did not succeed in promoting their artistic agenda. Yet according to Christopher Mount (1994–95), former director of typography at the Museum of Modern Art, "psychedelic poster art is the only graphic design movement that originated in the U.S."

The Psychedelic Shop closed on October 4. Two days later, Wilson opened an exhibition of his posters at the University of California-Berkeley. Unfortunately the "Death of the Hippie" was declared the same day, and the Psychedelic Era began to wane, though its influence is certainly felt even today. Haight Ashbury had become a worn-out commercialized tourist destination like Fisherman's Wharf. Poster artists moved out of town turning to underground comics, album covers, drug art, and anti-war posters. The quality of poster art dropped off after the *Show*. Moscoso remembers: "By this time I'm starting to get tired of posters, gee, I'm tired of them. I'm with Rick Griffin, he had been a cartoonist before the posters, and we came up with a plan of doing a full-color magazine. We called it *Zap Comix*."

The *Joint Show '86* opened on June 17, 1986, a month and a year before the twentieth anniversary, at the 60's Poster Gallery on Columbus Ave. in San Francisco. All five artists from the original *Show* were in attendance to "slide back into the Psychedelic Sixties at our sensational poster signing soiree. Come celebrate with us the 19th Anniversary of the first JOINT SHOW...Sixties food, sixties fun, and sixties friends... eighties style." The following year, 1987, the Big Five collaborated on the 20th anniversary "Summer of Love" celebration poster.

Fifty years later, we can reflect on the Summer of Love and wonder in today's social-political climate why we cannot experience that again.

NOTES

1. This article is based on a presentation given at Breaking Convention IV, Greenwich, England on June 30, 2017. The full presentation with all posters shown may be viewed at: https://www.youtube.com/watch?v=wnhOBsJmfHs. In the presentation, as in this article, specific posters are labeled with their ClassicPosters.com identification number (FD: Family Dog concert posters for the Avalon Ballroom; BG: Bill Graham's Fillmore Auditorium concert posters).

2. Psychedelic posters may be viewed at ClassicPosters (https://www. classicposters.com), Wolfgang's Vault (https://www.wolfgangs.com), and in a number of poster collection books listed in the bibliography below.

3. Thanks to the Edwina Albright collection at the Smithsonian Archives of American Art for permission to reproduce the images.

BIBLIOGRAPHY

Anon. (2015), *The Spirit of the Sixties: Art as an Agent for Change*. Carlisle, PA: Dickinson College.

Anthony, G. (1980), *The Summer of Love: Haight Ashbury at its Highest*. San Francisco: Last Gap Press.

Ashbolt, A. (2007), 'Go Ask Alice': Remembering the Summer of Love Forty Years Later. *Australasian J. Amer. Studies* 26(2), pp. 35–47.

Berkeley BARB archives: http://www.berkeleybarb.net/archives.html; July 14 and 28, 1967 issues: http://voices.revealdigital.com/cgi-bin/independentvoices?a=cl &cl=CL1&sp=BFBJFGD&ai=1&e [Accessed 19 April, 2018].

Gastaut, A., and Criqui, J-P. (2005), *Off the Wall: Psychedelic Rock Posters from San Francisco*. London: Thames on Hudson Publ.

Grunenberg, C, ed. (2005), *Summer of Love: Art of the Psychedelic Era*. London: Tate Publ.

Grunenberg, C., and Harris, J. (2005), *Summer of Love: Psychedelic Art, Social Crisis, and Counter Culture in the 1960s*. Tate Liverpool Critical Forum Vol. 8. Liverpool, England: Liverpool Univ. Press.

Grushkin, P. (1987), *The Art of Rock: Posters from Presley to Punk*. New York: Abbeville Press.

Lemke, G. (1999), *The Art of the Fillmore, 1966–71*. New York: Thunder's Mouth Press.

McCelland, G. (1980), *Rick Griffin*. New York: Perigee.

Moscoso, V. (2005), *Sex, Rock and Optical Illusion*. Seattle: Fantagraphics.

Mount, C. (1994–1995), *Typography and the Poster*. [museum exhibit]. New York: Museum of Modern Art.

Mouse, S. (1993), *Freehand: The Art of Stanley Mouse*. Berkeley CA: SLG Books.

Owens, T., and Dickson, D. (1999), *High Art: A Listing of the Psychedelic Posters*. London: Sanctuary

Sculatti, G., and Seay, D. (1985), *San Francisco Nights: The Psychedelic Music Trip, 1965-68*. New York: St Martin's Press.

Tomlinson, S., Medeiros, W., and Atkinson, D. (2011), *High Societies: Psychedelic Rock Posters from Haight Ashbury*. San Diego CA: San Diego Museum of Art.

Urquhart, R. (2010), Victor Moscoso. *Grafik* [online] (181), Available at: https://www.grafik.net/category/archive/victor-moscoso [Accessed 19 April, 2018].

Weller, S. (2012), Suddenly that Summer. *Vanity Fair* [online] 54(7), Available at: https://www.vanityfair.com/culture/2012/07/lsd-drugs-summer-of-love-sixties [Accessed 19 April, 2018].

KETAMINE AS A NEW MANAGEMENT TOOL FOR PERSISTENT PHYSICAL AND MENTAL PAIN

THARCILA CHAVES

Glutamate is the predominant excitatory neurotransmitter in the mammalian central nervous system (CNS), acting at a range of different glutamate receptor types, including N-methyl-D-aspartate (NMDA) receptors. These receptors are essential for neuronal development, synaptic plasticity, learning, and cell survival (Duman, Aghajanian, 2012, Hashimoto, 2017). Recent discoveries indicate that NMDA receptor-mediated neurotransmission plays a key role in the pathophysiology of depression and chronic pain.

The rapid antidepressant effect of the NMDA receptor antagonist ketamine, in patients with treatment-resistant depression (TRD), is considered the most important advance in the pharmacotherapy of depression in 50 years (Duman, Aghajanian, 2012, Hashimoto, 2017, Lara, Bisol & Munari, 2013). Ketamine is well-known as an anaesthetic, extensively used in humans, including children. Recently, the fast-acting antidepressant response produced by ketamine has been demonstrated in patients who are resistant to conventional therapies. A continuous infusion of ketamine, at 0.5 mg/kg, over the course of 40 minutes, can take a person out of suicidal thoughts (DiazGranados et al., 2010), something no other drug can do. This is one of the reasons why its use is increasingly applied in emergency rooms.

Moreover, ketamine's role as a safe and effective strategy for treating pain in emergency departments has recently been expanding (Gao, Rejaei & Liu, 2016). Not only for acute pain, ketamine is also beneficial for treating chronic pain. The last few years of pain science strongly suggest that neurology is the most important factor in the majority of chronic pain cases. Pain is actively regulated by the brain. Therefore, medications that work in the CNS are promising for the treatment of patients coping with chronic pain.

EVERLASTING BLUES

Depression has surpassed HIV/AIDS, malaria, diabetes and war as the leading cause of disability worldwide (World Health Organization, 2012). A single dose of ketamine alleviates depressive symptoms within minutes in patients who have failed to respond to two or more conventional antidepressants, and the effects are sustained for one week to months (Zarate et al., 2006, Zarate et al., 2010, Berman et al., 2000, Krystal et al., 1994). Ketamine is also effective for bipolar depression (Diazgranados et al., 2010), it decreases suicidal ideation (DiazGranados et al., 2010, Thakurta et al., 2012) and has shown positive results in the treatment of other mental conditions, such as post-traumatic stress disorder (PTSD) (Albott et al., 2018, Hartberg, Garrett-Walcott & De Gioannis, 2018) and obsessive-compulsive disorder (OCD) (Pittenger, 2015, Niciu et al., 2013). Furthermore, ketamine has shown antidepressant effects in patients who do not respond to electroconvulsive therapy (ECT) (Ibrahim et al., 2011).

In 2000, Berman et al. reported a rapid antidepressant effect of ketamine in patients with depression (Berman et al., 2000). Subsequently, several randomised placebo-controlled studies have demonstrated that ketamine is effective in reducing depressive symptoms with manageable side effects, such as increased heart rate, dizziness, nausea and anxiety (Zarate et al., 2006, Zarate et al., 2010, Berman et al., 2000, Krystal et al., 1994). They can be managed with the concomitant use of benzodiazepines and ondansetron, for example. A very popular regimen applied in scientific investigation uses an intravenous infusion of 0.5 mg/ kg of ketamine during 40 minutes (thus, for a person weighing 70 kg, the total administered is 35 mg of ketamine). It is important to mention that this dose is way lower than the doses used to reach a K-hole (higher than 150 mg).

Recent studies have demonstrated that depression is associated with reduced size of brain regions that regulate mood and cognition, including the prefrontal cortex and the hippocampus, as well as neuronal atrophy (i.e. decreased neuronal synapses in these areas). Antidepressants can block or reverse these neuronal deficits, although typical antidepressants have limited efficacy and delayed response (Duman, Aghajanian, 2012). The available antidepressants take two weeks or more to produce any effect and are only moderately effective, leaving more than one-third of depressed individuals refractory to treatment.

Studies performed in animals have shown that ketamine rapidly induces synaptogenesis and reverses the synaptic deficit caused by chronic stress, generating its remarkable rapid antidepressant action. Ketamine quickly increases the number and function of synaptic connections, which has focused attention on synaptogenesis as a fundamental process for the treatment of depressive symptoms and also suggests that disruption of synaptogenesis and loss of connections underlies the pathophysiology of depression (Duman, Aghajanian, 2012).

STUBBORN PAIN

In Europe, one in five people suffers from chronic pain. It is the most common cause for people to utilise healthcare resources (Pain Alliance Europe, 2017). The International Association for the Study of Pain defines chronic pain as "pain without apparent biological value that has persisted beyond the normal tissue healing time (usually taken to be three months)" (Harstall, Ospina, 2003). There are no universally accepted treatment guidelines for treating it. This underlines the high burden that chronic pain places on society, and also the importance of developing individualised effective analgesic therapies that take into account the biopsychosocial approach to pain as an essential tool for managing it.

According to Ingraham (2017), "pain itself can change how pain works, resulting in more pain with less provocation". Therefore, pain modifies the way the CNS works, leading to more sensitivity, i.e. more pain. This process is called "central sensitisation" because it involves changes in the brain and spinal cord. Sensitised patients are not only more sensitive to stimuli that should hurt (hyperalgesia), but sometimes to ordinary touch as well (allodynia). Also, the pain in sensitised patients echoes, fading more slowly than in other people (wind-up pain) (Ingraham, 2017, Woolf, 2011). Therefore, these are the key symptoms of central sensitisation: (a) allodynia (pain in response to a non-noxious stimulus, such as pressure from clothing or the touch of a feather), (b) hyperalgesia (increased pain sensitivity to a nociceptive stimulus) and (c) wind-up pain (stronger and longer lasting pain) (Woolf, 2011, von Hehn, Baron & Woolf, 2012).

When a person feels pain that has no explanation (because there is no extra tissue damage), it means that the nervous system is damaged, rather than the tissues it is supposed to be reporting on. Central sensitisation is a distinct type of chronic pain, different than neuropathic pain. Neuropathic pain is pain caused by dysfunctional nerve fibres. Actual trauma to nerves is required by the definition of neuropathy, so central sensitisation cannot be neuropathic.

The changes represented by central sensitisation include a situation where low threshold afferents begin to produce pain, something they never normally do, and this helps to explain why low intensity or innocuous stimuli are painful, contributing to the allodynia, hyperalgesia and wind-up pain that occur in the vicinity of a peripheral injury (Woolf, Thompson, 1991).

Ketamine decreases central sensitisation at the level of the spinal cord (dorsal ganglion) and CNS, providing anti-hyperalgesia and anti-allodynia effects (Gorlin, Rosenfeld & Ramakrishna, 2016). Additionally, wind-up is prevented by administration of ketamine

(Woolf, Thompson, 1991, Warncke, Stubhaug & Jørum, 1997). Warncke et al. (1997) have demonstrated that ketamine attenuates hyperalgesia and abolishes wind-up pain, whereas morphine does not affect any of these parameters, confirming the involvement of NMDA receptors in central hyperexcitability (aka central sensitisation) (Warncke, Stubhaug & Jørum, 1997).

The NMDA receptor blockade caused by ketamine leads to decreases in acute pain, opioid tolerance, opioid-induced hyperalgesia, chronic and neuropathic pain (Gorlin, Rosenfeld & Ramakrishna, 2016, Kurdi, Theerth & Deva, 2014). Ketamine given intravenously in low (subdissociative, subanaesthetic) intravenous doses (0.1–0.3 mg/kg) provides effective analgesia with minimal side effects (Kurdi, Theerth & Deva, 2014, Motov et al., 2017).

Central sensitisation is intimately connected with pain catastrophizing—a pattern of negative cognitive-emotional responses to actual or anticipated pain that includes rumination about pain, magnification of pain, and feelings of hopelessness about pain (Sullivan, Bishop & Pivik, 1995, Taub et al., 2017). Fear of pain and pain avoidance also say a lot about the subjective aspect of pain. It is noteworthy how ketamine can act on all of those symptoms, producing overall relief from mental and physical pains.

SPECIAL K

Ketamine is still not approved for psychiatric or analgesic uses. The off-label use of ketamine, i.e. using it for different purposes than anaesthesia, is increasingly common in the medical setting. In order to treat patients who are refractory to treatment, health professionals are claiming compassionate reasons in order to obtain the authorisation to use ketamine as an antidepressant and/or analgesic.

Ketamine is an off-patent drug, which makes it cheap. This is one of the reasons why the pharmaceutical companies are not marketing it for depression or chronic pain yet. They are looking for ketamine derivatives: new molecules similar to ketamine, which they can put a patent on. An exception is Johnson & Johnson, who are working on an intranasal spray of esketamine to treat depression (Reardon, 2018). Esketamine is not a new molecule. Ketamine exists in two forms (in equal parts in a racemic mixture): the enantiomers R-ketamine and S-ketamine (aka esketamine). It is under debate which enantiomer can produce better results with fewer side effects. Most of the studies around this issue have been performed only in animals so far.

Even though the intranasal route of administration has its value because patients do not need a medical setting for using it, ketamine can be addictive and concern around abuse is present when a patient is self-administering a drug that is also used for recreational purposes.

Ketamine is a mood enhancer and its hedonistic use has spread everywhere. Nonetheless, it creates tolerance and its abuse liability makes it a scheduled drug. Ketamine abuse can lead to so-called K-bladder (damage to the bladder tissue, causing the K-cramps) and other urinary tract problems. In a very severe scenario, it can result in bladder removal (Huang et al., 2011, Stichting Mainline, 2017).

A PSYCHEDELIC TREATMENT ALREADY AVAILABLE

Today, if a person living with TRD and/or chronic pain wants to try therapeutic ketamine in Europe, they do not have many options (excluding the black market). There are some clinical trials going on (with inclusion criteria to fit in and the possibility of getting placebo instead of ketamine, among other limitations) and few possibilities of having it in a private clinic. Whether health insurance would cover the off-label use of ketamine is uncertain. On the one hand, because it is off-label, there is a reason for insurance companies to deny the refund. On the other hand, compassionate use could be a reason to claim for the refund.

Ketamine being an addictive substance, it requires a medical setting and professional monitoring of its use as an antidepressant and/or analgesic, which must be followed up closely. Even though the side effects are well tolerated, it is necessary to have trained people present during the ketamine infusion.

In the United States, ketamine clinics are increasingly popular, indicating that there is an urgent need for rapid-onset antidepressants for TRD and suicidality. Despite the palliative care and rehabilitation that are usually connected with pharmacotherapy in the treatment of chronic pain, 38% of the patients report not being satisfied with their treatments (Pain Alliance Europe, 2017). Hence the need to assist those patients who have not found a way to deal with their condition.

Undoubtedly, there is still a lot to be explored about the effects of ketamine in the human body and consciousness. But this is not a reason to ignore the fact that ketamine has the potential to help people now, with the knowledge that we already have. The failure of conventional therapies and the rise of the ketamine clinics might be the beginning of a new paradigm in mental and physical pain managements. Are the ketamine clinics the first legal modern psychedelic clinics?

REFERENCES

Albott, C.S., Lim, K.O., Forbes, M.K., Erbes, C., Tye, S.J., Grabowski, J.G., Thuras, P., Batres-Y-Carr, T.M., Wels, J. & Shiroma, P.R. 2018, "Efficacy, Safety, and Durability of Repeated Ketamine Infusions for Comorbid Posttraumatic Stress Disorder and Treatment-Resistant Depression", *The Journal of clinical psychiatry*, vol. 79, no. 3, pp. 10.4088/JCP.17m11634.

Berman, R.M., Cappiello, A., Anand, A., Oren, D.A., Heninger, G.R., Charney, D.S. & Krystal, J.H. 2000, "Antidepressant effects of ketamine in depressed patients", *Biological psychiatry*, vol. 47, no. 4, pp. 351-354.

Diazgranados, N., Ibrahim, L., Brutsche, N.E., Newberg, A., Kronstein, P., Khalife, S., Kammerer, W.A., Quezado, Z., Luckenbaugh, D.A., Salvadore, G., Machado-Vieira, R., Manji, H.K. & Zarate, C.A.,Jr 2010, "A randomized add-on trial of an N-methyl-D-aspartate antagonist in treatment-resistant bipolar depression", *Archives of General Psychiatry*, vol. 67, no. 8, pp. 793-802.

DiazGranados, N., Ibrahim, L.A., Brutsche, N.E., Ameli, R., Henter, I.D., Luckenbaugh, D.A., Machado-Vieira, R. & Zarate, C.A.,Jr 2010, "Rapid resolution of suicidal ideation after a single infusion of an N-methyl-D-aspartate antagonist in patients with treatment-resistant major depressive disorder", *The Journal of clinical psychiatry*, vol. 71, no. 12, pp. 1605-1611.

Duman, R.S. & Aghajanian, G.K. 2012, "Synaptic dysfunction in depression: potential therapeutic targets", *Science (New York, N.Y.)*, vol. 338, no. 6103, pp. 68-72.

Gao, M., Rejaei, D. & Liu, H. 2016, "Ketamine use in current clinical practice", *Acta Pharmacologica Sinica*, vol. 37, no. 7, pp. 865.

Gorlin, A.W., Rosenfeld, D.M. & Ramakrishna, H. 2016, "Intravenous sub-anesthetic ketamine for perioperative analgesia", *Journal of anaesthesiology, clinical pharmacology*, vol. 32, no. 2, pp. 160-167.

Harstall, C. & Ospina, M. 2003, *How prevalent is chronic pain?*.

Hartberg, J., Garrett-Walcott, S. & De Gioannis, A. 2018, "Impact of oral ketamine augmentation on hospital admissions in treatment-resistant depression and PTSD: a retrospective study", *Psychopharmacology*, vol. 235, no. 2, pp. 393-398.

Hashimoto, K. 2017, *The NMDA receptors*, Humana Press, Cham, Switzerland.

Huang, P.W., Meng, E., Cha, T.L., Sun, G.H., Yu, D.S. & Chang, S.Y. 2011, "'Walking-stick ureters' in ketamine abuse", *Kidney international*, vol. 80, no. 8, pp. 895.

Ibrahim, L., Diazgranados, N., Luckenbaugh, D.A., Machado-Vieira, R., Baumann, J., Mallinger, A.G. & Zarate, C.A.,Jr 2011, "Rapid decrease in depressive symptoms with an N-methyl-d-aspartate antagonist in ECT-resistant major depression", *Progress in neuro-psychopharmacology & biological psychiatry*, vol. 35, no. 4, pp. 1155-1159.

Ingraham, P. 2017, *Central sensitization in chronic pain*. Available: www. painscience.com/articles/central-sensitization.php [2017, March 21].

Krystal, J.H., Karper, L.P., Seibyl, J.P., Freeman, G.K., Delaney, R., Bremner, J.D., Heninger, G.R., Bowers, M.B.,Jr & Charney, D.S. 1994, "Subanesthetic effects of the noncompetitive NMDA antagonist, ketamine, in humans. Psychotomimetic, perceptual, cognitive, and neuroendocrine responses", *Archives of General Psychiatry,* vol. 51, no. 3, pp. 199-214.

Kurdi, M.S., Theerth, K.A. & Deva, R.S. 2014, "Ketamine: Current applications in anesthesia, pain, and critical care", *Anesthesia, essays and researches,* vol. 8, no. 3, pp. 283-290.

Lara, D.R., Bisol, L.W. & Munari, L.R. 2013, "Antidepressant, mood stabilizing and procognitive effects of very low dose sublingual ketamine in refractory unipolar and bipolar depression", *The international journal of neuropsychopharmacology / official scientific journal of the Collegium Internationale Neuropsychopharmacologicum (CINP),* vol. 16, no. 9, pp. 2111-2117.

Motov, S., Mai, M., Pushkar, I., Likourezos, A., Drapkin, J., Yasavolian, M., Brady, J., Homel, P. & Fromm, C. 2017, "A prospective randomized, double-dummy trial comparing IV push low dose ketamine to short infusion of low dose ketamine for treatment of pain in the ED", *The American Journal of Emergency Medicine,* vol. 35, no. 8, pp. 1095-1100.

Niciu, M.J., Grunschel, B.D., Corlett, P.R., Pittenger, C. & Bloch, M.H. 2013, "Two cases of delayed-onset suicidal ideation, dysphoria and anxiety after ketamine infusion in patients with obsessive-compulsive disorder and a history of major depressive disorder", *Journal of psychopharmacology (Oxford, England),* vol. 27, no. 7, pp. 651-654.

Pain Alliance Europe 2017, *Survey on chronic pain 2017: diagnosis, treatment and impact of pain,* Brussels.

Pittenger, C. 2015, "Glutamate modulators in the treatment of obsessive-compulsive disorder", *Psychiatric annals,* vol. 45, no. 6, pp. 308-315.

Reardon, S. 2018, "'Party drug' turned antidepressant approaches approval", *Nature reviews.Drug discovery,* vol. 17, no. 11, pp. 773-775.

Stichting Mainline 2017, *Mainline: drugs, gezondheid en de straat.*

Sullivan, M.J., Bishop, S.R. & Pivik, J. 1995, "The pain catastrophizing scale: development and validation.", *Psychological assessment,* vol. 7, no. 4, pp. 524.

Taub, C.J., Sturgeon, J.A., Johnson, K.A., MacKey, S.C. & Darnall, B.D. 2017, "Effects of a pain catastrophizing induction on sensory testing in women with chronic low back pain: A pilot study", *Pain Research and Management,* vol. 2017.

Thakurta, R.G., Das, R., Bhattacharya, A.K., Saha, D., Sen, S., Singh, O.P. & Bisui, B. 2012, "Rapid response with ketamine on suicidal cognition in resistant depression", *Indian journal of psychological medicine,* vol. 34, no. 2, pp. 170-175.

von Hehn, C.A., Baron, R. & Woolf, C.J. 2012, "Deconstructing the neuropathic pain phenotype to reveal neural mechanisms", *Neuron,* vol. 73, no. 4, pp. 638-652.

Warncke, T., Stubhaug, A. & Jørum, E. 1997, "Ketamine, an NMDA receptor antagonist, suppresses spatial and temporal properties of burn-induced secondary hyperalgesia in man: a double-blind, cross-over comparison with morphine and placebo", *Pain,* vol. 72, no. 1-2, pp. 99-106.

Woolf, C.J. 2011, "Central sensitization: implications for the diagnosis and treatment of pain", *Pain,* vol. 152, no. 3, pp. S2-S15.

Woolf, C.J. & Thompson, S.W. 1991, "The induction and maintenance of central sensitization is dependent on N-methyl--aspartic acid receptor activation; implications for the treatment of post-injury pain hypersensitivity states", *Pain,* vol. 44, no. 3, pp. 293-299.

World Health Organization 2012, , *Depression – fact sheet number 369.* Available: http://www.who.int/mediacentre/factsheets/fs369/en/ [2014, July 7th].

Zarate, C.,Jr, Machado-Vieira, R., Henter, I., Ibrahim, L., Diazgranados, N. & Salvadore, G. 2010, "Glutamatergic modulators: the future of treating mood disorders?", *Harvard review of psychiatry,* vol. 18, no. 5, pp. 293-303.

Zarate, C.A.,Jr, Singh, J.B., Carlson, P.J., Brutsche, N.E., Ameli, R., Luckenbaugh, D.A., Charney, D.S. & Manji, H.K. 2006, "A randomized trial of an N-methyl-D-aspartate antagonist in treatment-resistant major depression", *Archives of General Psychiatry,* vol. 63, no. 8, pp. 856-864.

TO SLEEP, PERCHANCE TO TRIP: IS DREAMING A NIGHTLY PSYCHEDELIC EXPERIENCE?

JOSIE MALINOWSKI, ENZO TAGLIAZUCCHI, CHRISTOPHER TIMMERMANN, & ROBIN CARHART-HARRIS

INTRODUCTION

Is dreaming a nightly psychedelic experience? The comparison between night-time dreaming and psychedelic consciousness has been made widely, but only recently begun to be explored in psychedelic and dream science. A recent review paper (Kraehenmann, 2017) systematically compared the two states, concluding that "psychedelics acutely induce dreamlike subjective experiences" (p. 1032). There are two main aims of this chapter. First, we will review the comparison of dreaming and psychedelic consciousness, adding some new insights, especially in light of recent research into the phenomenology of dimethyltrptamine (DMT) and narrative analyses of psychedelic experiences. Second, we will consider some theoretical implications of this comparison, especially in terms of the therapeutic potential of dreams and psychedelics, and some wider social/cultural implications of the similarities between the two states.

A BRIEF COMPARISON OF DREAM AND PSYCHEDELIC CONSCIOUSNESS

Kraehenmann notes the following similarities across dreaming and psychedelic consciousness. Both states of consciousness involve: (1)

internally-generated, vivid visual imagery (a "dream" while asleep and an "hallucination" while awake); (2) activation of emotional centres of the brain, and recall of emotional memories; (3) decrease in logical thinking and concomitant increase in fluid, associative, and metaphorical modes of thinking; and (4) changes to the sense of self and to body boundaries, occasionally resulting in nondual awareness.

He noted some differences too: that geometric forms are common in psychedelic experiences but not dreams from rapid-eye-movement (REM) sleep; that dreams are less interactive with the external world; and that REM dreams lack metacognition. But even these differences may not be so great. Geometric shapes may occurring during hypnagogia (dreams experiencing during sleep onset) and hypnopompia (dreams experienced when transitioning to wakefulness) (Bresloff et al., 2002), just as geometric shapes are most likely during initial breakthrough in psychedelic experiences; dreams often incorporate stimuli from the external world such as loud sounds (Nielsen, 2018) or cutaneous sensations (Nielsen, 1993); and in REM-sleep lucid dreams awareness of the dream state is attained.

In addition to the similarities outlined by Kraehenmann (2017), some other crossovers are worth noting. First, both dreams and psychedelic experiences make the return of suppressed or repressed thoughts more likely. For dreams, this idea goes back to Freud (1900/1997) but has only recently been experimentally evidenced (e.g. Wegner et al., 2004). In psychedelic consciousness, the notion that a psychedelic explorer may face the conscious return of unprocessed, suppressed, or traumatic memories dates back to early psychedelic research (e.g. Busch & Johnson, 1950), but has not yet been experimentally researched. However, it has been hypothesised that the healing potential of ayahuasca for trauma is due to the return of suppressed trauma when ingesting this DMT-based psychedelic (Inserra, 2018). In addition, psychedelics have been shown to lead to psychological insight (Carbonaro et al., 2018), as has therapy with dreamwork (over and above therapy without dreamwork) (e.g. Hill, 2018).

Second, both dreams and psychedelic experiences have the potential to be intensely spiritual, impactful and transformative experiences. Jung

(1948) describes "big" dreams, also known as "archetypal" dreams, which include magical, mythical, and spiritual elements, intense emotions, a sense of profundity, feelings of awe, and encounters with strange creatures, such as mythological creatures or wild animals. They are seen as wholly different to "little" dreams, which are more common and usually relate in some way to our own waking lives ("day residue"— Freud 1900/1997), and often feature worries or concerns from waking life. In contrast, "big", impactful dreams lead to a deepening of the dreamer's perception of themselves (Kuiken, Lee, & Singh, 2006). Likewise psychedelic experiences often involve some element of the magical, mystical, or spiritual; for example, in Turton, Nutt, & Carhart-Harris (2014), 6 out of 15 participants described their laboratory-based psilocybin experience as "spiritual", three described it as "mystical", six described a sense of "awe", and one said that their experience would "change the way you look at life" (p.27).

Third, both the dream state and the psychedelic state have long histories of being compared with psychosis. All three states share multiple similarities, such as hallucinations (called "dreams" when asleep), and disordered, illogical cognitions. It has been suggested (Carhart-Harris, 2007), that all three states, along with the "dreamy state" of temporal lobe epilepsy, share a common neural substrate: a medial temporal lobe corollary of pontine-geniculate-occipital (PGO) waves that correlate with REM sleep and may be a piece of the puzzle in how dreams and wakeful dream-like states are generated (Gott, Liley, & Hobson, 2017). In relation to the second point above, it is worth noting that experiences that are considered pathology by some may be considered spiritual by others (British Psychological Society, 2017), perhaps because of the mystical quality of and/or the special knowledge or insights afforded by these experiences.

In the next section, we provide a comparison of the dream state with one particular psychedelic: dimethyltrptamine (DMT).

PHENOMENOLOGICAL SIMILARITIES BETWEEN DREAMING AND THE DMT STATE

In both dreaming and the DMT state an "internal generation of a world-analogue" (Siclari and Tononi, 2016)—meaning an immersion is an analogue world, separate but as immersive and "convincing" as this one—occurs alongside a de-afference or disconnection from external stimuli (Nir and Tononi, 2010; Strassman, 2001). In the DMT state, users usually report an immersion into an "alternative reality or dimension" (Timmermann et al., 2018) which feels more "real" than that of waking experiences (Cott and Rock, 2008; Strassman et al., 1994b) and similarly, dreams are usually felt as an imagined world or virtual reality (Siclari and Tononi, 2016). Furthermore, while visual images are frequently reported (Kahan and Claudatos, 2016; Strassman, 1995; Szára, 1956) emotional, vestibular and somatic reactions are also (but less) commonly identified in both states (Kahan and Claudatos, 2016; Schredl, 2010; Strassman, 2001; Strassman et al., 1994a).

Reduced or complete loss of awareness of the external environment has been noted for both the DMT (Gouzoulis-Mayfrank et al., 2005; Strassman et al., 1994a) and dream states (Nir and Tononi, 2010), while a sense of familiarity with the alternative environment can ensue in both conditions, regardless of the bizarre nature of the content of these experiences (Siclari and Tononi, 2016; Strassman, 2001). These characteristics suggest that in both dreaming and the DMT experience, there might be reduced levels of metacognitive abilities such as reflexive insight (Fox et al., 2013; Kahan and Claudatos, 2016; Rechtschaffen, 1978). Relatedly, volitional and decision-making abilities have been found to be impaired in the DMT state (Gouzoulis-Mayfrank et al., 2005; Strassman et al., 1994a).

Another notorious feature that is commonly reported following DMT-use is an encounter with "beings" or "entities" that appear to communicate with users (Sai-Halász et al., 1958; Strassman, 2001) and drinking of ayahuasca (a brew that contains DMT, which has been used by various indigenous groups for hundreds of years in the Amazon) can lead to subjectively-felt encounters with sentient "beings", usually described as "spirits" by indigenous practitioners (Luna and Amaringo, 1999; Shanon, 2002). In a similar vein, contents in dreams can include interactions with other beings, although these are more often identified as humans (Siclari et al., 2017; Wolman and Kozmová, 2007)—which is not the case with DMT. In both states these interactions can have a "mentalizing" feature (beings encountered appear to have a mind and intentions of their own; Strassman, 2001; Fox et al., 2013) and a significant emotional character, which may be of a threatening or frightening nature (Cott and Rock, 2008; Fox et al., 2013; Strassman, 2001; Valli et al., 2005).

NEUROBIOLOGICAL OVERLAPS

Neurobiological similarities between REM-sleep dreaming and the psychedelic state have been the topic of a review (Carhart-Harris, 2007) and commentary (Carhart-Harris & Nutt, 2014). Put concisely, it has been proposed that both states entail a switch to a fundamental, perhaps ontogenetically and phylogenetically primitive mode of brain and mind function, characterised by a greater predominance of limbic activity, including oscillatory activity most closely associated with the limbic system, such as hippocampal theta activity (Carhart-Harris et al., 2014). Part of the evidence base for this includes the observation that electrical stimulation of relevant medial temporal lobe structures can induce after discharges of oscillatory activity in the theta range alongside dreamlike subjective experiences—including apparent recollections of remote, sometimes childhood memories (Barbeau et al., 2005). We have recently observed the emergence of theta oscillations during the peak of the DMT experience, and this has also been observed with 5-MeO-DMT (Acosta-Urquidi, 2015). Increased limbic activity under psilocybin has also been detected with fMRI (Tagliazucchi et al., 2014). Future work is required to better examine the association between limbic activity and the psychedelic experience, which can be challenging due to limitations in the depth resolution of neuroimaging measures such as EEG and

MEG and poor temporal resolution with fMRI. We hope, however, that a combination of these techniques may serve to overcome some of these limitations, something we are presently exploring in the context of DMT. Speculations about DMT release during sleep being responsible for REM sleep episodes were made in the mid-1980s (Callaway, 1980) and although we are sceptical about this particular hypothesis, it is interesting nonetheless. Intravenous LSD during sleep was found to induce REM sleep (Torda, 1968), as has LSD given just before sleep onset (Muzio et al., 1966) and intensified dreaming was also found when LSD was introduced into sleep (Torda, 1968). In the future, we intend to assess whether IV DMT may have the same REM-promoting effect if administered during NREM sleep. Assessing this via simultaneous EEG and fMRI may be particularly interesting.

In the next section, we continue our comparison of dream and psychedelic consciousness through the narrative analysis method.

NARRATIVE ANALYSIS OF DREAMS AND PSYCHEDELIC CONSCIOUSNESS

Dream narratives are among the earliest written documents in human history (Grunebaum, Caillois et al. 1966). From ancient cultures (e.g., Sumerian, Assyrian, Egyptian) to present day societies, dream narratives have been ascribed different meanings, such as pre- and retrocognition, communion with spirits of the dead and with deities, remote viewing, time travel, and as causing or influencing future events (Pick & Roper 2004). It is interesting to note that many of these uses and interpretations have been given as well to the experiences elicited by "hallucinogens", especially by classic psychedelics (Schultes, Hofmann et al. 2001). In modern times, the interpretation of dream narratives has become widespread in the context of different psychoanalytical theories, which postulate a relationship between dream content and unconscious thoughts and emotions (Pick & Roper 2004). It has been proposed that the psychedelic state could represent a gateway to the unconscious (Carhart-Harris, Leech et al. 2014).

The analysis of dream reports (collected in the form of "dream journals") has also been employed in the context of scientific inquiry. Such analysis required the development of algorithmic or semi-algorithmic tools to allow experimenters to perform unbiased measurements of the contents, semantics and complexity of dream narratives. To cite an example, the link between the physiological and phenomenological aspects of REM sleep episodes was found not only by means of technical developments (e.g. whole-night sleep EEG) but also by analytical tools applied to dream reports (Foulkes 1962). Currently, automated tools known as natural language processing (NLP) can be applied to very large corpora of annotated dream reports such as DreamBank (http://www.dreambank.net/) and Dreamjournal (http://dreamjournal.net/), to reveal recurring topics and investigate how they relate to the individual characteristics of the dreamers (Domhoff and Schneider 2008).

In comparison, the scientific analysis of free narratives of drug-induced experiences has received less attention. This is in spite of large databases that have accumulated thousands of reports over decades, e.g. Erowid Experience Vaults (http://erowid.org/experiences/) and the Bluelight forum (http://www.bluelight.org/vb/content/). As in the case of retrospective analysis of dream narratives, the study of drug-induced phenomenology using first-person reports presents substantial disadvantages related to lack of control or knowledge of the experimenter over important variables such as the identity of the drug and its dose. However, these analyses also present a crucial advantage: they enable research that would be otherwise impossible due to ethical reasons, unreasonable legislation, or a combination of both. While the recent "psychedelic renaissance" emerged to some extent due to a relaxation of drug laws for a small set of substances, a systematic evaluation of the phenomenology of hundreds of natural and synthetic hallucinogens is (and most likely will remain) impossible to perform in a controlled laboratory setting (Nutt, King et al. 2013).

The availability of online resources enables a "comparative phenomenology" of dreams and drug-induced experiences based on the systematic and automated analysis of free narratives (Hobson 2001). Tools such as Latent Semantic Analysis (LSA) enable researchers to measure the similarity between these texts, not only in terms of common groups or ordered sets of contiguous words (n-grams), but also in terms of shared semantic concepts (Landauer, Laham et al. 2004). For instance, the sentences "the garden was full of flowering roses" and "a vase with daisies sits on the table" have no words in common, yet LSA identifies them as similar since they both refer to the same concept (flowers). Sanz and Tagliazucchi applied LSA to measure the semantic similarity between narratives of drug-induced experiences in the Erowid corpus and dream reports of different self-reported lucidity in the Dream journal corpus (Sanz and Tagliazucchi 2018).

Although the results suggest that neither psychedelics, dissociatives, nor deliriants can fully reproduce all features of dream phenomenology, the authors found that reports of LSD-induced experiences ranked first in terms of their similarity to dreams of high-lucidity, while plants of the Datura genus surpassed LSD when considering low-lucidity dreams. Overall, reports of experiences induced by dissociatives (e.g. ketamine, methoxetamine, PCP) ranked first in terms of their similarity to dream reports, followed by deliriant agents (different plants rich in the tropane alkaloids atropine, hyoscyamine and scopolamine), serotonergic psychedelics and entactogens (e.g. MDMA). Dreams are highly dissociative brain states, which could underlie the similarity to the phenomenology induced by drugs such as ketamine or PCP (Morris and Wallach 2014). Conversely, drugs labelled as stimulants, sedatives, antipsychotics and antidepressants resulted in experiences bearing a very low resemblance to dreams. The most frequent words appearing both in the subjective reports of dreams and hallucinogens revealed that terms associated with perception ("see", "visual", "face", "reality", "colour"), emotion ("fear"), setting ("outside", "inside", "street", "front", "behind") and relatives ("mom", "dad", "brother", "parent", "family") were the most prevalent across both experiences.

SUMMARY OF SIMILARITIES BETWEEN DREAMING AND PSYCHEDELIC CONSCIOUSNESS

Research clearly shows that dreaming and psychedelic experiences may share multiple phenomenological features: vivid visual hallucinations; changes to bodily perceptions; intense emotions (some pleasant, some not so); changes to cognitive functioning, such that logic decreases but creativity and hyper-association increases; geometric shapes (rarer in dreams, but not unheard of); the loss of attention to external stimuli in the actual immediate sensorium, but with the potential for such stimuli to become incorporated into the hallucination or the dream; the return of suppressed memories, thoughts, or emotions; experiences that are located in space and time; social interactions within the experiences; spiritual/magical/mystical "big" and "awe-inspiring" experiences; and similarities with other dream-like states such as "psychosis".

Although there are also clear differences between dreaming and psychedelic experiences, the ability of psychedelics to induce dream-like states is of great importance both in terms of the therapeutic potential of sleep/dreaming/psychedelics, and in terms of wider societal implications. In this last part of the chapter, we review these implications.

THEORETICAL IMPLICATIONS

A major theory of sleep and dream function is the emotion-processing theory (e.g. Cartwright, 2011; Hartmann, 1996; Levin & Nielsen, 2007, 2009; Malinowski & Horton, 2015; Vandekerckhove and Cluydts, 2010; Walker & van der Helm, 2009). These theories posit that during REM sleep (as reflected by the subjective mental state of dreaming), cognition is much more hyperassociative, fluid, and creative than it is during waking states. Some waking states, such as daydreaming and mindwandering, may share some of these qualities, but dreaming is at the far end of the spectrum (Fox et al., 2013). The theories further suggest that at least one of the functions of this kind of cognition is to process, or work through, emotional memories and experiences from our waking lives, so that the intensity of the emotion we initially felt during the experience is gradually, over time, turned down, so that we feel less strongly about it in the future.

Much research converges to support this theory, such as: 1) we preferentially dream of emotional experiences (Schredl, 2006; Malinowski & Horton, 2014); 2) we dream especially of unpleasant thoughts that we've tried to suppress (Wegner et al., 2004; Malinowski et al., 2018); 3) REM sleep helps us to regulate our mood (Short & Louca, 2015); and 4) REM sleep reduces our reactivity to emotional stimuli (both negative (Franzen et al., 2009) and positive (Gujar et al., 2011). These studies, and many other lines of evidence, all point to the notion that REM sleep and dreams process our emotional waking-life memories. Walker and van der Helm (2009) describe this process as "overnight therapy".

Sleep and dreaming are also altered in individuals with mood disorders, such as depression. Depressed individuals experience shortened REM latency (it takes less time for them to enter REM following sleep onset), and greater REM duration (length of REM cycle) and density (amount of rapid eye movements per REM cycle) (Palagini et al., 2012). All of these differences point to an intensification of REM sleep in those experiencing depression, and disrupted REM may precede and predict an oncoming depressive episode. Disturbed REM is further evidenced by neuroimaging findings: during REM sleep, depressed individuals experience elevated metabolic activity in temporal and occipital cortices (Palagini et al., 2012), and the efficacy of some antidepressants may derive from their ability to inhibit this activity (Nofzinger, 2004). In terms of dreams, individuals with the highest levels of depression and suicidality tend to have the most nightmares (Ağargün et al, 1998). Depressed individuals also tend to lack the kind of hyperassociative dreaming seen in normal REM dreams (Cartwright et al., 1984; Cartwright et al., 2006).

Likewise, there are now several studies that evidence the emotion-processing, therapeutic potential of psychedelics. Psilocybin reduces end-of-life (Griffith et al., 2016) and cancer-related (Ross et al., 2016) depression and anxiety, and depressive symptoms even in individuals with treatment-resistant depression (Carhart-Harris et al., 2016). Reduction in depression symptoms in treatment-resistant patients is related to decreased blood flow in the temporal cortex, including in the amygdala, as well as a presumed decrease in default mode network (DMN) integrity acutely, followed by an increase post-acutely (Carhart-Harris et al., 2017). The authors suggest this may be understood as a kind of "reset" effect, whereby the initial disintegration of the DMN, enhancing the global connectivity of the brain, and its subsequent re-integration enables normal service to resume. Given that dreams of depressed individuals lack hyperassociativity (Cartwright et al, 1984; Cartwright et al., 2006), it would be expected that this quality of dreaming would be recovered following psychedelic therapy. Roseman, Nutt, & Carhart-Harris (2018) found that the efficacy of psilocybin for treatment-resistant depression was correlated with the mystical/spiritual nature of the experience, and with ego-dissolution. These qualities of the psychedelic experience align closely with the "big" dreams described by Jung (1948).

A formal comparison of the quality of the psychedelic experience and its efficacy for depression treatment on the one hand, and the quality of dream experiences and their efficacy for day-to-day emotion-processing on the other, is currently lacking. However, the following intriguing points may be noted, and may warrant further investigation:

1. "Normal" REM dream cognition and psychedelic neurobiology point to a "hyperassociative", global connectivity in the brain, whereas dreams during depression lack this hyperassociativity;

2. REM sleep in depression involves hyperactivity in some brain areas, including the amygdala, and the classic psychedelic psilocybin reduces amygdala blood flow one day after treatment and this reduction is related to a reduction in depression symptoms;

3. Although the research is underdeveloped, there are early

indications and anecdotal accounts that both dreams and psychedelic experiences bring forth unprocessed, unwelcome thoughts and memories that individuals suppress or repress in waking/non-psychedelic consciousness.

Taking these three points together, we may speculate that by inducing a "big", mystical/spiritual, hyper-connective dream-like experience in individuals for whom REM sleep and dreaming is disturbed and often very unpleasant, psychedelics may facilitate the processing of unpleasant thoughts/memories and thereby achieve a therapeutic effect on a much bigger scale than regular—bizarre and emotional, but not usually intensely mystical—dreams do on a nightly basis. Fox et al. (2013) said that typical night dreams are a more intensified version of daydreams and mind-wandering. Perhaps psychedelics, and "big" dreams, are an even more intensified version of this. With specific reference to psychedelics, the ability to process the dreamlike content while awake and also remember this content afterwards may allow the "waking-dreamer" to derive more insight and understanding from the experience than would otherwise occur in a night dream—particularly if the opportunity for epistemic development is emphasised before and after the psychedelic experience, e.g. by the "trip sitter/s" or "guides".

SOCIETAL IMPLICATIONS

"I have a dream"
– Martin Luther King Jr., 1963

The legislation against psychedelic drugs, and even against conducting scientific research with psychedelics, that formed part of the backlash against their rising popularity in 1960s counterculture had incredible success in convincing the public that these naturally occurring chemicals, which have been used in human religion and culture far further back than recorded history can reach, are dangerous. The tide is beginning to turn once again on this, with study after study now being published showing the medicinal and healing potential of psychedelics (and other currently illicit drugs). Likewise, the psychedelic renaissance is once again beginning to take on a wider political consciousness, with one study finding that a dose of psilocybin reduces authoritarian views (Lyons & Carhart-Harris, 2018), and psychedelic experiences forming part of the new consciousness-raising movement Psychedelic Socialism / Acid Communism (Gilbert, 2017). Understanding that psychedelic consciousness is not only natural to human consciousness (it is something we all do every night, several times) but also functional and progressive (it may help us to process our emotional/traumatic experiences and reduce rigid, authoritarian views) adds weight to this ongoing psychedelic revolution.

CONCLUSION

Dream consciousness and psychedelic consciousness overlap in many ways. The ability of psychedelic drugs to bring about emotional healing may be akin to the life-altering but rare "big" dreams that individuals may experience during sleep, or, more generally, to the everyday emotion-processing that occurs during sleep, reflected in our dreams. Psychedelics states of consciousness and "big" dreams may be an "intensified" version of normal, "little" dreams, which are themselves an intensification of daydreaming and mind-wandering. Understanding the links between the psychedelic and dream state may help to demystify the psychedelic experience to some extent, allowing us to better appreciate it as a fundamental brain/mind-state that we all experience, at some level, every night.

REFERENCES

Acosta-Urquidi, J. (2015). 'QEEG studies of the acute effects of the visionary tryptamine DMT'. *Cosmos and History: The Journal of Natural and Social Philosophy*, 11(2), 115–129.

Ağargün, M. Y., Çilli, A. S., Kara, H., Tarhan, N., Kincir, F., Öz, H. (1998). 'Repetitive and frightening dreams and suicidal behavior in patients with major depression'. *Comprehensive Psychiatry*, 39 (4) 198–202. doi.org/10.1016/S0010-440X(98)90060-8.

Barbeau, E., Wendling, F., Régis, J., Duncan, R., Poncet, M., Chauvel, P., & Bartolomei, F. (2005). 'Recollection of vivid memories after perirhinal region stimulations: synchronization in the theta range of spatially distributed brain areas'. *Neuropsychologia*, 43(9), 1329–1337. doi:10.1016/j.neuropsychologia.2004.11.025

Bresloff, P. C., Cowan, J. D., Golubitsky, M., Thomas, P. J., & Wiener, M. C. (2002). 'What geometric hallucinations tell us about the visual cortex'. *Neural Computation*, 14, 473–491.

Busink, R. & Kuiken, D. (1996). 'Identifying Types of Impactful Dreams: A Replication'. *Dreaming*, 6(2), 97–119.

Busch, A. K., & Johnson, W. C. (1950). 'L.S.D. 25 as an aid in psychotherapy; preliminary report of a new drug'. *Dis Nerv Syst*, 11(8), 241–243.

Callaway, J. C. (1980). 'A proposed mechanism for visions of dream sleep'. *Medical Hypotheses*, 26, 199–124.

Carhart-Harris, R. (2007). 'Waves of the unconscious: The neurophysiology of dreamlike phenomena and its implications for the psychodynamic model of the mind'. *Neuropsychoanalysis*, 9(2), 183–211.

Carhart-Harris, R. L. et al. (2016). 'Psilocybin with psychological support for treatment-resistant depression: an open-label feasibility study'. *Lancet Psychiatry*, https://doi.org/10.1016/S2215-0366(16)30065-7

Carhart-Harris, R., et al. (2017). 'Psilocybin for treatment-resistant depression: fMRI-measured brain mechanisms'. *Scientific Reports*, 7: 13187. doi: 10.1038/s41598-017-13282-7

Carhart-Harris, R. L., Leech, R., Hellyer, P. J., Shanahan, M., Feilding, A., Tagliazucchi, E., & ... Nutt, D. (2014). 'The entropic brain: A theory of conscious states informed by neuroimaging research with psychedelic drugs'. *Frontiers In Human Neuroscience*, 8

Carhart-Harris, R., & Nutt, D. (2014). 'Was it a vision or a waking dream?' *Front. Psychol.*, doi.org/10.3389/fpsyg.2014.00255.

Cartwright, R. (2011). *The Twenty-Four Hour Mind: the Role of Sleep and Dreaming in Our Emotional Lives*. Oxford: Oxford University Press.

Cartwright, R. D., Luten, A., Young, M., Mercer, P., and Bears, M. (1998). 'Role of REM sleep and dream affect in overnight mood regulation: a study of normal volunteers'. *Psychiatry Res.* 81, 1–8.doi:10.1016/S0165-1781(98)00089-4

Cartwright, R., Agargun, M. Y., Kirkby, J., & Friedman, J. K. (2006). 'Relation of dreams to waking concerns'. *Psychiatry Research* 141, 261–270.

Cott, C., and Rock, A. (2008). 'Phenomenology of N,N-Dimethyltryptamine Use: A Thematic Analysis'. *J. Sci. Explor.* 22, 359–370.

Domhoff, G. W. and A. Schneider (2008).'Studying dream content using the archive and search engine on DreamBank.net'. *Conscious Cogn* 17(4): 1238–1247.

Euston, D. R., Tatsuno, M., & McNaughton, B. L. (2007). 'Fast-forward playback of recent memory sequences in prefrontal cortex during sleep'. *Science*, 318, 1147–1150.

Fox, K. C., Nijeboer, S., Solomonova, E., Domhoff, G. W., & Christoff, K. (2013). 'Dreaming as mind wandering: Evidence from functional neuroimaging and first-personcontent reports'. *Frontiers in Human Neuroscience*, 7, 412. http://dx.doi.org/10.3389/fnhum.2013.00412.

Foulkes, W. D. (1962). 'Dream reports from different stages of sleep'. *J Abnorm Soc Psychol* 65: 14–25.

Franzen, P. L., Buysse, D. J., Dahl, R. E, Thompson, W., & Siegle, G. J. (2009). 'Sleep deprivation alters pupillary reactivity to emotional stimuli in healthy young adults'. *Biological Psychology*, 80 (3), 300–305.

Freud (1900/1997). *The Interpretation of Dreams.* London: Wordsworth Classics.

Gilbert, J. (2017, Sept.). *Psychedelic socialism: The politics of consciousness, the legacy of counterculture, and the future of the left.* Retrieved from https://jeremygilbertwriting.files. wordpress.com/2017/09/psychedelic-socialism2.pdf.

Gott, J. A., Liley, D. T. J., & Hobson, J. A. (2017). 'Towards a functional understanding of PGO waves'. *Frontiers of Human Neuroscience*, 11(89), 1–12.

Gouzoulis-Mayfrank, E., Heekeren, K., Neukirch, a, Stoll, M., Stock, C., Obradovic, M., et al. (2005). 'Psychological effects of (S)-ketamine and N,N-dimethyltryptamine (DMT): a double-blind, cross-over study in healthy volunteers'. *Pharmacopsychiatry* 38, 301–311. doi:10.1055/s-2005-916185

Griffiths, R. R. et al. (2016). 'Psilocybin produces substantial and sustained decreases in depression and anxiety in patients with life-threatening cancer: A randomized double-blind trial'. *Journal of Psychopharmacology*, 30(12), 1181–1197. doi: 10.1177/0269881116675513

Grunebaum, G. E. v., R. Caillois and Gustave E. von Grunebaum Center for Near Eastern Studies. (1966). *The dream and human societies.* Berkeley, University of California Press.

Gujar, N., Yoo, S-S. H., Hu, P., & Walker, M. P. (2011). 'Sleep deprivation amplifies reactivity of brain reward networks biasing the appraisal of positive emotional experiences'. *The Journal of Neuroscience*, 31(12), 4466–4474.

Hartmann, E. (1996). 'Outline for a theory on the nature and functions of dreaming'. *Dreaming*, 6(2), 147–170.

Hill, C. (in press). 'Benefits of dreamwork in psychotherapy'. In R. J. Hoss & R. P. Gongloff (Eds.), *Dreams: Understanding biology, psychology, and culture, Vol 2* (pp. xx-xx). ABC-CLIO.

Hobson, J. A. (2001). *The dream drugstore : chemically altered states of consciousness*. Cambridge, Mass., MIT Press.

Inserra, A. (2018). 'Hypothesis: The psychedelic ayahuasca heals traumatic memories via a sigma 1 receptor-mediated epigenetic-mnemonic process'. *Frontiers in Pharmacology*, 9(300), 1–13.

Kahan, T. L., and Claudatos, S. (2016). 'Phenomenological features of dreams: Results from dream log studies using the Subjective Experiences Rating Scale (SERS)'. *Conscious. Cogn.* 41, 159–176. doi:10.1016/j.concog.2016.02.007.

Kahan, T. L., & LaBerge, S. L. (1996). 'Cognition and metacognition in dreaming and waking: Comparisons of first and third-person ratings'. *Dreaming*, 6(4), 235–249.

Kraehenmann, R. (2017). 'Dreams and psychedelics: Neurophenomenological comparison and therapeutic implications'. *Current Neuropharmacology*, 15, 1032–1042.

Kraehenmann, R., D. Pokorny, L. Vollenweider, K. H. Preller, T. Pokorny, E. Seifritz and F. X. Vollenweider (2017). 'Dreamlike effects of LSD on waking imagery in humans depend on serotonin 2A receptor activation'. *Psychopharmacology* (Berl) 234(13): 2031–2046.

Kron, T., & Brosh, A. (2003). 'Can Dreams During Pregnancy Predict Postpartum Depression?' *Dreaming*, 13 (2), 67–81.

Kuiken, D., Lee, M., & Eng, T., & Singh, T. (2006). 'The Influence of Impactful Dreams on Self-Perceptual Depth and Spiritual Transformation'. *Dreaming*, 16(4), 258–279. DOI: 10.1037/1053-0797.16.4.258

Jung, C. G. (1948). 'On the nature of dreams'. In R. F. C. Hull (Trans.), *Dreams* (pp. 69–84). London: Routledge.

Landauer, T. K., D. Laham and M. Derr (2004). 'From paragraph to graph: latent semantic analysis for information visualization'.*Proc Natl Acad Sci USA* 101 Suppl 1: 5214–5219.

Levin, R. & Nielsen, T. A. (2007). 'Disturbed dreaming, posttraumatic stress disorder, and affect distress: a review and neurocognitive model'. *Psychological Bulletin*, 133(3), 482–528.

Levin, R. & Nielsen, T. A. (2009). 'Nightmares, bad dreams, and emotion dysregulation'. *Current Directions in Psychological Science*, 18(2), 84–88.

Luna, L. E., and Amaringo, P. (1999). *Ayahuasca Visions: The Religious Iconography of a Peruvian Shaman*. North Atlantic Books.

Malinowski, J., & Horton, C.L. (2014) 'Emotion but not stress modulates the incorporation of waking experiences into dreams'. *Dreaming*, 24(1), 18–31.

Malinowski, J. E. & Horton, C. L. (2015). 'Metaphor and hyperassociativity: the imagination mechanisms behind emotion assimilation in sleep and dreaming'. *Frontiers in Psychology*, 6 (1132), 1–19.

Malinowski, J. E., Carr, M., Edwards, C. L., Ingarfill, A., & Pinto, A. (2018). *The effects of dream rebound: Evidence for emotion-processing theories of dreaming*. Manuscript submitted for publication.

Morris, H. and J. Wallach (2014). 'From PCP to MXE: a comprehensive review of the non⬚ medical use of dissociative drugs'. *Drug Testing and Analysis* 6(7–8): 614–632.

Muzio, J. N., Roffwarg, H. P., and Kaufman, E. (1966). 'Alterations in the nocturnal sleep cycle resulting from LSD'. *Electroencephalogr. Clin. Neurophysiol.* 21, 313–324. doi: 10.1016/0013-4694(66) 90037-X

Nichols, D. E. (2016). 'Psychedelics'. *Pharmacol Rev* 68(2): 264–355.

Nir, Y. and G. Tononi (2010). 'Dreaming and the brain: from phenomenology to neurophysiology'. *Trends Cogn Sci* 14(2): 88–100.

Nielsen, T. (1993.) 'Changes in the kinaesthetic content of dreams following somatosensory stimulation of leg muscles during REM sleep'. *Dreaming*, 3(2), 99–113.

Nielsen, T. (2018). 'Microdream neurophenomenology: A paradigm for dream neuroscience'. In K. Cristoff & K. C. R. Fox (eds), *The Oxford Handbook of Spontaneous Thought: Mind-Wandering, Creativity, and Dreaming*. Oxford: Oxford Library of Psychology.

Nir, Y., and Tononi, G. (2010). 'Dreaming and the brain: from phenomenology to neurophysiology'. *Trends Cogn. Sci.* 14, 88–100. doi:10.1016/j.biotechadv.2011.08.021.Secreted.

Nofzinger, E. A. (2004). 'What can neuroimaging findings tell us about sleep disorders?' *Sleep Med*, 5, Suppl 1:S16–22.

Nutt, D. J., L. A. King and D. E. Nichols (2013). 'Effects of Schedule I drug laws on neuroscience research and treatment innovation'. *Nat Rev Neurosci* 14(8): 577–585.

Palagini L., Baglioni, C., Ciapparelli, A., Gemignani, A., & Riemann, D. (2013). 'REM sleep dysregulation in depression: State of the art'. *Sleep Medicine Reviews*, 17(5):377–90. doi: 10.1016/j.smrv.2012.11.001

Pick, D. and L. Roper (2004). *Dreams and history : the interpretation of dreams from ancient Greece to modern psychoanalysis.* London ; New York, Routledge.

Preston, G. C., C. Brazell, C. Ward, P. Broks, M. Traub and S. M. Stahl (1988). 'The scopolamine model of dementia: determination of central cholinomimetic effects of physostigmine on cognition and biochemical markers in man'. *J Psychopharmacol* 2(2): 67–79.

Rechtschaffen, A. (1978). 'The single-mindedness and isolation of dreams'. *Sleep* 1, 97–109

Roseman, L., Nutt, D., & Carhart-Harris, R. (2018), 'Quality of Acute Psychedelic Experience Predicts Therapeutic Efficacy of Psilocybin for Treatment-Resistant Depression'. *Frontiers in Pharmacology*, 8(974), 1–10. doi: 10.3389/fphar.2017.00974.

Ross, S., et al. (2016). 'Rapid and sustained symptom reduction following psilocybin treatment for anxiety and depression in patients with life-threatening cancer: a randomized controlled trial'. *Journal of Psychopharmacology*, 30(12) 1165–1180. doi: 10.1177/0269881116675512.

Sai-Halász, A., Brunecker, G., and Szára, S. (1958). 'Dimethyl-tryptamin : ein neues Psychoticum'. *Psychiatr. Neurol.* (Basel). 135, 258–301.

Sanz, C. and E. Tagliazucchi (2018). 'The Experience Elicited by Hallucinogens Presents the Highest Similarity to Dreaming within a Large Database of Psychoactive Substance Reports'. *Front Neurosci* 12: 7.

Schredl, M. (2006). 'Factors affecting the continuity between waking and dreaming: emotional intensity and emotional tone of the waking-life event'. *Sleep & Hypnosis*. 8(1), 1–5.

Schredl, M. (2010). 'Dream content analysis: Basic principles'. *Int. J. Dream Res.* 3, 65–73. doi:10.11588/ijodr.2010.1.474.

Schultes, R. E., A. Hofmann and C. Rätsch (2001). *Plants of the gods: their sacred, healing, and hallucinogenic powers.* Rochester, Vt., Healing Arts Press.

Shanon, B. (2002). 'Ayahuasca visualizations: a structural topology'. *J. Conscious. Stud.* 9, 3–30.

Short, M. A., & Louca, M. (2015). 'Sleep deprivation leads to mood deficits in healthy adolescents'. *Sleep Medicine*, 16, 987–993.

Siclari, F., and Tononi, G. (2016). 'Sleep and Dreaming', in *The Neurology of Consciousness*, eds. S. Laureys, O. Gosseries, and G. Tononi (Elsevier Ltd), 107–128.

Strassman, R. J. (1995). 'Human psychopharmacology of N,N-dimethyltryptamine'. *Behav. Brain Res.* 73, 121–124. doi:10.1016/0166-4328(96)00081-2.

Strassman, R. (2001). *DMT: the spirit molecule.* Rochester, Vermont: Park Street Press.

Strassman, R. J., Qualls, C. R., Uhlenhuth, E. H., and Kellner, R. (1994a). 'Dose-response study of N,N-dimethyltryptamine in humans. II. Subjective effects and preliminary results of a new rating scale'. *Arch. Gen. Psychiatry* 51, 98–108. doi:10.1001/archpsyc.1994.03950020022002.

Strassman, R. J., Qualls, C. R., Uhlenhuth, E. H., and Kellner, R. (1994b). 'Dose-Response Study of N,N-Dimethyltryptamine In Humans. II. Subjective effects and preliminary results of a new rating scale'. *Arch. Gen. Psychiatry* 51, 98–108.

Szára, S. (1956). 'Dimethyltryptamin: Its metabolism in man; the relation of its psychotic effect to the serotonin metabolism'. *Experientia* 12, 441–442. doi:10.1007/BF02157378.

Tagliazucchi, E., Carhart⊠Harris, R., Leech, R., Nutt, D., & Chialvo, D. R. (2014). 'Enhanced repertoire of brain dynamical states during the psychedelic experience'. *Human Brain Mapping*, 35(11), 5442–5456. doi:10.1002/hbm.22562

Timmermann C., Roseman L., Schartner M., Williams L., Erritzoe D., Muthukumaraswamy S., Leech R., Nutt D., Carhart-Harris R. (2018). *Dynamic shifts in experience and brain activity induced by DMT.* Paper presented at the Association for the Scientific Study of Consciousness meeting. Krakow.

Torda, C. (1968). 'Contribution to serotonin theory of dreaming' (LSD infusion). *N.Y. State J. Med.* 68, 1135–1138

Toro, G. and B. Thomas (2007). *Drugs of the Dreaming: Oneirogens: Salvia divinorum and other dream-enhancing plants*, Simon and Schuster.

Turton, S., Nutt, D. J., & Carhart-Harris, R. L. (2014). 'A qualitative report on the subjective experience of intravenous psilocybin administered in an fMRI environment'. *Current Drug Abuse Reviews*, 7(2), 117–127.

Valli, K., Revonsuo, A., Pälkäs, O., Ismail, K. H., Ali, K. J., and Punamäki, R. L. (2005). 'The threat simulation theory of the evolutionary function of dreaming: Evidence from dreams of traumatized children'. *Conscious. Cogn.* 14, 188–218. doi:10.1016/S1053-8100(03)00019-9.

Vandekerckhove, M., & Cluydts, R. (2010). 'The emotional brain and sleep: an intimate relationship'. *Sleep Medicine Reviews*, 14, 219–226.

Walker, M. P. & van der Helm, E. (2009). 'Overnight therapy? The role of sleep in emotional brain processing'. *Psychological Bulletin*, 135(5), 731–748.

Wegner, D. M., Wenzlaff, R. M., & Kozak, M. (2004). 'Dream rebound: The return of suppressed thoughts in dreams'. *Psychological Science*, 15, 232–236. http://dx.doi.org/10.1111/j.0963-7214.2004.00657.x

Wolman, R. N., and Kozmová, M. (2007). 'Last night I had the strangest dream: Varieties of rational thought processes in dream reports'. *Conscious. Cogn.* 16, 838–849. doi:10.1016/j.concog.2006.09.009.

DARK RETREAT & PSYCHEDELICS— A FEMTHEOGEN?

REGINA U. HESS

RECONNECTING WITH OUR PRIMORDIAL DIVINE FEMININE FOUNDATION

With its goals of enhancement of self-realization and training of all senses through entering altered states of consciousness[1], the ancient high-level practice of prolonged darkness meditation, used for example as a secret practice in Tantric Buddhism can be found across a wide range of spiritual and indigenous traditions. The crucial factor in dark meditation is to keep the eyes open, as this potentiates the experience. This can be achieved either with a blindfold that leaves enough space inside to leave the eyes open—or in a room that is entirely dark. Prolonged darkness meditation is not at all comparable to closing one's eyes as not to see. Frustrating the brain that wants to produce vision is what evokes a profound expanded state of consciousness.

Mantak Chia, a South-Asian expert in dark retreat for decades, suggests that in prolonged darkness a biochemical reaction in the brain might cause the syntheses of extraordinary molecules such as DMT, which can induce altered states of perception. According to Chia[2], the darkness actualizes successively higher states of consciousness, that might correlate with the synthesis and accumulation of psychedelic chemicals in the brain to the level of an endogenous psychedelic experience. However, to date these assumptions have not been confirmed in research findings. At higher levels, ingested or endogenously produced psychotropic substances are associated with producing spiritual visions, and transcendent and mystical experiences. 5-MEO-DMT for example is found in large quantities within the venom of the toad known as *Bufo alvarius*. This amphibian remains buried underground[3] in an inert state for long periods of time, a state reminiscent of the darkness and void of existence of a prolonged dark retreat.

There is a largely forgotten dimension to the darkness and this is the fertile darkness of the womb of creation: the Divine Feminine and the cyclical nature of humans, of certain plants and animals, and of the moon[4]. A process of conception is involved, a process of gestation, and a process of birth. It is here in the darkness that the magic of the Sacred Feminine occurs: the mysteries of life in their cyclical nature. It is in the absence of light that we humans undergo a spectacular metamorphosis into a body-mind-spirit unity before being birthed into the world on our planet. In cultural, religious, and scientific terms, darkness is seen as primal and as such is within us all. From a mythological viewpoint, reflected in many creation myths, the primal or primordial ground is associated with the experience of oneness with God, in the darkness where all is one. Darkness is associated with the Great Mother[5], the spirit of the night and giver of life assumed as "Nature itself, the great mystery of the unbroken unity"[6].

PSYCHEDELIC EXPERIENCE AS A FORM OF YOGA

Psychedelic substances—*psychedelics* (from the Greek word *psyche* for "mind", "soul" and *delos* meaning "visible" or "manifest")—have also been called *entheogens, psychotomimetics*, and *hallucinogens*. Depending on the context[7] they are termed medicines, drugs, tools, props, et cetera. Psychedelics may expand the mind, or manifest more of it, actually enabling the mind[8] to process information from novel, multiple, or even parallel perspectives[9]. Another view says psychedelics expand the "holes in the sieve", or "reducing valve"[10] of ordinary consciousness, so that more information is received, both from within and without the sensory nervous system. A further perspective sees psychedelics as merely disrupting, or perturbing, normal brain chemistry rather than actually "expanding consciousness"[11], so that psychedelic visions are actually a natural response to entopic neurochemical chaos. Still another view says they are dangerous drugs of abuse about which there can be no discussion.

Psychedelics remained largely undiscovered in the West until the late nineteenth century. From 1901–02, in his landmark lecture series on *The Varieties of Religious Experience*[12], American psychologist Williams James described his experience with nitrous oxide, a psychedelic compound used as an analgesic in medicine. Some years later, in 1952, Aldous Huxley published a record of his experimentation with mescaline, a psychedelic derived from a cactus local to Central and North America. He reported seeing a bouquet of flowers "shining with their own inner light and all but quivering under the pressure of the significance with which they were charged".[13]

Why are we so fascinated by psychedelics? Perhaps because they seem to occasion transformative experiences that help us to see the world differently, and thus help us to adapt and grow? These experiences can be especially useful in times of disorder or trauma. The enhancement of psychospiritual growth through the use of altered states of consciousness with endogenic and exogenic induction methods constitutes one main area of interest within the field of transpersonal psychology, and is perhaps simply a newer term for an older pursuit—such as yoga.

Among the factors leading to the widespread proliferation of yoga in the West is the translation into English of Patanjali's *Yoga Sutras* as a philosophical, yet also practical guide to the attainment and practice of yoga. Sutra 4.1 is relevant to the investigation of psychedelics. It speaks of "the subtle attainments" of yoga, i.e. advanced practices, saying: "The subtle attainments can be achieved through birth, herbs/drugs, mantra, or austerities."[14] According to Sutra 4.1, some individuals are simply inborn with natural abilities to achieve "subtle attainments"; others have to work at it through mantra and other austerities, such as *asanas*, fasting and abstaining from pleasures. However, many people need more help, according to Patanjali. In some instances, something a little extra is needed to help the practitioner achieve the subtle attainments. In the West, where materialism and "monophasic"[15] consciousness predominates, psychedelic 'props' may be particularly useful. Indeed, psychedelics guru Timothy Leary himself referred to LSD as "modern yoga".[16]

PSYCHEDELIC INITIATION RITES IN DARK CAVES—THE ELEUSINIAN MYSTERIES

Myths and sagas from all around the world refer to the mystery of darkness. In Buddhism, practices involving darkness relate to the end of suffering.[17] The disciple who wishes to embody spiritual power must undergo extended periods of solitude in silence and darkness, seen as periods of gestation in darkness during which the mythical fruits can grow. Ancient oracle sites in Greece such as the Oracle of Delphi[18] or the Oracle of Poseidon, also called the Oracle of the Souls, used dark caves and subterranean labyrinths at temples where initiates and visitors entered altered states of consciousness.

The Eleusinian Mysteries are a famous example of initiation. The paradigm uniting life and death was the seed implanted into the ground, entrusted in the darkness of the earth, in the expectation that it would return and sprout, without which there could be no life here in the realm above. The initiates experienced a journey of the spirit to a reality in a parallel dimension establishing pathways of communication and reciprocal visitation that defined the terms for humankind's relationship with Gaia. The initiates were offered the opportunity to identify themselves with the most basic cycles of nature at the deepest level of their existence. The great hall of initiation at Eleusis was an architectural similitude of a cave, a metaphor which can be traced back to the Paleolithic times when humans rose as *"Homo spiritualis"*. The cave was the womb of Gaia—the vulva to a world beyond and a gateway for birth into this realm of ordinary living[19]. The cave offered a release from ordinary seeing. On the night of the great Mystery, the initiates returned to the hall of the sanctuary, after their spiritual journey to Eleusinian mysteries. They experienced themselves reborn and returned to their chthonic family. The valence of death became positive through personal experience. The visionary experience in the Eleusinian sanctuary and the gathering and use of magical entheogens is well documented. It includes the symbol of the opium poppy capsule—narcosis as induced by opium as symbolic of death. The initiates were exposed to a glimpse of a transcendent reality by the ingestion of a powerful psychoactive drink called *kykeon* (mix) possibly derived from ergot (*Claviceps purpurea*). Ergot is a fungus that infects both wild grains such as wild fleabane and cultivated grains such as barley. It contains LSA alkaloids—with an impact similar to LSD—which are also found in Mesoamerican morning glory or Hawaiian baby woodrose seeds. The mushroom was seen as the fermentation of the earth.

TOWARDS A NEW ELEUSIS

Shortly before his death, Swiss chemist Albert Hofmann, the discoverer of LSD wrote: "Only a new Eleusis could help mankind to survive the threatening catastrophe in Nature and human society and bring a new period of happiness." Hofmann saw the crisis that we humans have created by our destruction of our planet Gaia and the possible extinction of our species. By "a new Eleusis", he was proposing to heal the dangerous separation of humankind's individual consciousness from its natural immersion in the surrounding environmental universe.[20]

C.G. Jung diagnosed modern Western civilization as having a cultural complex—a dissociative disorder—which he ascribed to the separation of our human nature from Nature as a whole[21][22]. He assumed interconnectedness as a living animated reality—as a primordial foundation that carries our archaic knowledge. Entering altered states of consciousness, such as those induced by darkness meditation and psychedelics, can help us to revive our archaic knowledge and integrate it into our modern psyche, and to reconnect with our primordial Divine Feminine foundation.

THE ARCHETYPE OF DEATH AND REBIRTH

We are identified with the ego structures that we developed to navigate the world and which are solidified after adolescence. Depending on the dose, psychedelics can have an ego-dissolving impact.[23] This might be associated with a death–rebirth experience in a literal and metaphorical sense of experience. The disidentification with our ego structures and layers of conditioning allows an opening to something larger, often with an intense spiritual quality. This mysterious source has many names. From an archetypal psychology perspective it is termed Self. The Self is beyond any archetype, for it is the primal unity from which archetypes flow. In dissolving ego, we can open ourselves up to the primordial energies of Self. As the process progresses, the ego emerges again, but in reconstituted form. It takes time and repeated experience for transformation[24]. Beneficial as it may be, there are many contraindications that have to be taken seriously for every individual. Engagement with the Self is important at a personal and collective level. It can include greater openness to the qualities of love, harmony and co-operation. The term *femtheogen*[25] expresses how psychedelics can enhance the feminine principle to act as a bridge between ego and Self. Positively-charged high archetypal penetrance states can amplify our perception of beauty in what Huxley called the "positive transfiguration"[26]. Hofmann felt that many people were without any innate access to the realization of beauty, and that a psychedelic experience could give them a visionary experience of nature[27]. Many of us need to go through shadow processing of conditioning, traumas, and comforts through death-rebirth experiences for transformation. In order to make use of these experiences, we need an enquiring and open mindset, a safe and supportive setting and the tools to process and integrate the material into the consciousness so that it can be useful to us in our daily lives. Experience without integration can be an opportunity lost.

CIVILIZING OUR BARBARIC SELF

Endogenously and exogenously induced consciousness-expanding practices have been used for thousands of years by many cultures around the world in ritualistic applications to enhance and assist spiritual and psychological development, healing and wellbeing[28]. Natural examples of expanded states of consciousness include birth, near-death, death, and extreme experiences. Endogenously induced, i.e. non substance-based methods of consciousness-expansion, can include dreams, holotropic breathwork, dark retreat, trance, dance etc. Exogenous induction methods may include the use of psychedelic substances such as LSD, psilocybin, mescaline, and entactogens such as MDMA. When administered responsibly within a skilled setting, both endogenous and exogenous induction—can have a great medicinal, therapeutic, spiritual and social potential. Scientific studies have demonstrated that mind-expanding substances—when used wisely— are not only non-addictive and non-toxic but can be of great value for opening our minds and hearts, for evoking healing processes, and for facilitating mystical experiences involving a deeper interconnectedness of body-mind-spirit, with others, with Nature and with the cosmos.

Maxwell[29] suggests that our barbaric self is in need of civilizing. Healing the fragmentation that is at the root of the current world crisis requires an integrated epistemology—a "deep science" that integrates both the rational knowledge of scientific empiricism and the intuitive knowing of spiritual experience—what Anderson[30] terms "Sacred Science". All is seen as sacred—as an I–Thou relationship instead of an I–it relationship. Here we enter the eye of the needle. It requires heroic action on all our parts—individually, collectively, and globally[31]. In the fierce urgency of Now, if a genuine planetary wisdom-culture fully emerges and becomes stable, taking radical responsibility for transformation and social change for the restoration of the wholeness of the Earth in harmony with humanity, then the turning of the wheel may become the great participatory planetary transition[32 33 34].

We humans have responsibility—not power. May we civilize our barbaric Self by remedying our lost connection with Nature—to create, all together, a life-honouring civilization on Earth. May we restore our relationship with Nature to reintegrate our archaic mind into our modern soul. Let this be a spiritual task—like the initiates finding their way to a New Eleusis—a sanctuary of the fertile Divine Feminine darkness as our primordial foundation elaborately intertwined with endogenic and exogenic psychedelic induction for initiation into modern rites of passage.

We have to ask ourselves again the primordial questions: What is life? What is the meaning of our human life? What are we doing on this beautiful but damaged planet? What are we doing to each other and with each other? The questions posed by mind-expanding substances are the age-old questions of meaning and transcendence— can we learn to become responsible for our existence? This is truly an ecstatic adventure.[35]

Towards a New Eleusis—An Ecstatic Femtheogen Adventure.

ENDNOTES

1. The topic of dark retreat has been dealt with in more detail in this book chapter: Hess, R.U. (2017a). 'The ancient practice of dark retreat meditation: An endogenous psychedelic and Divine Feminine encounter'. *Implications From Transpersonal Theory, Research, and Practice*. Chapter 4. In McMullin, Hess, and Boucouvalas (Eds.) (2017*)*. *Metamorphosis Through Conscious Living. A Transpersonal Psychology Perspective*. Cambridge, UK: Cambridge Scholars Publishing.

2. Chia, M. (2014). *Endless Cosmic Orgasm. Dark room Retreat for Lucid Living, Lucid Dreaming & Lucid Death*. Los Angeles, CA: DolphinOlogy Inc.

3. Martinez-Cordero, M. A. (2018). The Convergence of Healers and Explorers of Consciousness at 3rd Global Transpersonal Symposium 'From Inner Peace to World Peace', Veracruz, Mexico. *Integral Transpersonal Journal Volume X*, Number X, 2018, 138-147

4. Hess see 1

5. Lowenthal, M. (2003). *Dawning of clear light. A Western Approach to Tibetan Dark Retreat meditation*. Charlottesville, VA: Hampton Road Publishing

6. Lowenthal see 4

7. Weisbecker, T. J. (2017) 'Hallucinogenic metamorphosis: An overview of hallucinogen-induced transformative mystical experience'. In McMullin, Hess, & Boucouvalas (Eds.) (2017). *Metamorphosis Through Conscious Living: A Transpersonal Psychology Perspective*. Cambridge, UK: Cambridge Scholars Publishing.

8. Weisbecker see 6

9. Kent, J. L. (2010). *Psychedelic Information Theory: Shamanism in the Age of Reason*. Seattle, WA: PIT Press/Supermassive.

10. Huxley, A. (1952). 'The Doors of Perception'. *Mental, 98*. pp. 13-15.

11. For example Tart, C. T. (1975). *States of Consciousness* (p. 206). New York, NY: EP Dutton.

12. James, W. (2015). *The varieties of religious experience*. Open Road Media.

13. Huxley, A. (1952). 'The Doors of Perception'. *Mental, 98*. p. 9.

14. Dass, R. (1971). *Be Here Now*. San Cristobal, NM: Lama Foundation; Dass, R. (2010). *Be Love Now: The Path of the Heart*. New York, NY: HarperOne.

15. Fadiman, J. (2011). *The Psychedelic Explorer's Guide: Safe, Therapeutic, and Sacred Journeys*. Rochester, VT: Park Street Press, Inner Traditions/Bear & Co.

16. For example (a) Savage, C. (1968). Psychedelic therapy. In *Research in Psychotherapy Conference*, 3rd, May-Jun, 1966, Chicago, IL, US. American Psychological Association; (b) Kurland, A. A., Unger, S., Shaffer, J. W., & Savage, C. (1967). Psychedelic therapy utilizing LSD in the treatment of the alcoholic patient: A preliminary report. *American Journal of Psychiatry, 123*(10), 1202-1209; (c) Pahnke, W. N., Kurland, A. A., Unger, S., Savage, C., Wolf, S., & Goodman, L. E. (1970). Psychedelic therapy (utilizing LSD) with cancer patients. *Journal of Psychoactive Drugs, 3*(1), 63-75.

17. Heaven, R., & Buxton, S. (2005). *Darkness Visible. Awakening Spiritual Light Through Darkness Meditation*. Rochester, VT: Destiny Books.

18. Delphys is a Greek word meaning "womb", and the oracle is the process of uncovering secret wisdom and knowledge.

19. Ruck, C. A. P. (2017). The Gaia project: Restoring ancient mysteries. In Sessa, B., Luke, D., Cameron A., King, D. Tollan, A. & Wyrd, N. (2017). *Breaking Convention: Psychedelic Pharmacology for the 21st Century*. London, UK: Strange Attractor Press, pp. 217-228

20. Ruck, C. A. P. (2017) see 17

21. Sabini, M. (2014). 'The Earth has a Soul. Sabini, M.' (2016). *The Earth Has a Soul. C. G. Jung on Nature, Technology and Modern Life*. Berkeley, California, USA: North Atlantic Books.

22. Hess, R. U. (2018, forthcoming). Book Review. The Earth has a Soul. C. G. Jung on Nature, Technology and Modern Life by Meredith Sabini (2016). Berkeley, California, USA: North Atlantic Books. xvi + 252 pp, paperback, $ 18,95. *The Humanistic Psychologist, Special Issue: 60 years Transpersonal Psychology*.

23. Read, T. (2017). 'Psychedelics and Numinous Experiences'. In Sessa, B., Luke, D., Cameron A., King, D. Tollan, A. & Wyrd, N. (2017). *Breaking Convention: Psychedelic Pharmacology for the 21st Century*. London, UK: Strange Attractor Press, pp. 287-296

24. Ruck, C. A. P. (2017) see 17

25. Papaspyrou, M. (2015). 'Femtheogenes'. In Dickens, R., Read, T. (Eds). (2015). *Out of the Shadow*. London, UK: Muswell Hill Press.

26. Huxley, A. (1977). *Moksha*. Rochester, Vermont: Park Street Press, p. 204

27. Walsh, R. & Grob, C. (Eds.) (2005). *Higher Wisdom: Eminent Elders Explore the Continuing Impact of Psychedelics*. NYC, NY: State University Press, p. 51

28. Hess, R. U. (2017b). 'Embodying the sacred at the threshold of life and death, wounding and healing'. In Jahrsetz, I.B., Hess, R.U., Miller, J., & Pervötz, R. (Eds.) (2017). *The Intimacy of Consciousness Exploration and Transpersonal Psychotherapy: Coming Home*. Cambridge, UK: Cambridge Scholars Publishing.

29. Maxwell 2013. Maxwell, T. P. (2003). Integral spirituality, deep science, and ecological awareness. *Zygon, 38*(2), 257-276.

30. Anderson, R. (2017). Toward a sacred science—Reflecting forward. *The Humanistic Psychologist*. Advance online publication. http//dx.doiorg/10.1037/hum0000079

31. Hess, R. U. (2018, forthcoming) see 22

32. Korten, T. (2007). *From Empire To Earth Community*. Oakland, CA: Berrett-Koehler Publishers

33. Macy, J. (2007). *World as Lover, World as Self: Courage for Global Justice and Ecological Renewal*. Berkeley, CA: Parallax Books.

34. Raskin, (2016). Raskin, P. (2016). *Journey to Earthland: The Great Transition to Planetary Civilization*. Boston, MA: Tellus Institute

35. Metzner, R. (Ed.) (1968/2015). 'The Ecstatic Adventure'. NYC, NY: Macmillan Publishing. [modified in e-mail, 2015]. In Passie, T. & Permantier, P. (2016). *Harry C. Kane. Mandala of Life*. Solothurn, Switzerland: Nachtschatten Publishers. p.17.

THE ANECHOIC DARKROOM AS A PSYCHEDELIC STATE

DAVID LUKE, CHRISTOPHER TIMMERMANN, MENDEL KAELEN & BETH BELL-LANGFORD

Darkroom retreats are an ancient esoteric practice among many different cultural lineages, such as various sects of Tibetan Buddhism and among the Kogi tribe of Columbia. Among the Nyingmapa and the Bönpo Buddhist traditions such practices, sometimes entailing entering into darkness for forty-nine days or more, are usually reserved for advanced practitioners and are considered a preparation for death (e.g., Achard, 2008).

Alternatively, the Kogi identify selected children from their communities, those divined at birth to become shamans, and raise them for either the first nine or eighteen years of their life entirely in the dark environment of a cave. With nothing but enough background ambient light so that their eyes develop normally, they never see the outside world in daylight for all that time. They are nurtured and the world outside is described to them in vivid detail, to enhance the power of their active imagination to see the world and, when they emerge, some of them as adults, the world they see for the first time is supposedly as they have imagined it (Davis, 1996). It's possible that this prolonged confinement in dark space during their formative years has profound effects on the neurobiological development of their brain (Durwin, 2001), perhaps through the overproduction of nocturnal brain chemicals made in the pineal gland, such as melatonin, and, according to Strassman's (2001) as yet unproven and controversial hypothesis, endogenous DMT, a potent psychedelic molecule that is produced naturally in the human body.

The academic study of sensory deprivation was explored quite extensively in the 1950s and 1960s, by pioneers of consciousness research like John Lilly (1977) who developed the flotation tank in 1954. Suspending the body in dense salt-infused temperature-controlled water and immersed in near silence and darkness, the flotation tank is able to reduce much of the external sensory stimulation of gravity, sound, light, and ambient temperature. Lilly reported many psychological and physical benefits to the flotation tank, such as accelerated rest and rejuvenation relative to ordinary sleeping, and noted the profound nature of the visual hallucinations that occurred.

Much of the work conducted by other researchers during that era tended to focus instead on the psychopathological features of prolonged sensory deprivation—such as hallucinations—and sensory deprivation was used as a model of psychosis. However, the findings of such research were invariably mixed and it became apparent that experiences in confined spaces were heavily contingent upon psychological priming, as was aptly demonstrated by Orne and Scheibe (1964) who found that the presence of a panic button and an 'emergency tray' with drugs and medical instruments in view greatly enhanced negative cognitions. The parallels here with psychedelics is served by the adage that experiences are derived not just from the 'substance' but also the 'set and setting', i.e., the person's prior state of mind and the conditions in which they have the experience (Leary, Litwin & Metzner, 1963).

With the commercial development of personal flotation tanks in the 1980s, the negative connotations of sensory deprivation began being replaced with reports of spontaneous addiction cessation (Suedfeld & Coran, 1989), the gaining of personal insights and the positive enhancement of mood (Suedfeld & Borrie, 1999), though the research into the hallucinatory effects of sensory deprivation has generally waned since the 1960s.

Of note, one of the current project's research scientists, David Luke, teamed up with artists Blue Firth and Mark Pilkington in 2010 to explore darkroom experiences in a supposedly haunted room at the Royal Academy of Arts in London as part of an art–science collaboration

(Luke, Firth & Pilkington, 2013). Spread across eight groups, one hundred people sat in silence and near-total darkness for 30 minutes in the allegedly haunted room fitted with blackout blinds. All the participants were informed that the room was supposedly haunted and about a quarter reported possibly or definitely having an inexplicable sense experience, with 7% of the whole group reporting that they possibly or definitely had a genuine paranormal experience (such as seeing an apparition). The certainty of having such experiences was found to be related to the reported number of prior labile temporal lobe symptoms, which are related to epilepsy, although those with such symptoms may not necessarily experience full epileptic seizures.

THE SOUND OF SILENCE

During the 1940s, the acoustics expert Leo Beranek named and developed the first anechoic chamber. Such chambers are suspended and insulated rooms or compartments that are both shielded from external sound waves and lined with materials inside that absorb reflections of sound and deaden echoes from within. These chambers have primarily been used in the study of acoustic engineering, and very little research has been conducted looking at the psychological properties of such chambers until recently. As with the early sensory deprivation work, the limited psychological research with anechoic chambers has utilised these environments as safe methods for inducing 'psychotic-like experiences' in order to study them in a controlled manner.

These recent studies of darkroom anechoic chambers have found that even short periods (only 15 or 25 mins) in these environments tended to increase the experience of perceptual distortions, such as faces and shapes, and even the sensed presence of an evil entity. Such effects were more elevated for hallucination-prone individuals and for those scoring higher on the personality trait of schizotypy, which is associated with a great tendency to have unusual experiences and psychotic-like symptoms (Daniel, Lovatt & Mason, 2014; Mason & Brady, 2009).

SCIENCE MEETS SENSATION

The scientists working on the current project were approached by the artist Haroon Mirza to work collecting psychological data for his anechoic darkroom installation entitled 'Chamber for Endogenous DMT (Collapsing the Wave Function)'. Haroon was interested in exploring whether the altered state induced by the darkroom anechoic chamber was in any way similar to psychedelic experiences induced through substances like DMT, even speculating that the experiences might be due to elevated levels of endogenous DMT, i.e. that which is made within the body.

Within the confines of the gallery environment we were unable to do the full biochemical assaying necessary to detect and monitor levels of DMT in the body, but we were able to administer various psychological measures to help us identify and understand the kinds of experiences induced by the chamber in an exploratory manner. Further, we were able to administer a number of other psychological measures before volunteers entered the chamber to establish which personality traits of individuals would predict the kinds of experiences they would have, given that experiences are usually complex interactions of traits and states. That is, that the person's underlying psychology and biology interacts with the situational factors (i.e. set, setting or substance) of the altered state. In the current study, the setting (Haroon's exhibition and staff at the gallery) and the substance (one to two hours in the darkroom anechoic chamber) remained constant.

METHODS

Numerous visitors to the gallery tried the chamber, and data was collected from 49 volunteers during the exhibition. Most of the participants spent two hours in the chamber though a few spent a little less time in there, and others a little longer. Times ranged from 60–255 minutes (mean = 116 mins).

Participants were briefed about the nature of the study and gave their informed consent to take part. First they completed a number of psychological profile measures. Upon entering the chamber they were reminded that they could leave at any time should they wish. They were supplied with a torch if they needed to leave although all they had to do was call out as they were constantly monitored by a microphone inside the chamber. They were provided with some soft cushions to sit or lie on, but they were requested to avoid falling asleep. Once their allotted time was complete (decided before entering by the participant) they were collected from the chamber and after a moment in an acclimatisation anteroom they then completed a number of psychological measures to assess their experience. All but one participant—who asked to leave shortly after entering—stayed inside the chamber for their allotted time. The study was given ethical approval by the University of Greenwich Departmental Research Ethics Committee for Psychology.

PRE-CHAMBER MEASURES

A number of self-report questionnaire personality measures were used to predict experiences in the anechoic darkroom induced state. These included the Modified Tellegen Absorption Scale (MODTAS; Jamieson, 2005), and the Iowa Interview for Partial Seizure-like Symptoms (IIPSS; Roberts, 1999).

The MODTAS measures the psychological construct called 'absorption' which refers to the individual's openness to a variety of cognitive, perceptual, and imagistic experiences as well as vivid imagery, synaesthesiae, and intense involvement in aesthetics and nature. Absorption has been found to be strongly associated with fantasy proneness, and modestly associated with both openness to experience and hypnotic susceptibility (Roche & McConkey, 1990). Absorption was also found to be the best of a wide range of predictor variables of the psychological features of the altered state induced by psilocybin, the active ingredient in magic mushrooms (Studerus, 2013).

The IIPSS measures various different sensory, cognitive and affective phenomena that may be related to disturbances of the temporal lobe and is used to help identify the presence of partial seizure-like symptoms typical of epilepsy. Previous research has found that IIPSS scores can predict inexplicable or reportedly paranormal-like (e.g. apparitions) sensory experiences in darkroom states (Luke, Firth & Pilkington, 2013) but can also predict performance on psi tasks of clairvoyance and precognition in relation to geomagnetic activity (Roney-Dougal, Ryan & Luke, 2014).

POST-CHAMBER MEASURES

A number of self-report questionnaire state measures were used to classify experiences following time spent in the anechoic darkroom induced state. These included the Mystical Experiences Questionnaire (MEQ; Maclean, Leoutsakos, Johnson & Griffiths, 2012), the Five Dimensions of Altered States (5D-ASC; Dittrich, Lamparter & Maurer, 2010—though used as 11 dimensions in the current research), the researchers' own devised Darkroom Visual Analogue Scale (DVAS), and a qualitative self-report section where participants wrote an account of their subjective experience in the chamber.

The MEQ was developed for assessing the occurrence of mystical experiences and was utilised in research exploring such experiences with psilocybin, whereby approximately 55–61% of high dose psilocybin recipients reported 'complete mystical experiences' (e.g., Griffiths, Richards, McCann & Jesse, 2006). MEQ scores have also been found to predict better outcomes from psychedelic-assisted psychotherapy using psilocybin to treat tobacco smoking cessation and end-of-life related depression and anxiety. The MEQ assesses features of the mystical experience along four factors: mystical experience, positive mood, transcendence of space and time, and ineffability (the inability to fully render the experience into language).

The 5D-ASC is a measure of altered states of consciousness and has been widely used in identifying the psychological features of psychedelic experiences. Factors assessed with the 5D-ASC include the experience of unity, spiritual experience, anxiety, impaired cognition, synaesthesia and visual imagery. This measure was augmented by the researchers' own scale (DVAS) which was devised to explore various psychological phenomena such as the experience of geometric visual percepts (called 'entoptics'), out-of-body experiences, distortions of time, sensed presences of other beings, and emotional changes.

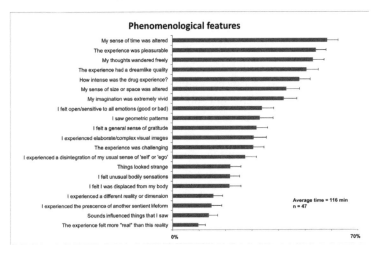

Figure 1: Percentage of respondents reporting various phenomena of altered states

RESULTS

Sleepy and dreamy

On the whole nearly all participants had some odd phenomena to report, although one or two of those who were very experienced in meditation did not find the experience to be especially different to their usual practice. According to the subjective written reports about 25% of volunteers had a dreamlike quality to their experience and most suspected that they fell asleep for at least part of their time inside.

Falling alseep is not surprising because it can be difficult to remain conscious in such circumstances, especially when at least 10% reported that they could not tell if their eyes were open or shut. Those reporting dream-like experiences or suspecting that they fell asleep reported being significantly more sleepy before entering the chamber than those who did not report dream-like experiences ($p = .017$).

Visual imagery

The most common experience was the perception of visual images, primarily coloured shapes (about 50%), often described as mist or clouds of colour or flashes of light, and about 13% reported the perception of colourful geometric patterns (entoptics), though a few (7%) only saw shapes in black and white, or exotic shades of grey. For some (5%) they reported being able to see their limbs when they moved them, although it is supposed that this was a hallucination due to expectation and kinaesthetic feedback about the position of one's body; a kind of visual phantom limb experience. Since we initially reported this phenomena (Luke, Timmermann, Kaelen & Bell-Langford, 2018), one of the study participants who experienced it conducted his own investigations (Jelfs, 2018) and discovered the effect to be entirely illusory (as other people's limb movements cannot be seen while one's own can) and discovered that the phenomena was first reported in 1970 by Hofstetter as 'phantom visual imagery'.

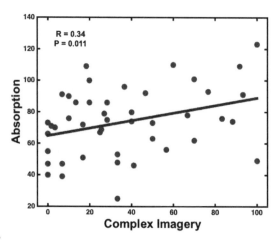

(Left Facing Page, Bottom) *Figure 2: Scattergram to show the degree of correlation between the prior personality trait of Absorption and the reported degree of complex imagery in the darkroom*

Assessing the relationship between pre- and post-chamber measures, complex imagery was correlated with absorption ($r = .34$, $p = .011$), and elementary imagery was correlated with absorption ($r = .34$, $p = .011$) and temporal lobe lability (TLL) ($r = .38$, $p = .006$). The perception of entoptics, specifically, was only correlated with TLL, as measured by both the DVAS ($r = .36$, $p = .007$) and the 5D-ASC entoptics items ($r = .45$, $p = .001$).

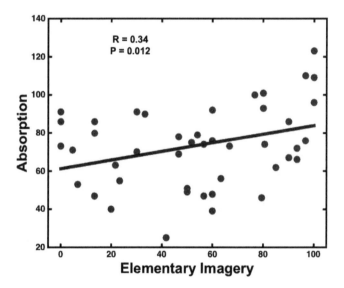

(Above) *Figure 3: Scattergram to show the degree of correlation between the prior personality trait of Absorption and the reported degree of elementary imagery in the darkroom*

Of sound, body, and mind

About 20% of participants reported auditory hallucinations, which primarily consisted of buzzing and humming sounds seemingly emanating from inside their head. Those reporting buzzing/humming sounds scored significantly higher on absorption (p = .014). One participant ascribed the buzzing to tinnitus, although buzzing and humming sounds often accompany the early stages of out-of-body experiences (OBEs), which were also reported by 5% of participants, with a further 5% reporting changed perceptions of one's body, and 5% reporting the perceived disappearance of one's body. Changes in body perception, however, were not accompanied by the perception of buzzing and humming sounds in these cases. Furthermore, the DVAS and 5D-ASC items relating to OBEs did not correlate with either absorption or TLL. Additionally, one person reported that their body had gone numb, whereas about 8% experienced 'energy' moving within their body, identified as kundalini (an experience of energy rising up the spine following esoteric yogic practices) by one person.

Ominous numinous

Perhaps surprisingly, 10% of participants reported the sensed presence of a sentient being in the room that they perceived to be threatening, although for one participant the presence changed to being non-threatening, and one other person experienced only a non-threatening presence. Such experiences are common with sleep paralysis, a relatively common experience that occurs between waking and sleeping whereby the person is paralysed (as though they are sleeping) but feel as though they are consciously awake.

Curiously, however, *none* of the reports of sensed presence in the chamber came from the 25% of the sample who reported dream-like experiences or who suspected that they had fallen asleep, although it is possible that those experiencing the sensed presence in the chamber had actually drifted into hypnagogia but had not realised (as seemingly occurs with sleep paralysis). Nevertheless, no one reported the experience of paralysis so these sensed presences are most likely not caused by sleep paralysis experiences but may be related to them.

Exploratory analysis of the predictor variables found that those reporting sensed presences had 66% more temporal lobe symptoms than those that did not experience a sensed presence (statistically significant at p = .032). Furthermore, those experiencing threatening presences reported more than twice as many affective temporal lobe symptoms as those not reporting threatening presences (statistically significant at p = .028) and significantly more temporal lobe symptoms overall (p = .036), indicating that non-clinical epileptic symptoms (termed temporal lobe lability) are possibly related to the experience of sensed presence in darkrooms. However, in a prior study both temporal lobe lability and absorption were found to be only indirectly related to sleep paralysis, as all these factors are related to an increased vividness of dream and hypnagogic imagery (Spanos et al., 1995). However, exploring responses to the specific DVAS item of 'sensed presence' in the chamber this was not found to be correlated to TLL scores, but was correlated with absorption (r = .34, p = .01).

Contracted hours

Changes to the perception of time were quite prevalent, with 23% reporting the complete loss of a sense of time and a further 15% reporting that the time went much faster than they expected in the chamber. Perhaps surprisingly those reporting that time had contracted scored significantly *lower* (p = .033) on the measure of absorption than those that did not experience time contraction.

Only one person reported that time dilated (slowed down) in the chamber, making a total of 41% of participants commenting on changes in time-perception in their written reports. However, acknowledging that their 'sense of time was altered' on the DVAS measure was reported by 96% of participants, with the mean percentage of the most imaginable alteration in sense of time being 58%. Similarly, 100% of participants reported changes in space-time on the MEQ. When asked on the 5D-ASC if they experienced 'past, present and future as a unity' 39%

responded that this had occurred more than usually, with a mean percentage increase of 14% more than usual.

The DVAS item that 'sense of time was altered' was not correlated with absorption but was correlated with sensory temporal lobe symptoms ($r = .43$, $p = .0016$) as was the MEQ changes in space-time subscale ($r = .38$, $p = .005$). The MEQ space-time subscale was also correlated with absorption ($r = .38$, $p = .006$), as was the DASC item of experiencing 'all time as one' ($r = .45$, $p = .001$).

Mystical chamber

Only two of the thirty-nine participants providing written subjective accounts explicitly reported having a spiritual experience in the chamber. One of these also scored above 60% of the total maximum on all four factors of the MEQ, qualifying them for having a 'complete mystical experience' (as defined by the developers of the MEQ). In total there were only two out of forty-seven participants completing the MEQ that qualified for a complete mystical experience, although two others were just shy of this standard by small amounts (5 and 11%) on only one of the four factors, but exceeded 60% on the other three factors.

Equivalent percentages of complete mystical experience in a sample are expected with about 70 µg/kg of psilocybin (a small dose). Nevertheless, the mystical experience factor of the MEQ demonstrated a weak correlation with time spent in the chamber ($r = .30$, $p = .02$) so duration could be thought of as somewhat relative to psychedelic dosage and presumably the longer spent in the chamber the more mystical experiences and greater depths of altered consciousness would be expected. The overall average mystical experience score for the whole sample was 47% and, as with psilocybin-induced experiences scores on the MEQ, were highly significantly correlated with absorption scores ($r = .58$, $p = .000012$).

(Right Facing Page, Top) *Figure 4: Mean scores across the sample (N=49) on the four subscales of the Mystical Experience Questionnaire regarding their experience in the darkroom*

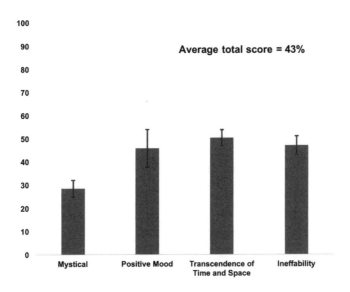

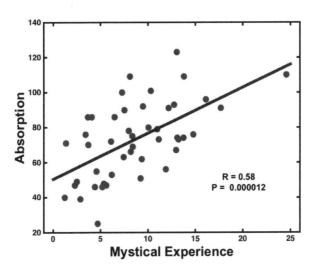

(Above) *Figure 5: Scattergram to show the degree of correlation between the prior personality trait of Absorption and the reported percentage of mystical experience (overall MEQ scores)*

Chamberdelic?

Comparing the profile of chamber experiences with that of psychedelically induced experiences it can be seen that they share many of the same phenomenological features, such as the induction of visual hallucinations (including entoptics), changes in the perception of time, space and one's body, and enhanced positive mood. Strong psychedelic experiences, especially with DMT, ayahuasca and psilocybin can also give rise to encounters with seemingly sentient and discarnate entities (Luke, 2017), and although these effects were not reproduced in the chamber a proportion of participants did have distinct (and disturbing) feelings of a sensed presence, if not full-blown entity encounters.

Some of the missing features typical of psychedelic experiences were essentially lacking from the written accounts, however, such as the experience of synaesthesia, impaired cognition, and changes in the meaningfulness of one's experience. Nevertheless, it should be noted that the primary type of synaesthesia reported as induced by psychedelics is where auditory stimuli produces concurrent visual percepts (Luke & Terhune, 2013), so such experiences would likely be absent in an anechoic chamber. Furthermore, as with psychedelic experiences (with psilocybin), absorption was found to be a good predictor of experience, and in some respects the degree of altered consciousness was equivalent to the largest clinical dose (315 µg/kg) of psilocybin (Studerus, 2013) or a reasonably strong oral dose (150 µg) of LSD (Liechti, Dolder & Schmid, 2017), at least in terms of the percentage scores for elementary imagery.

(Right Facing Page, Top) *Figure 6: Showing the overall mean percentage for the sample (N=49) for overall intensity of the various 11D-ASC subscales of altered states of consciousness*

Altered States of Consciousness Questionnaire

Complex imagery was also a strong feature and equates to about a moderate dose of psilocybin (about 160 µg/kg) or oral LSD (about 75 µg), as does insightfulness, blissful state, the experience of unity and impaired cognition.

Disembodiment is also at about the same level for psilocybin (about 160 µg/kg) and somewhat weaker for LSD (about 50 µg). Experiences of changed meaning are roughly equivalent to a weak dose of psilocybin (about 60 µg/kg) or LSD (about 50 µg), with synaesthesia being somewhat weaker again (about 80 µg/kg psilocybin or 30 µg LSD).

Spiritual experience, however, was on a par with a reasonably strong dose of psilocybin (260 µg/kg) or moderate dose of LSD (about 100 µg), and levels of anxiety were quite high in terms of dose (about 340 µg/ kg psilocybin or 200 µg LSD) indicating that the chamber produced more anxiety relative to the degree of altered consciousness than do classic psychedelics.

CONCLUSION

In conclusion it might be said that approximately two hours in the anechoic darkroom is capable of inducing genuine psychedelic-like experiences, with features of the altered state ranging in equivalence to weak, moderate and even strong psychedelic experiences, depending on the specific phenomenon. As with psychedelics, the psychological construct of absorption was shown to predict the depth of experiences participants had, and temporal lobe lability was able to predict some other phenomena that absorption did not, such as entoptics and sensed presences. As a final caveat, the statistical analyses reported here are merely exploratory and have not been corrected for multiple analyses, and so should be taken as indicative rather than evidential until further replications can be conducted.

ACKNOWLEDGEMENTS

With thanks to Haroon Mirza for inviting us to collaborate on this art–science project, to the staff of the Zabludowicz Gallery for guiding participants through the darkroom process, and to the participants for bravely taking part.

REFERENCES

Achard, J-L. (2008). *Enlightened Rainbows: The Life and Works of Shardza Tashi Gyeltsen.* Leiden: Brill.

Daniel, C., Lovatt, A., & Mason, O. J. (2014). 'Psychotic-like experiences and their cognitive appraisal under short-term sensory deprivation'. *Frontiers in Psychiatry, 5*(106), 1-8.

Davis, W. (1996). *One river: Science, adventure and hallucinogenics in the Amazon basin.* London: Simon & Schuster.

Dittrich, A., Lamparter, D., & Maurer, M. (2010). '5D-ASC: Questionnaire for the assessment of altered states of consciousness. A short introduction' (3rd ed.). Zurich, Switzerland: PSIN PLUS.

Durwin, J. (2001). *Dreamtime: Psycho-biological methodology and morphogenesis in the shamanic tradition.* Unpublished manuscript, Arizona State University.

Griffiths, R. R., Richards, W. A., McCann, U., & Jesse, R. (2006). 'Psilocybin can occasion mystical-type experiences having substantial and sustained personal meaning and spiritual significance'. *Psychopharmacology, 187*, 268-83.

Hofstetter, H. W. (1970). 'Some observations of phantom visual imagery'. *American Journal of Optometry and Archives of the American Academy of Optometry, 47*, 361-366.

Jamieson, G. A. (2005). 'The modified Tellegen absorption scale: A clearer window on the structure and meaning of absorption'. *Australian Journal of Clinical and Experimental Hypnosis, 33*, 119-139.

Jelfs, J. (2018). 'Investigating "phantom visual imagery' in an anechoic darkroom—anecdotal report'. In E. Neilson (Ed.), *For a partnership society—Haroon Mirza* (pp.158-159). London: Zabludowicz Collection.

Leary, T., Litwin. G. H., & Metzner, R. (1963). 'Reactions to psilocybin administered in a supportive environment'. *Journal of Nervous and Mental Disease, 137*, 561-573.

Liechti, M.E., Dolder, P.C. & Schmid, Y. (2017) 'Alterations of consciousness and mystical-type experiences after acute LSD in humans'. *Psychopharmacology, 9-10*, 1499-1510.

Lilly, J. C. (1977). *The Deep Self.* New York: Simon & Schuster.

Luke, D. (2017). *Otherworlds: Psychedelics and Exceptional Human Experience.* London: Muswell Hill / State University of New York Press.

Luke, D., Firth, B., & Pilkington, M. (2013, September). *The Men (and Women) Who Stare at (Sheep and) Goats: Beliefs, Expectations, Experiences, Neurology and Gender in Haunt Site Vigils.* Paper presented to the International Conference of the Society for Psychical Research, University of Swansea, 6th September.

Luke, D., & Terhune, D. B. (2013). 'The induction of synaesthesia with chemical agents: A systematic review'. *Frontiers in Psychology, 4,* 753.

Luke, D., Timmermann, C., Kaelen, M., & Bell-Langford, B. (2018). 'The anechoic darkroom as a psychedelic state' (2018). In E. Neilson (Ed.), *For A Partnership Society— Haroon Mirza* (pp.148-157). London: Zabludowicz Collection.

Maclean, K. A., Leoutsakos, J.-M. S., Johnson, M. W., & Griffiths, R. R. (2012). 'Factor analysis of the Mystical Experience Questionnaire: A study of experiences occasioned by the hallucinogen psilocybin'. *Journal for the Scientific Study of Religion, 51*(4), 721–737.

Mason, O. J., & Brady, F. (2009). 'The Psychotomimetic Effects of Short-Term Sensory Deprivation'. *Journal of Nervous and Mental Disease, 197*(10), 783-785.

Orne, M. T., & Scheibe, K. E. (1964). 'The contribution of nondeprivation factors in the production of sensory deprivation effects: The psychology of the "panic button"'. *Journal of Abnormal and Social Psychology, 68*(1), 3-12.

Roberts, R. J. (1999). 'Epilepsy spectrum disorder in the context of mild traumatic brain injury'. In N.R. Varney and R. J. Roberts (Eds.) *The evaluation and treatment of mild traumatic brain injury* (pp.209-247). Hillsdale, NJ: Lawrence Erlbaum.

Roche, S., & McConkey, K. (1990). 'Absorption: Nature, assessment, and correlates'. *Journal of Personality and Social Psychology, 59*(1), 91–101.

Roney-Dougal, S., Ryan, A., & Luke, D. (2014). 'The relationship between local geomagnetic activity and psychic awareness'. *Journal of Parapsychology, 78*(2), 235-254.

Spanos, N. P., McNulty, S. A., DuBreuil, S. C., Pires, M., & Burgess, M. F. (1995). 'The frequency and correlates of sleep paralysis in a university sample'. *Journal of Research in Personality, 29,* 285-305.

Strassman, R. (2001). *DMT: The Spirit Molecule: A Doctor's Revolutionary Research into the Biology of Near-death and Mystical Experiences.* Rochester, VT: Park Street Press.

Studerus, E. (2013). *Psilocybin-induced Altered States of Consciousness: Tolerability, assessment, and prediction.* Saarbrücken, Germany: Südwestdeutscher Verlag für Hochschulschriften.

Suedfeld, P., & Borrie, R. A. (1999). 'Health and therapeutic application of chamber and floatation restricted environmental stimulation therapy' (REST). *Psychology and Health, 14,* 545-566.

Suedfeld, P., & Coran, S. (1989). 'Perceptual isolation, sensory deprivation, and REST: Moving introductory psychology texts out of the 1950s'. *Canadian Psychology/Psychologie Canadienne. 30*(1), 17-29.

BLAKE'S ARTISTIC VISION AND THE PERILS OF DUALISTIC CONSCIOUSNESS

GEORGE ERVING

William Blake's influence upon "psychedelic literature" has been well noted by authors such as Aldous Huxley, Alan Watts, Allen Ginsberg, and Timothy Leary, who drew inspiration from Blake's artistic vision because it seemed to anticipate their own consciousness-changing experiences that erased the apparent boundaries between self and other, body and soul, human and divine. Blake's works also suggested that such heightened states of awareness are not the exclusive preserve of saints, mystics, shamans, or madmen whose claims were to be vindicated at the end of human history, but rather that such states of awareness are available to anyone at any time, if only they would "cleanse the doors of perception" to experience "the infinite" and "the eternal" that are ever-present but hidden by the dualistic assumptions and beliefs that are intrinsic to the Western materialist worldview.

Beginning with his earliest writings, Blake is consistently preoccupied with the possibility of attaining non-dualistic consciousness, but also with the deeply imbedded cultural beliefs that prevent such vision. For example, one sees this tension in the famous passage from Blake's early work *The Marriage of Heaven and Hell* (1790), which provided the title for Huxley's account of his mescaline experience, as well as the rock group The Doors with their name:

The ancient tradition that the world will be consumed in fire at the end of six thousand years is true, as I have heard from Hell. || For the cherub with his flaming sword is hereby commanded to leave his guard at the Tree of Life, and when he does, the whole creation will be consumed, and appear infinite and holy, whereas it now appears finite and corrupt. || This will come to pass by an improvement of sensual enjoyment. || But first the notion that man has a body distinct from his soul, is to be expunged; this I shall do, by printing in the infernal method, by corrosives, which in Hell are salutary and medicinal, melting apparent surfaces away, and displaying the infinite which was hid. || If the doors of perception were cleansed every thing would appear to man as it is: infinite. || For man has closed himself up, till he sees all things thro' the narrow chinks of his cavern.[1]

Here, Blake's narrator playfully endorses the biblical account of the apocalypse that will occur at the end of history, but only to subversively appropriate it for his own purpose by suggesting that the "infernal method" of relief etching used to inscribe the plate's words and images has in itself the capacity to provoke an apocalyptic moment anytime they are read. Such moments are portals through which the reader may pass to experience an undifferentiated consciousness that delights in sensual experience, rejects the distinction between body and soul, and recognizes time and space as conceptual illusions. Blake thus offers his literary art as an opportunity for readers to "cleanse the doors of perception", free the mind from its self-enclosed cavern, and recognize that the Self is not ontologically separate from the world it experiences.

What has been less well understood by authors in the psychedelic tradition is that Blake also provided a deeply insightful analysis of the cultural, political, and historical forces that prevent such experiences, both in his day and in ours. As one might surmise from the above passage, his critique centers on the materialist worldview that had gained widespread currency in late eighteenth-century Europe as a result of three major conceptual developments: first, the advent of Newtonian physics, which viewed nature as ultimately reducible to inert, corpuscular particles of matter subject to mathematically precise laws of motion; second, the emergence of empirical method as the presumptive authority by which all claims to truth should be evaluated; and third, John Locke's empirical psychology, articulated in his *An Essay Concerning Human Understanding* (1690), which asserted that all knowledge originates in sensory information gleaned from our encounters with the material world. In what follows, I'd like to explain how, for Blake, the widespread acceptance of these ideas encouraged the human spirit to "close itself up, till it sees all things [only] thro' the narrow chinks of its cavern", and to suggest in particular how the illusory dualism of Self and Other produced by such occluded vision conditions the psychology of envy, rivalry, and violence that aims both at others and at oneself.

BLAKE'S REJECTION OF MATERIALISM

Blake's works participate in the "Romantic Movement", which rebelled against the Neoclassical celebration of Reason as the ultimate arbiter of truth by finding justification in a new authority—that of an inner voice that gave expression to the creative imagination. However, what sets Blake apart from other British Romantic Period writers is his rejection of the notion that this inner authority is the voice of nature. For Wordsworth and the young Coleridge, the creative imagination is able to forge moments of communion with the natural world whose existence otherwise stands outside and beyond itself; but for Blake, the creative imagination recognizes that "nature", when viewed as something external to the self, even when it's perceived in spiritual terms, is the product of an illusion rather than a source of comfort and belonging. As he remarks in his annotations to Wordsworth's *Poems*, "I see in Wordsworth the Natural Man rising up against the Spiritual Man Continually [...] Natural Objects always did & now do Weaken and deaden & obliterate Imagination in me" [E665].[2] For Blake, Wordsworth's attachment to Nature was merely a new manifestation of Enlightenment materialism that was anathema to his non-dualistic vision of the Self, and he consequently directed his artistic energy toward realizing a different goal, which was "To open the Eternal Worlds, to open the immortal Eyes Of Man inwards into the Worlds of Thought: into Eternity / Ever expanding in the Bosom of God, the Human Imagination—".[3]

Blake's negative appraisal of Nature begins with his attack on the model of the mind proposed by Locke, who along with Francis Bacon and Isaac Newton he often identifies as one of the chief architects of the Self's alienation. As Blake argues in his early work, "There Is No Natural Religion", Locke's formulation of the mind (wherein all our thoughts and thus our human identity originate in sensory impressions received from the external world) renders the Self a passive receptacle of experience, incapable of imagining or desiring anything other than what experience dictates. Such a being must necessarily find itself resigned to a crippling fatalism. Blake further argues that the Lockean Self must experience itself as fragmented. In its acts of self-examination the mind splits in two, as observer and observed, thus importing the logical dichotomy between internal and external into its own structure so that the Self finds its thoughts to be like strangers in its own home. To make matters worse from Blake's perspective, Locke had defined personal identity only as acts of remembered consciousness, thus fragmenting the Self further by ignoring the underlying roles played by its imaginative, emotional, and corporeal elements. For Blake, this mistaken understanding of the Self as alienated, passively determined, and internally fragmented—ideas enforced by the religious, political, and social institutions of his time—is the key source of what he refers to as our "fallen" condition.

Imaginative vision, by contrast, actively shapes the world it inhabits, dissolves the apparent dualisms of Self and Other, and finds expression through its coordinating efforts with the intellect, the passions, and the body. As his rebellious Devil in *The Marriage of Heaven and Hell* proclaims:

Man has no body distinct from his soul; for that call'd Body is a portion of Soul discern'd by the five Senses [the chief inlets of Soul in this age].

Energy is the only life and is from the Body and Reason is the bound or outward circumference of Energy. Energy is eternal delight.[4]

Blake's Devil does not mean, however, to deny the value of Reason, for creative energy would take no particular form (i.e., have no circumference) without it. But if Reason, from its cultural position of privilege, were to supplant imaginative energy, its bounding circumference would contract to a vanishing point and thus bring about its own demise. For Blake, creative imagination, or what he often calls the "poetic genius", instead embraces a productive tension between Reason and Energy, and between all mutually constitutive binary pairings (man/woman, lightness/darkness, positive/negative, self/other, gay/straight, cis/trans, etc.). His artistic vision doesn't, for example, do away with the body/soul distinction in favor of a synthesizing third term, as with the Hegelian dialectic. Rather, his vision conserves the individuality of each element, while also stressing their interdependence. As he proclaims,

Without Contraries is no progression. Attraction and Repulsion, Reason and Energy, Love and Hate, are necessary to Human existence. [But] from these Contraries spring what the religious call Good & Evil. *Good is the passive that obeys Reason. Evil is the active springing from Energy. Good is Heaven. Evil is Hell.* [my emphasis][5]

It is the followers of institutional and "natural religion" (i.e., those, such as deists, who have sought to reconcile Scripture with a materialist view of nature) who stand opposed to "progression" (and thus unwittingly to "Human existence") because they view conceptual dyads such as Reason and Energy in morally hierarchical terms. Here, "the religious" wish to demote and ultimately extinguish "energy" (political, artistic, sexual) in favor of an intellectual and spiritual passivity that by following the dictates of "reason" will supposedly lead to salvation. Such logic, however, fails to recognize that to destroy either term of the dyad is to destroy the whole. Blake names this misguided attempt to privilege one term at the expense of the other a "Negation", and views this habit of mind as the true source of evil. To be clear, evil is not the inferior term in a good/evil binary; rather, evil results from the attempt to morally rank aspects of consciousness so that the supposedly undesirable elements are repressed and threatened with extinction. For Blake, Locke's idea of the Self depended upon such negations (such as the superiority of mind over body, of reason over imagination), which fragment and constrict consciousness, leaving the Self in the bewildered and forlorn state expressed by one of his characters, who laments, "I am like an atom / A Nothing left in darkness—yet I am an identity—I wish & feel & weep & groan—Ah terrible, terrible!" [6]

Blake's pervasive concern, then, is to expose the ways in which the widespread adoption of Locke's beliefs about the "natural self" had made the human subject profoundly unhappy in its own subjectivity, and to use his literary art to awaken a true self-understanding that frees us from the imprisoning logic of negation.

FRAGMENTED CONSCIOUSNESS, MIMESIS, AND ENVY

In what follows, I'd like to briefly describe how Blake dramatizes what he believed were the *behavioral* consequences of self-alienation and fragmented consciousness in the first of his three major epic poems (or what he called "prophecies"), entitled *The Four Zoas: [Or] The torments of Love & Jealousy in the Death and Judgement of Albion the Ancient Man* (1797–1805). This extraordinarily complex psychodrama narrates the fall and redemption of Albion, who simultaneously symbolizes the psychological landscape of a single individual, the troubled spirit of ancient Britannia in its current political relations with Napoleonic France, and the archetypal struggle of consciousness to dissolve the subject-object distinction imposed by sense perception and reason when they are uncoupled from the promptings of the passions, the wisdom of the body, and the work of imaginative vision. Albion represents a passive consciousness that has fallen into a "slumber of materialism", one that lasts for most of the poem's nine "nights" while his psychic faculties (the four "Zoas" of Reason, Imagination, Emotion, and Corporeal awareness) cease to work in cooperative opposition and wage war with one another. Albion's eventual awakening, figured as the reintegration of these parts into a functional whole, is brought about largely by the heroic efforts of Los, the Zoa of creative imagination, in his moments of apocalyptic epiphany that overcome the illusion that divides body and soul, self and other, the human and the divine.

Here however, I wish to focus on Blake's insights into the psychology of the divided psyche as described in the first four of the work's nine nights. These describe the fallen condition of each Zoa in its dualistic worldview that privileges the Self and falls prey to the illusion of self-sufficiency. Each Zoa declares itself to be god and master and yet each finds itself frustrated, despairing, and haunted by feelings of emptiness while secretly envying the appearance of autonomy it imagines the Other possesses. Their plight dramatizes the fundamental condition of humankind's fallen condition—the inability to recognize that the Self's true nature is *inter-dividual*. Blake refers to this failure as the condition of "Selfhood" (taken literally as the state of limited vision that results from donning a hood—the hood of materialist beliefs that violate the doctrine of contraries, especially by valorizing reason and denigrating creative energy). In Blake's myth, Albion had once upon a time, or rather in the state of eternity that transcends time, experienced his fully realized Self before succumbing to the spiritual slumber of alienated Selfhood that has been the waking "reality" of modern world history reaching back at least to the Enlightenment.

For Blake, the alienated Self must always be governed by desire for the people and things from which it feels itself separated. Desire, after all, presupposes absence—e.g., one desires food when one's stomach is empty—and one then attempts to fill the emptiness by negating the food as such and assimilating it to oneself in the act of eating. Desire for affection, for love, or more fundamentally for recognition (the desire to be desired), likewise presupposes a kind of emotional emptiness that often triggers a similar attempt to "negate" and assimilate another's desire. One might even say (following a line of thinking that reaches from Hegel through Alexandre Kojève) that desire defines the Self insofar as the Self's ontological status is the result of its assimilating actions. You are what you eat; you are what satisfies your desire.

Most importantly for Blake, the desires of the alienated self were ultimately responsible for the envy, rivalry, and violence he witnessed in the world—between individuals, families, communities, and nations, but also within the psyche of each person enslaved by "mind-forged manacles" of the materialist worldview and its intrinsic dualisms. In this regard, he seems to have anticipated the theories of René Girard in recognizing that desire is often based upon the illusion of autonomy: one tends to believe one's desires are self-generated, and that they are the authentic expression of self-sovereignty when in fact they are *imitative*: one desires what one sees another desire. Moreover, the desiring subject fails to recognize that by imitating what another desires, his imitation is actually aimed at the *being* of the other. The imitating subject wishes not only to be *like* the one who models what to desire, but at some unacknowledged level to *be* the model. Why? Because the model, as Other, *seems* to possess an authenticity that is secured by his apparently self-generated and self-satisfied desire, and thus an enviable self-sufficiency that attracts the subject. The plight of the subject, then, is a series of unhappy delusions: first, that he is a Self separated from other selves; second, that he is the author of his own desires, when in fact he imitates, often unawares, those of others; third, that he is not attracted to these others, when in fact he is because they appear to the authors of their own desires and thus appear to possess a self-sufficiency, a fullness of being, the subject feels is missing in himself.

These delusions create the conditions for conflict. When the envious subject attempts to imitate the Other by reaching for the same object the Other desires, the two become rivals, and each comes to regard the other with both fascination and hatred. As Girard remarks,

The subject is torn between two opposite feelings toward his model—the most submissive reverence and the most intense malice. This is the passion we call hatred. Only someone who prevents us from satisfying

a desire which he himself has inspired in us is truly an object of hatred. The person who hates first hates himself for the secret admiration concealed by his (sic) hatred. In an effort to hide this desperate admiration from others, and from himself, he no longer wants to see in his [model] anything but an obstacle.[7]

Typically, rivals hide their feelings of fascination and envy from one another, and especially from themselves, by projecting an image of superior self-sufficiency, either through contempt or affected indifference. Thus each views the other in terms of absolute difference; hatred only sees otherness, but it is fueled by the repression of a deeper, unacknowledged sameness that becomes increasingly frustrating as the rivalry intensifies. An accelerating feedback loop ignited by the tension between fascination and loathing, and the frustration of finding sameness where there should be difference, builds toward a climactic moment of violence that finally obliterates all apparent distinctions. For Blake, each subject's attempt to negate the other and stand victorious ironically results in the sacrifice of the separate identity and self-sufficiency it most seeks to secure.

THE PSYCHOLOGY OF VIOLENCE IN THE FOUR ZOAS

The psychology of rivalry I've just described illuminates the key confrontations between various Zoas that drive the plot of Blake's poem. For example, in "Night V", envy appears as a contagion that infects each character and brings them into violent conflict. I pick up the narrative with the birth of Orc (the Zoa of the passions which in its fallen state symbolizes the energy of violent revolution) to his quarrelsome parents Los (the expression of the Creative Imagination in its fallen state) and Los's mate Enitharmon. Fearful that the adolescent Orc plots his death, father Los violently binds Orc to a rock with "the chain of Jealousy" (*Four Zoas,* 341). When Los later attempts to free his son he finds that the chain has woven itself into his son's limbs so completely that Orc becomes jealousy's manifest expression. Orc's howlings of rage travel across vast psychic spaces to awaken the Zoa Urizen (the symbol of Reason in its fallen state, the limiter of creative energy) who despite having experienced a troubled prophetic vision in which he sees himself forced to serve the adolescent Orc (ibid. 326), cannot resist his fascination with Orc's distressed howlings. As Urizen descends into Orc's caves, he beholds a world of violent "fire, rage, [and] blood [, and discovers] "howling Orc whose awful limbs cast forth red smoke & fire" (352–3). Urizen's response, however, is not one of fear or horror, but of envy, though he affects studied indifference: "Urizen approached not near but took his seat on a rock / And rang'd his books around him brooding Envious over Orc" (353), and, a few lines later, "Urizen fixed in Envy sat brooding & coverd with snow / His book of iron on his knees" (353).

Their ensuing exchange develops according to the dynamics of mimetic rivalry I've described. Each expresses contempt for the other while concealing his own envy. Each views the other in terms of absolute difference, yet their dialogue becomes increasingly symmetrical, as each, fettered by envy, postures as autonomous and demands the other's subordination. Urizen mocks Orc's predicament; Orc affects nonchalance. Urizen lies that he has initiated their conversation purely out of pity (354); Orc sneers at Urizen as a self-enslaved "groveling demon of woe" (354) and acts "as if in Joy of [his violent] prison" (354). In a remarkable passage just preceding the violent climax of their standoff, Blake brings into close relation the key concepts we have been discussing that result from fragmented consciousness—desire, envy, deceit, and the illusion of autonomy:

> *Urizen envious brooding sat & saw the secret terror [Orc] Flame high in pride & laugh to scorn the source of his own deceit | Nor knew the source of his own but thought himself the Sole author Of all his wandering Experiments in the horrible Abyss.* (356)

The referential ambiguity of the pronoun "his" indicts both Urizen and Orc as self-deceived: each denies his fascination with the other and fails to recognize the mimetic origins of his behavior. Thus if Urizen and Orc are

> not in accord [as Girard would note] it is not because they are too different ... but [rather] because they are too alike. Yet the more they grow alike, the more different they imagine themselves and the sameness by which they are obsessed appears to them as an absolute otherness.[8]

With each successive failure to assert a decisive difference, the tension builds to a violent crisis in which violence itself becomes the object of desire. Urizen "ma[kes] Orc / In Serpent formed compelled [to] stretch out & up the mysterious tree [... so] that he might draw all human forms / Into submission to his will nor [did he know] the dread result" [that he would be drawn into limitless cycles of reciprocal violence] (Four Zoas, 356). Rather than signaling Urizen's victory, Orc's crucifixion and metamorphosis into a serpent signifies the fusion of the two adversaries into undifferentiated violence, whose historical consequences are to be seen in the policies of government ministries and state religion that sanction unregulated child labor, the slave trade, and military aggression motivated by the desire for imperial supremacy. Clearly for Blake, the psychodynamics of Selfhood apply to the behavior of nations as well as individuals, for his poetry describes how in each case "Desire clings to violence and stalks it like a shadow because violence has become the signifier of divin[e sovereignty]."[9]

It is this deeply pervasive but largely unrecognized link connecting violence with the Lockean view of the Self that animates Blake's artistic vision. For, as I have tried to suggest, Blake sought to expose as delusional and dangerous the pervasive notion of the Self as an isolated subjectivity situated in a material universe. He saw that such limited self-understandings were at the root of intra- and inter-personal fragmentation, and that in their obedience to the logic of negation rather than the productive opposition of contrarieties they must inevitably succumb to the patterns of violent mimetic rivalry that characterize Albion's protracted nightmare, and the reality of human history.

ENDNOTES

1. Blake, William. *The Marriage of Heaven and Hell*, in *The Complete Poetry and Prose of William* Blake, ed. David Erdman (UC California Press, 1982), plate 14, p. 39.

2. Blake, William. "Annotations to Wordsworth's *Poems*, in *The Complete Poetry and Prose of William* Blake, ed. David Erdman (UC California Press, 1982), p. 665.

3. Blake, William. *Jerusalem: The Emanation of the Giant Albion*, in *The Complete Poetry and Prose of William* Blake, ed. David Erdman (UC California Press, 1982), p. 147.

4. Blake, William. *The Marriage of Heaven and Hell*, in *The Complete Poetry and Prose of William* Blake, ed. David Erdman (UC California Press, 1982), plate 4, p. 34.

5. Blake, William. *The Marriage of Heaven and Hell*, in *The Complete Poetry and Prose of William* Blake, ed. David Erdman (UC California Press, 1982), plate 3, p. 34.

6. Blake, William. *The Four Zoas: The Torments of Love & Jealousy in the Death and Judgement of Albion the Ancient Man*, in *The Complete Poetry and Prose of William* Blake, ed. David Erdman (UC California Press, 1982), p. 302.

7. Girard, Rene. *Deceit, Desire, and the Novel* (Johns Hopkins UP, 1962), pp. 10–11.

8. Ibid. p. 106.

9. Girard, Rene. *Violence and the Sacred* (Johns Hopkins UP, 1972), p. 151.

PSYCHEDELIC ROMANTICISM: GINSBERG, BLAKE AND WORDSWORTH

LUKE WALKER

> *The notion that man has a body distinct from his soul, is to be expunged; this I shall do, by printing in the infernal method, by corrosives, which in Hell are salutary and medicinal, melting apparent surfaces away, and displaying the infinite which was hid. If the doors of perception were cleansed every thing would appear to man as it is: infinite. For man has closed himself up, till he sees all things thro' narrow chinks of his cavern.*
>
> William Blake, *The Marriage of Heaven and Hell*, 1793.

William Blake, a marginal figure in his own lifetime (1757–1827), attained the status of presiding deity within the transatlantic counterculture of the 1960s. This aspect of Blake's reception history has sometimes been treated with embarrassment by scholars of Romanticism, but in recent years it has gained increased attention; see for example the 2017 exhibition *William Blake and the Age of Aquarius*, and its beautifully produced companion book (Eisenman, 2017).

If it is easy to perceive Blake's visual influence on the swirling organic style of 1960s psychedelic concert posters, it is equally clear why his poetry and prose seemed so meaningful to the psychedelic pioneers of the mid twentieth century. In the lines quoted above, Blake prescribes a method by which humanity can perceive 'the infinite' through opened 'doors of perception'; surface reality must be melted away, using an acid which is medicinal. As anyone with an interest in psychedelic history will be aware, these lines gave Aldous Huxley the title for his groundbreaking trip report *The Doors of Perception* (1954), and Jim Morrison a name for The Doors. Moreover, while there is no evidence that the visionary Blake ever used any drugs beyond an occasional pint of beer, a recognizable drug culture existed amongst other Romantic writers such as Samuel Taylor Coleridge, Thomas De Quincey and Humphry Davy, which paralleled that of the 1960s.

Growing interest in this set of interwoven psychedelic and literary histories was apparent at Breaking Convention 2017, with papers by George Erving on the radical non-dualism of Blake's philosophy and Neşe Devenot on Huxley's Romantic inheritance, as well as my own talk, adapted below, on Allen Ginsberg's psychedelic readings of Blake and Wordsworth. The time therefore seems ripe for the concept of 'Psychedelic Romanticism' to take its place within the current psychedelic renaissance, as well as within the field of Romantic reception studies.

GINSBERG AND BLAKE

Over the course of a few days in the summer of 1948, as a twenty-one-year-old student at Columbia University, Allen Ginsberg had a series of consciousness-expanding experiences which were by turns blissful, absurd and frightening. They were not only Blakeian in the sense that they seemed to mirror Blake's own visionary experiences, but also in the sense that they were directly linked to, and even stimulated by, Blake's poetry. Later, Ginsberg began to refer to these 1948 events as his 'Blake vision' (in the singular), even though during these multiple experiences Blake's presence was manifested in a primarily auditory form, as Ginsberg heard the voice of Blake reciting poetry to him.

There are discrepancies between some of Ginsberg's various accounts of the Blake vision, but according to most versions, the initial ecstatic part of the vision occurred while he was reading a specific Blake poem, 'Ah! Sun-flower' from *Songs of Experience*, and in a sense the vision was a reading of that poem. It involved a sudden understanding of the poem's combination of particularity and universality; Ginsberg felt an intense self-identification with both the 'Sun-flower' itself, 'Seeking after that sweet golden clime', and the 'Youth' in the poem, who 'pined away with desire', at the same time as realizing that the poem, in Ginsberg's words, 'expressed some kind of universal longing for union with some infinite nature' (Ginsberg, 2001: 36–37).

This first ecstatic vision was followed the same day by two further experiences, brought on by reading two more poems from *Songs of Experience*, 'The Little Girl Lost' and 'The Sick Rose'. As with 'Ah! Sun-flower', Ginsberg again experienced an intense and overwhelming sense of identification with the central character of 'The Little Girl Lost', a girl called Lyca, while also interpreting the poem in universal terms:

I suddenly realized that Lyca was me, or Lyca was the self... 'If her heart does ache / Then let Lyca wake'—wake to what? Wake to the same awareness I was just talking about—of existence in the entire universe. The total consciousness then, of the complete universe. (Ginsberg, 2001: 39)

His vision of 'The Sick Rose' was much darker: 'I experienced "The Sick Rose," with the voice of Blake reading it, as something that applied to the whole universe, like hearing the doom of the whole universe, and at the same time the inevitable beauty of doom' (2001: 38). Other visions in the following days, which centred around Blake's poems 'London' and 'The Human Abstract', became increasingly paranoiac: 'it was the same depth of consciousness or the same cosmical awareness but suddenly it was not blissful at all but it was *frightening*. Some real serpent fear entering the sky... like a hand of death coming down on me' (2001: 44).

It is clear from Ginsberg's descriptions that these were not just experiences of 'hearing voices', but also of sudden and complete consciousness expansion. Yet while the vision was in every respect a classic psychedelic experience, it was not drug-induced. In fact, according to Ginsberg himself, his early experiments with a range of psychedelic drugs—beginning with his first peyote trip in 1952 and continuing through his first use of LSD in 1959 and first uses of ayahuasca and psilocybin in 1960—were primarily focused on recapturing or recreating the essence of what he referred to as his 'natural' Blake vision. The vision was a source of inspiration to him personally and to the other Beats, leading him to adopt Blake as a poetic and spiritual 'guru'. As I have argued elsewhere, Ginsberg's insistent proselytizing on Blake's behalf was the key reason why 1960s counterculture gained an intrinsically Blakean character, so that the 1948 Blake vision deserves to be treated as one starting point for the 'long 1960s'.

In the years immediately after the visions, Ginsberg theorized that the words of Blake's poems contained a hermetic effectiveness in and of themselves, by which the listener might transcend bodily, material reality. Blake's words could be mystical catalysts, and if he learnt their secret Ginsberg might gain the same power. 'Poetry is the secret formula for / miracles', he concluded in an unpublished poem from this period (Ginsberg, 1977: 197).

However, from the early 1960s onwards, Ginsberg also began to see the Blake vision as a kind of burden. In a further link with Romantic poetry, he half-jokingly described the vision as an albatross around his neck: like Coleridge's Ancient Mariner, Ginsberg felt the need to explain his visionary experience to all those he met (Ginsberg, 2001: 35). As Ginsberg's commitment to Buddhism deepened during the 1960s and 1970s, he realized that his mental attachment to the Blake vision—including his obsessive quest to recover its essence through psychedelics—was a form of suffering or 'dukkha'. He explicitly signalled this shift in attitude within his 1963 poem 'The Change', composed following a long stint in India, in which he vowed to abandon the body-mind dualism that had underpinned his visionary quest up to this point. The solution was not to abandon Blake, nor to abandon psychedelics, but rather to pay renewed attention to the embodied, material aspects of the experience. This eventually resulted in an understanding of poetry as a *material* catalyst for psychedelic experience, so that Blake's poems were understood not as secret codes, but as universal mantras or even as tabs of acid, their effects available to all readers and listeners. This was an important shift from Ginsberg's earlier understanding of the 1948 vision, in which he had believed himself to be individually chosen to receive the spirit of Blake, just as Blake himself had received the spirit of his poetic guide Milton. Under the influence of the non-theistic religion of Buddhism, he came to understand the Blake vision less as an external, spiritual visitation from God or Blake, and more as an internal, embodied event. Much later in his life, Ginsberg even suggested that the voice arrived from the future as much as the past: 'the voice of Blake, the ancient saturnal voice, is the voice I have now. I was imagining my own body consciousness' (Ginsberg, 1974: 21).

This shift in Ginsberg's interpretation of the 'psychedelic Blake' solidified further after 1968 when he began the twin practices of setting Blake's poems to music and engaging in long Buddhist and Hindu mantra-chanting sessions. Now he realized that it was precisely the bodily, physical effects of rhythmic sound and breathing patterns which might cause a chemical change in the mind similar to that achieved through psychedelics. This did not mean that he became reductionist or wholly materialist in his thinking on this topic; he still believed that psychedelic experiences, whether triggered by the words, rhythms and breaths of poetry, or by plants and chemicals, were far more than mere 'hallucinations'; they were of profound importance for an understanding of existence itself. But it did mean that, having let go of his earlier obsessive attachment to his personal Blake vision, and of his attempts to use drugs to recreate it or to decipher a mystical meaning, he was now in a position to explicitly make the chemical connection between poetry and psychedelic substances.

In 1965, Ginsberg speculated that 'certain combinations of words and rhythms actually had an electrochemical reaction on the body, which could catalyze specific states of consciousness. I think that's what probably happened to me with Blake' (Ginsberg, 2001: 31). In a 1971 interview, he took this idea further, explaining how the visionary experience accessed via psychedelics or poetry is not so much the experience of a secret, transcendent other universe, but rather the normative state that society must return to:

Western civilization has certainly come to this funny kind of contradictory point where finally its technology has produced a chemical which catalyzes a consciousness that finds the entire civilization leading up to that chemical pill absurd, because the consciousness was always there all along with the animals in the forest, or when you were huntin' the animals in the forest... The function of Blake art or Blake's art, is to catalyze that experience in other people... as a psychedelic universal cosmic consciousness... So you find in Blake or in any good poetry a series of vowels which if you pronounce them in proper sequence with the breathing indicated by the punctuation... will get you high physiologically (Ginsberg, 1974: 17–23).

PSYCHEDELIC WORDSWORTH

While Ginsberg considered Blake to be his 'guru', his interest in the links between psychedelic consciousness and Romantic poetry also extended beyond Blake. In 1967, during a break from the Dialectics of Liberation conference at London's Roundhouse, Ginsberg made a weekend trip to Wales, where he visited Tintern Abbey in the Wye Valley, a site made famous by William Wordsworth's poem, then continued on to the more remote Llanthony Valley, where he took LSD on a hillside, and while still high began to draft one of his great poems of the 1960s, 'Wales Visitation'.

He later (rather flippantly) referred to 'Wales Visitation' as 'my first great big Wordsworthian nature poem' (Kramer, 1970: 22), and the poem makes reference to Blake, to Wordsworth, and to Tintern Abbey itself. Indeed, as I have argued elsewhere, the poem is not merely Wordsworthian in tone, but represents a very conscious, philosophical engagement with Wordsworth's 'Lines Written a Few Miles Above Tintern Abbey' (Walker, 2013). Furthermore, Ginsberg's LSD-inspired 'Wordsworthian nature poem' must be seen as part of his broader interest in explicitly psychedelic readings of Wordsworth, representing a second, often overlooked element of Ginsberg's psychedelic Romanticism, alongside Blake.

Although Wordsworth and Blake are very different poets—not least, as Ginsberg himself often pointed out, in terms of their politics— Ginsberg found a psychedelic sensibility within Wordsworth's poems such as 'Tintern Abbey', where Wordsworth famously attempts to define and evoke

> *a sense sublime*
> *Of something far more deeply interfused,*
> *Whose dwelling is the light of setting suns,*
> *And the round ocean, and the living air,*
> *And the blue sky, and in the mind of man,*
> *A motion and a spirit, that impels*
> *All thinking things, all objects of all thought,*
> *And rolls through all things.*

In a 1975 lecture, Ginsberg claimed that Wordsworth 'had visited Tintern Abbey and had some sort of psychedelic experience' (Ginsberg, 2011a). Although he was not suggesting that Wordsworth's experience was drug-inspired, Ginsberg's use of the word 'psychedelic' does indicate a direct parallel between the experience that led Wordsworth to write 'Tintern Abbey' and his own LSD trip that inspired 'Wales Visitation'. Ginsberg also frequently drew attention to the 'drug culture' within which Wordsworth wrote, even if, unlike his friends Coleridge and Davy, he did not partake. '*What went on,*' Ginsberg wondered, 'in the Humphry Davy household on Saturday midnight, when Coleridge arrived by foot, through the forest, by the lakes?' (Ginsberg, 2001: 44).

During the 1960s, as a leading representative of the counterculture, Ginsberg was often called upon to publicly discuss the effects of psychedelic drugs such as LSD and defend their use. Not only did he make specific comparisons with Wordsworth's poetry, he often made the point that the epiphanic visions experienced during an LSD trip were just as 'natural' as those described by Wordsworth in the 1790s. Within months of composing 'Wales Visitation', Ginsberg read the poem in its entirety during a PBS television interview with conservative ideologue William Buckley, patiently (but also provocatively) explaining that it was 'written in Wales, high on LSD. Fifth hour of LSD for those who are specific technologists in this', before going on to claim that the LSD vision was 'a natural thing. I cited Blake and Wordsworth as having that natural vision' (Ginsberg, 2001: 90). By 1968, the linking of Blake with drugs had become a 1960s commonplace, but it is significant that Ginsberg goes beyond this well-established Blakean psychedelic trope, to suggest links between Wordsworth's poetry and the psychedelic experience.

In another television interview conducted in the 1990s, Ginsberg again linked Wordsworth with psychedelics, explaining that 'the psychedelic experience, whether with peyote, or LSD, or psilocybin… might catalyze a very similar sense of infinity, or expansiveness, or "panoramic awareness" we call it, which you find in Wordsworth's "Sonnet on Westminster Bridge" or his moment on top, when he steps out of the mist in *The Prelude*' (Ginsberg, 2011b).

While both of these interviews took place after Ginsberg's composition of 'Wales Visitation', we can identify them as belonging within a series of public statements made by Ginsberg in similarly formal and even inquisitorial settings, in which he draws on Wordsworth to explain and justify the use of psychedelic drugs. Significantly, this trope dates back to before the 1967 LSD trip that inspired 'Wales Visitation'. In a remarkable testimony given during a special US Senate hearing on drugs in 1966, Ginsberg described a recent LSD trip in which

> *I saw a friend dancing long haired before green waves, under cliffs of titanic nature that Wordsworth described in his poetry... I accept the evidence of my own sense that, with psychedelics as catalysts, I have seen the world more deeply at specific times. And that has made me more peaceable.* (Ginsberg, 2000, 72–73).

Here Ginsberg not only explicitly equates his LSD vision with a Wordsworthian version of the sublime, but also follows this with what sounds very much like a paraphrased version of lines 48–50 of 'Tintern Abbey':

While with an eye made quiet by the power
Of harmony, and the deep power of joy,
We see into the life of things.

In these and other statements, Ginsberg again defines within a psychedelic context Wordsworth's poetic vision of what he and Coleridge called the 'One Life', a concept which lies at the centre of Romanticism; he also makes it clear that he sees no essential difference between his own spontaneous 'Blake vision' of 1948, the visionary experiences described by Wordsworth, and an LSD trip. For Ginsberg, Romanticism, whether of the Blakeian or Wordsworthian variety, is inherently psychedelic; in making this claim, he locates the Beat movement and 1960s counterculture within a Romantic context, while also defining Blake and Wordsworth through the context of their countercultural reception.

BIBLIOGRAPHY

Eisenman, SF. (ed.) (2017) *William Blake and the Age of Aquarius*. Princeton, NJ: Princeton University Press.

Ginsberg, A. (1974) *Allen Verbatim: Lectures on Poetry, Politics, Consciousness*. Edited by Ball, G. New York: McGraw-Hill.

Ginsberg, A. (2011b) BBC Face to Face Interview, 1994. *The Allen Ginsberg Project*. Available at: https://allenginsberg.org/2011/11/bbc-face-to-face-interview-1994-asv21/ (Accessed 15/07/18).

Ginsberg, A. (2000) *Deliberate Prose: Selected Essays 1952–1995*. Edited by Morgan, B. Harmondsworth: Penguin.

Ginsberg, A. (1977) *Journals Early Fifties Early '60s*. Edited by Ball, G. New York: Grove Press.

Ginsberg, A. (2001) *Spontaneous Mind: Selected Interviews 1958–1996*. Edited by Carter, D. London: Penguin.

Ginsberg, A. (2011a) Wordsworth - 1975 Naropa Class. *The Allen Ginsberg Project*. Available at: https://allenginsberg.org/2011/11/wordsworth-allens-1975-naropa-class-2/ (Accessed 15/07/18).

Kramer, J. (1970) *Paterfamilias: Allen Ginsberg in America*. London: Victor Gollancz.

Walker, L. (2013) Allen Ginsberg's 'Wales Visitation' as a neo-Romantic response to Wordsworth's 'Tintern Abbey'. *Romanticism*. 19(2) pp. 207–217.

THE FEELING & THE FIELD: PSYCHEDELIC ANALOGIC & THE POETICS OF EXPERIENCE

SAM KNOT

In which the literary metaphor undergoes metamorphosis into something of its own antithesis: a form of psychedelic straight-talk.

'Bard Nameless as the Vast, babble to Vastness!' So says Allen Ginsberg in 'Wales Visitation', his 1967 poem about an acid trip in the Black Mountains. *Babbling to vastness* is a pretty neat way to encapsulate the act of psychedelic poetry! But perhaps primarily our attention is being drawn to the associated *state of namelessness*: it is here we find our metaphorical ground, the fertile dirtiness from which sprouts these 'orchards of mind language manifest human' (Ginsberg).

We return to a state of namelessness, both in the psychedelic experience and as be-mused poets, when we see beyond language as merely the habit of thinking we already know what it is we are talking about. In tripping we encounter language alive, as something that emerges in and as experience itself, being the many ways existence says itself. This is a realm of novelty and inspiration, where the only facts seem to be feelings, and meaning can complete us without ever finishing itself off. Here we find a mode of language we have to give ourselves up to: we cannot really pin it down or simply reduce it to itself.

The dominant cultural trend, at least when it comes to saying anything of real importance, is to prioritise the literal mode of words meaning only the thing to which they directly refer. A neat and tidy approach like this can enable us to use language as a formal system with which we can prove stuff (logic, in other words) but this will only take us so far: language as a whole is a much trickier beast, and sitting right at the core of its infinite capacity for tricks is metaphor, a thing possessed of such primordial shape-shifting categorical fluidity that it tends to challenge the very act of its own definition.

Aristotle, circa 350 BCE, gives our earliest definition in his *Poetics*, stating in the broadest sense that metaphor consists of the transference of names, either associatively along lines of species and genus, or comparatively via proportion or analogy. We have since refined his definition to classify the first instance as metonymy, reserving metaphor for the second, and this distinction has become something of a binary pair we can use to organise our thoughts, not only in linguistics and literary theory, but also in cognitive science and even psychology (perhaps other places as well). In many cases it can be quite straightforward to tell a metonym (English is my tongue) from a metaphor (these words are butterflies), and yet there are ways we might read certain metonyms metaphorically, and of course metaphor relies (at least in part) upon metonymic (categorical/associative) relationships for its functionality (even in subverting such); and so metaphor complexifies this relationship, making it hard to know exactly where one might start and the other end. In this way it can appear that, in attempting to analyse something that goes right to the roots of human meaning-making, we might court meaninglessness as well.

Aristotle writes of metaphor as being underlain by a kind of analogical equation: A is to B as C is to D, stating that we need only give two terms in order to infer the others, and also that one of the terms might refer to some nameless quality. An example he gives is the line: 'sowing around a god-created flame', making the point that, while scattering seeds is called sowing, the action by which the sun scatters its rays has no proper name of its own. So that, as well as helping us to talk about nameless or novel things, metaphor might fire our imaginations to reinvigorate established senses (a starry gardener?) revealing what can otherwise become hidden behind well-used words. Thus with effective metaphor experience can be renewed and ideas reborn, and this is one way we could make the literary metaphor itself a metaphor for the psychedelic experience, which could then lead us to say that all poetry (or the good stuff at least!) might be effectively psychedelic.

Such analogical acts of moving meaning about illustrate quite clearly the standard etymological derivation of *meta-phor* (from the Ancient Greek) as *carrying over*. We might also note an established directionality to this transference: we tend to transfer meaning from something familiar or sensory to something novel or conceptual. Such directionalities are often uncovered by metaphor research: it is deeply fascinating to me how they are suggestive of certain asymmetries in the ways we think (at the very least), for instance there are hierarchies in how our senses interact within language and how we apply them to the world (*I see all there is to feel*), and there is the relationship between space and time, in which we tend to apply spatial metaphors to time but not vice versa, making their relationship asymmetrical (at least cognitively) and yet (at least conceptually) we might consider them co-emergent. Thus *metaphorical space* becomes something of a star player here, being both imagination's unreachable limit and its inexplicable essentiality, allowing our psychedelic poets to communicate an embodied emptiness, gifting them the ethereal concrete of this psychedelic now in which to invoke (mind/time/imagination) at play with the sort of intentional absence (space!) by which poetry shares power.

So—space is anything but nothing, and yet nothing is ultimately what it brings to mind—perhaps 'most concretely' space is difference: but even this suggests a certain absence (and absence, in something of a conundrum, can be rather easy to miss). Our modern dictionary definition states that metaphor is: 'a figure of speech in which two things that are not literally connected are compared for effect'. Well, I am taking the dictionary at its word here, but perhaps the only things that *are* literally connected are words and their definitions (or else everything might be)? Thus the dynamic role of difference in metaphor is largely dismissed when framed purely in terms of *non-literality*, and our focus on the similarities involved begins to seem somewhat belligerent. Metaphor arguably derives its imaginative power (its ability to shake us up, to say so much with so little) most profoundly from the degree of difference that can be present: the gaps that open up. So, rather than saying *not literally connected,* perhaps we should be saying *sufficiently different* instead?

Regardless, the flipside of this is that the start of our standard definition is rather a lot of fun: *metaphor is a figure of speech.* Here we have stumbled across a multi-dimensional pun that neatly introduces us to the modern meaning of *meta,* this notion of something referring to itself: *figure of speech* is in itself a metaphor, and here it occurs inside something of a metaphor about metaphor, and just to go one dizzying step deeper: the word metaphor can itself be seen as a metaphor: it uses the etymological image of *carrying over* in order to concretise its conceptual nature. Of course in formal terms this is worryingly meaningless stuff, its self-referential nature can give rise to infinite recursion: *the horror! Metaphorical turtles all the way down!* But this kind of thing is only really a problem for logical robots: if we can do something with this notion of *a figure of speech*, if we can respond to it imaginatively—explore it a little—then talking about metaphor with recourse to further metaphors might actually get us somewhere in quite a meaningful way.

Now, before we get to the poetry in earnest (and in order to really put the *figure* into these *figures of speech*) I need to make explicit one more approach to metaphor that is massively relevant to our understanding of the psychedelic literary metaphor: this is the idea of cognitive or conceptual metaphor, most notably explored by Lakoff and Johnson in *Metaphors We Live By* (1980). I ask you to briefly ponder the following phrases: *I am high. I am getting spun out. Okay now I am centred. You have grounded me. I figured it out. I have gotten to grips with it. I see what you mean. Man that is far out.* These are just a few examples of the cognitive metaphors that are so staggeringly widespread in our speech, so deeply embedded in our day-to-day communications, that they can sometimes be a little slippery to get a hold of. Perhaps we might notice quite quickly the metaphorical component of such common expressions as *falling in love* or being so angry our *blood boils*—but the idea can be subtler than that—we might talk about something being *out of sight*, and this could carry the implication of a deeper underlying metaphor of, for instance, *sight as container*. What I aim to put across most clearly here is the sense in which such metaphors are not merely tricks of language but somehow express the very structures of thought: they reveal how we understand the world in terms of our own embodied experiences— our language is literally figurative—*our bodies fields of feelings in which language makes senses.*

So let us return to this vast namelessness, inside and out, which could be considered as the literal suspension of what is *noun* (known!) or else the utter *verb*-alisation of everything. This is the condition for the possibility of language embodying itself. It is here that language reveals its primary nature as an act of disclosure. Only later, when the poetry is over, can language be considered literally as representation. Thus the bearded bard, when he tells himself to *babble*, this is a euphemism for poetry—to talk from experience full of innocence, to be the babbling brook using its own body to tell of its travelling paths. Here we allow language to be its most primal self, making human being poet. This self-effacement (for Ginsberg's poem is anything but babble!) is thus a form of permission: to be merely *babbling on* we can allow ourselves the ultimate freedom to say what we please and to go where we need—and this is the condition for the possibility of psychedelic poetry.

*

We now begin our exegesis in earnest, in introducing the other poem under current consideration, Michael McClure's 'Peyote Poem', written in 1955. It opens thus:

> *Clear—the senses bright—sitting in the black chair—Rocker— / the white walls reflecting the color of clouds / moving over the sun. Intimacies! The rooms // not important—but like divisions of all space / of all hideousness and beauty. I hear / the music of myself and write it down // for no one to read.*

And so, along with *babbling to vastness*, we now have a fair idea of what the act of psychedelic poetry might entail! *I hear the music of myself and write it down for no one to read.* This is a very fertile phrase. To begin with we could take it quite literally (if only for the sake of breaking a rule): McClure might be hearing the sounds of his own biology going about its business—the gurgle of his belly or the hum of his ears, maybe even the fizz of his neurons—and all these potential perceptions would be inevitably orchestrated in experience, conducted through himself and thus somewhat literally musical. But I think the deeper sense we get—*the music of myself*—is of noticing thought itself come to being: being aware of swathes of feeling that move through us, wordless ideas that might then determine themselves in writing. This keys us in to the notion that we might consider this poem a score, and so not only is it not the music: here we are talking about something that is not even words.

It is also interesting to note that, as with written music, this instant translation of trans-imaginative sensation will be somehow different and yet somehow the same each time it is performed. Thus a poem (like life) can have many meanings, and not all of them will be merely opinions, even if they happen to logically contradict or shift over time. Henri Bortoft, in *Taking Appearance Seriously* (2012), talks about this in terms of 'the dynamical unity of self-differencing.'

Also, we are writing *for no one to read*. And so here we are again, giving ourselves permission to say whatever we need, to be completely uncensored, to bring forth poetry for the sheer psychedelic feck of it! But more than that, we have conjured the presence of an absence: in writing *for no one to read* we are performing an action for no one to do, which is to say that no one might be someone too, and this speaks directly to us, as readers, for if we are reading this then we must be that no one, and for sure we are no longer entirely ourselves!

Psychedelic poetry delights in apparent paradox; it is a happily oxymoronic thing, filled with sophisticated stupidities—and while we might find such absurdities fun to trip over, at the same time they present us with no real stumbling block. This comfort with contradiction seems to manifest primarily in the context of embodying a certain spaciousness, thus we return again and again to this primordial interplay of space and body, the nameless and the namer, the unspeakable speaking.

Before moving on let us examine the first metaphor, which is in the form of a simile:

The rooms not important—but like divisions of all space of all hideousness and beauty.

Upon these white walls we watch the colours of cloud shadows dance; by virtue of this spatial division, this blank plane, we see projected a compressed drama of our solar system, of sun and earth and atmosphere and eyes, and it is intimate—it is all right here—but these particular divisions of space (our very own walls and windows) are not particularly important: they are instances of some universal action by which space is distinguishing itself, which in turn speaks to our sense of aesthetics (the ways we distinguish hideousness and beauty) and this cosmic insight is simply par for the course, a mere side-effect of paying attention. This is not your average literary metaphor! To me it seems as much a phenomenological observation as any kind of rhetorical device. In other words figures of speech such as these can appear as a natural consequence of reporting from a place that is upstream in our perceptual processes; a place where everything is happening as one, at once, but where this already means at least a few different things: we are immediately the medium; we no longer see things as we are habituated to, as if they were already there—we catch them in the very act of appearing. This is a realm in which subject and object have yet to distinguish themselves from each other; hence many psychedelic paradoxes might only be paradoxical after-the-fact.

'I smile to myself. I know // all that there is to know. I see all there // is to feel. I am friendly with the ache / in my belly. The answer // to love is my voice. There is no Time! / No answers. The answer to feeling is my feeling. // The answer to joy is joy without feeling.' (McClure).

Such a passage seems to me replete with something like sleight-of-hand metaphors: feelings beg questions to which they themselves become the answers; joy is answered by the transcendence of its own emotional nature, which is our witnessing it—our being beside ourselves with joy—yet this is not two separate things; this is joy in its completeness. We have seen that one of the standard ways of talking about literary metaphor is in terms of there being a state of tension between two things that are not literally connected but only juxtaposed for communicative purposes, but here we see that psychedelic metaphor can sometimes (even simultaneously) be considered *a textually unfolding instant of one thing in self-tension.*

Here is my favourite example of such a self-transformation: 'SPACIOUSNESS / And grim intensity—close within myself. No longer / a cloud / but flesh real as rock.' (McClure). These lines hint at a subtle reversal of the normal movement of metaphor (in which a sensory image proceeds towards an abstract concept), although we can see that here, in the image of cloud becoming flesh becoming rock. The abstraction to which this transfers is a transformation that simultaneously conveys a movement back in the other direction: it is as if space had become merely a conceptual thing, and here we witness its ingress back into flesh, and this space-flesh concrete as rock, in the sense that now we can actually grasp it: we are no longer just thinking about space, it is present as an aspect of our being embodied.

★

With this dynamic in mind let us slip back into the Ginsberg trip:

> *All the valley quivered, one extended motion, (...) a giant wash (...) a wavelet of Immensity, (...) Roar of the mountain wind slow, sigh of the body, (...) one Majesty the motion (...) white fog poured down (...) on the mountain's head—(...) mixing my beard with the wet hair of the mountainside, smelling the brown vagina-moist ground, (...) One being so balanced, so vast, that its softest breath moves every floweret in the stillness on the valley floor, (...) lifts trees on their roots, birds in the great draught (...) Groan thru beast and neck, a great Oh! to earth heart*

So, here we have a metaphorical act of personification (and a very old one at that) but there is a subtle genius to this portrayal of 'Mother Nature' that we might not notice at first: in talking out the body of the mountain-person not once is there any reference to mind. The entire scene is unified, animated, brought to life by virtue of One Great Breath—not through any notion of consciousness—certainly nothing that resembles thought as we ordinarily think it. The mountain is the head and body of nature as engaged in meditation, focused on breath— which is our breath too—and so it is through the feeling of our own no-mind (our own experiences of being conscious in wider senses) that we might begin to understand the ways in which nature is—well, let us just say the ways in which nature is! *Mind the gap!*

Here we see the idea of embodied cognition that underlies conceptual metaphor, and yet it seems to be turning itself inside out: in being aware of our breath we can know without really having to think about it that at no point are our bodies entirely our own—*yet this is what we are*—our cognition embodied in ever-more-enveloping forms of embodiment. This is not necessarily to say 'microcosm-macrocosm' or 'as above, so below' (in other words it is not primarily a statement of romantic identification) it is more like stating that *everything shares an interfacing nature* (which could also be the revelation of a phenomenological ontology) being as bodies that distinguish ourselves in, and as spectra of, space. One Great Breath embodies this space sensationally brought to life, and all meaning needs this space to breathe, to be. This field of feeling is outside and inside and all throughout—it is the very abyss made immanent—and so ours is a world of phenomenal gaps: spaces that reveal in and as themselves a variety of substances and properties—yet fundamentally these spaces will not be closed—*such primordial gap-ness might only be displaced.*

Thus we come to another way of seeing the 'explanatory gap' (as introduced by Joseph Levine in 1983) that has been a problem in theory of mind (and for materialist philosophies more generally): this is a tension between brain-based mechanisms and mind-based experiences—quantification and qualia—or what we might think about poetically in terms of a play between body and space: *in a very real sense anything that bridges the 'explanatory gap' becomes metaphor.* Thus for poets it is not a problem! It is the infinitely expressive *self*-explanatory gap: a form of permission given necessarily as limit, a sort of continual *no*-ing that all-ways says *yes*.

Let us finish the breath:

The great secret is no secret / Senses fit the winds, / Visible is visible, (...) Heaven breath and my own symmetric / Airs wavering thru antlered green fern / drawn in my navel, same breath as breathes thru Capel-Y-Ffn, / Sounds of Aleph and Aum / through forests of gristle, / My skull and Lord Hereford's Knob equal, / All Albion one. (Ginsberg).

When I first saw this line: *Visible is visible,* I thought: Shit! Here I am trying to make a case for psychedelic metaphor and the poem I chose ends with an anti-metaphorical metaphor! *What doth this mean?!* And then I noticed that McClure's poem, which is a completely different poem in so very many ways, curiously enough performs the same sort of trick: 'The room is empty of all but visible things. // THERE ARE NO CATEGORIES! OR JUSTIFICATIONS! // I am sure of my movements I am a bulk / in the air.' (McClure). Such that both poems seem to present the psychedelic experience as a journey beyond metaphor—and so I realised that, due to the imaginative nature of the experience, this must be none other than the radical acceptance of metaphor, or in some sense its fulfilment. Such a process seems to stem quite naturally from giving ourselves the permission to be performatively psychedelic—to act imaginatively and flow—and so the psychedelic poet seems to reveal something of the nature of what our bodies tell us we are: *enshrined openings.* Our bodies tell us that language tells us that metaphor tells us that: Being is always seeing through, and this seeing through is a seeing *to*, too.

★

Visible is visible. I find it somewhat amusing that these words have the same literal structure as the primary proposition in formal logic: A is A, but that in actual fact they point to a transcendence of this law of the same. These words say that what it means for things to be visible has in itself become visible. So not A is A, nor simply A is not-A, nor necessarily A is to B as C is to D; but more like A-Z, a.k.a: any of these if you so very please—but any, always, never only! This is the imaginative limit that allows us to say what we like, which is how we can be free while continuing to exist, meaning meaning cannot be exhausted, though in itself this can exhaust us, this ultimate spaciness of our bodies, these cosmically anarchic ways we are ruled by nothing, being always in the presence of that-which-is-neither-here-nor-there, the irreducible unexpandable imaginative simplexi-tease of this primordially positive negation—the utter wHoliNess of 0ursElves! This is the very essence of the innateness of structure as well as the opportunity for deconstruction—and so metaphor, like the psychedelic experience itself, is meta-structural: in exploring it we become more aware of our own perceptual and conceptual processes, by which we realise knowledge as grounded dynamically in the body, which leads us to say that truth, in a very primordial sense, necessitates *self-disclosure*. Language is a self-differencing hologrammatic unity that rearranges itself according to what is being said, which is what beings say/Being says. This is the metaphorical heart of psychedelic analogic, being *merely poetry, in other words*.

SOURCES

Aristotle. (350 BCE). *Poetics.* S. Butcher trans. [online] The Internet Classics Archive. Available at: classics.mit.edu/Aristotle/poetics.html [Accessed 6th May 2018].

Bortoft, H. (2014). *Taking Appearance Seriously: The Dynamic Way of Seeing in Goethe and European Thought.* 2nd ed. Edinburgh: Floris Books.

Ginsberg, A. (1994). *Planet News 1961–1967.* 9th ed. San Francisco: City Lights Books.

McClure, M. (2011). *Of Indigo And Saffron: New and Selected Poems.* Berkeley/Los Angeles/ London: The University of California Press.

Lakoff, G. and Johnson, M. (1980). *Metaphors We Live By.* 1st ed. [ebook]. Chicago and London: The University of Chicago Press.

Levine, J. (1983). Materialism and Qualia: The Explanatory Gap. *Pacific Philosophical Quarterly,* 64, pp. 354–361.

A SPELL ON THE TONGUE: THE USE OF HEIGHTENED SPEECH TO ALTER CONSCIOUSNESS

ERIC MADDERN

INTRODUCTION

Language has power. It is more than just a means of communication. When certain words are used in particular situations by gifted speakers at the right time they can transform receptive listeners. Those with ears to hear may be transported into another realm. They may be enchanted. They may feel uplifted, inspired, grateful and invigorated. They may be roused to act. They may feel love and see beauty. They may smile or laugh or gasp. They may be infused with the gift of divine power. Such 'heightened speech' has the capacity to touch places in the soul that other chatter does not reach. It is mind-altering and consciousness expanding.

I'd like to explore—as a practitioner rather than an academic—some of the time-honoured ways in which heightened speech has been used. The earliest examples are found in rituals done to cultivate and revere the sense of the sacred. They address the divine and also ensure cultural continuity and social cohesion. They may focus on rites of passage or purification, oaths of allegiance, healings, blessings, marriages, funerals and more. They take place in a context of participatory performance and make use of special music, song, dance, costume, food, symbolic acts and objects. Offerings or sacrifice may be part of it. But at the ceremony's core is the retelling of a sacred story, connecting the participant to the power of deities or ancestors and told through invocation and incantation; song and spell; prayer, preaching, praise, poem and prophesy. All use heightened speech. It is from such early rituals that theatre and most of the other arts have evolved.

Looking at the spectrum of the arts that make use of heightened speech we see that there is a literary-cultural end and a sacred end. The 'literary-cultural' end includes story, poetry, theatre and song. These are definitely expansive and potentially transformative forms, though they don't have the avowed intent of awakening the sacred or communing with the divine. However they often achieve this anyway. The sacred end of the high speech spectrum includes the avowedly spiritual practices of ritual, prayer, spell, blessing and prophecy.

I'd like to look at how some of these forms—from the spiritual to the cultural ends of the spectrum—use 'a spell on the tongue' to bring about an altered state of being. Perhaps at root what they do is simply open the gateway to the sacred, to the further reaches of human consciousness. This is particularly important in our time when so much of modern life is dominated by the profane. I cannot be comprehensive so am going to describe a few of the ways in which heightened speech is used to alter the state of mind. Some of my key examples will come from the Cymric tradition, as that is the mythic realm in which I am most steeped.

1. ORIGINAL RITUAL TRAVELS TO TIMELESS REALMS

So let's begin with primal or original ritual. In ritual everyone takes part, there is no audience. Often the language is out of the ordinary. It may include unusual or archaic forms of speech, it may not even be comprehensible, but in the context of a ritualised performance it has power. An actor-participant may become a mythic ancestor or play an archetypal role in a cultural foundation drama. S/he may have a painted body or wear a ceremonial mask and costume. S/he may chant or dance, 'becoming the person s/he was at the beginning of time'. The song-chant may be telling an ancient story. The rhythmic incantation may be repeating the names of god, thus transporting the chanter into an alpha state of bliss, into communion with mythic beings, giving a feeling of connectedness and transcendent identity. All who participate enter into a divine or sacred realm, becoming channels for a greater power.

EXAMPLE
Keeping the Dreaming Alive
One of my favourite examples of ritual is the sight I was privileged to see of Pitjantjatjara elders sitting cross-legged on the sand, rattling their boomerangs and singing ancient songs from the Dreaming in a cascading song-chant melody, while others, their bodies painted with ochre, vigorously danced and stamped the red earth. In such a way the land itself is energised and the people too draw spiritual strength from the earth and from their ancestors. And the Dreaming is kept alive.

2. PRAYER SPEAKS TO THE SACRED

Prayer often takes place within a ritual. It can be personal and intimate. It's the smaller self addressing the larger self, whether it be conceived as Ancestors, God, Great Spirit or The Universe. It might be Life, the Force that Drives the Green Fuse, the Generating Creativity of Evolution. Whatever it is, you are addressing oneness, wondrousness, infinity, eternity. Prayer is speaking to the gods and goddesses. It is addressing those higher beings, however they are seen or felt or imagined. It is talking up, offering gratitude and appreciation, giving one's self to the greatness. It may be asking for forgiveness or favour. It may express high hopes for healing, love and fulfilment. It may beseech divine aid to manifest a vision, great or small. It may simply be asking for help to live a worthy life.

EXAMPLES
The Lord's Prayer is probably the best-known example in Christian countries. Perhaps it is elevating for some; for many it may feel familiar and friendly, but for others endless repetition of it as a rote mutter may have rendered it somewhat meaningless.

What works better for me is this Tewa prayer:

Oh our Mother the Earth, oh our Father the Sky,
Your children are we, and with tired backs
We bring you the gifts that you love.
So weave for us a garment of brightness;
May the warp be the white light of morning,
May the weft be the red light of evening,
May the fringes be the falling rain,
May the border be the standing rainbow.
Thus weave for us a garment of brightness
That we may walk fittingly where birds sing,
That we may walk fittingly where grass is green,
Oh our Mother the Earth, oh our Father the Sky!

Such a prayer, especially when spoken outside in nature, is as effective a connector to sacred realms as anything.

3. PROPHECY CHANNELS THE DIVINE

Whereas in prayer the person speaks up to 'the gods', in prophecy 'the gods' speak down through the person. The prophet is thus thought to be channelling words that are divinely inspired, however 'divine' is conceived or experienced. Prophecy is an uncommon art these days. Perhaps the best-known modern prophet would be Martin Luther King who not only seemed to, but also claimed to, channel his 'dream' directly from God.

EXAMPLE
Merlin's Prophecy
There's a well-known story from Welsh tradition that culminates in a renowned passage of heightened speech. Vortigern, a usurper king, had fled from the Saxons and was trying to build a tower below the mighty summit of Snowdon. His walls kept collapsing and eventually an old druid said he must sacrifice a fatherless boy for his walls to stand. Such a child was found but, on the point of sacrifice, broke free from his captors

and *saw* the problem. Dragons! For this boy was none other than the young Merlin and he had 'the sight'. Red and white dragons, freed from an underground cavern, chased each other across the heavens before disappearing over the horizon. Merlin, infused by dragon power, fell into a prophetic trance.

This is supposed to have happened about fifteen hundred years ago and yet somehow a version of this prophecy has survived, presumably passed down by word of mouth until it was transcribed by Geoffrey of Monmouth in 1136 in *The History of the Kings of Britain*. It's full of strange and unfamiliar symbolism and yet some of it weirdly rings true to this day. It's an extraordinary example of speech uttered in an altered state or trance that can still be uplifting. As a 'myth-handler' I've taken some liberties adapting it. Here's the last part of my version of Merlin's Prophecy.

Though the Goddess be forgotten
there will come a time of plenty
when the soil will be fruitful beyond man's need.
The Fatted Boar will proffer food and drink;
the Hedgehog will hide his apples in London.
Underground passages will be built beneath the city.
Stones will speak; the sea to France will shrink
and the secrets of the deep will be revealed.

But beware the Ass of Complacency,
swift against goldsmiths, slow against ravenous wolves.
Oak trees shall burn and acorns grow on lime trees.
The Severn River will flow out through seven mouths.
Fish will die in the heat and from them serpents will be born.
And the health giving waters at Bath shall breed death

Then root and branch shall change places,
And the newness of the thing shall seem a miracle.
The healing maiden will return, her footsteps bursting into flame.

She will weep tears of compassion for the people of the land,
Dry up polluted rivers with her breath,
Carry the forest in her right hand, the city in her left,
And nourish the creatures of the deep.

With her blessing
Man will become like God
Waking as if from a dream:
Heart open and filled with light,
Radiant face, glowing like the rising sun,
Shining eyes, like twin silver moons,
Radiant ears, shimmering with song,
Shining lips, that dance over words,
Words of magic that burst into the air becoming swallows.
The soul shall walk out; the mind of fire shall burn.
And, in the twinkling of an eye, the dust of the ancients
Shall be restored.

In the *White Book of Rhydderch* one of the oldest surviving fragments of story says that: 'before it was taken or settled these islands were known as "Clas Myrddin"', Merlin's sacred enclosure. Whether there was one or many Merlins, there is undoubtedly a figure with that name in the collective unconsciousness of Britain who may once have been the high priest of the land; who is associated with the building of Stonehenge and the coming of Arthur; and who uttered an inspired prophecy which rings true even now. Any words attributed to this archetypal character, no matter how much they've been reshaped over the centuries, have an aura and are a prime ancient example of heightened speech.

4. BLESSING DISSEMINATES GOODWILL

Chanting is about becoming one with higher forces. Prayer involves beseeching the gods. Prophecy is channelling down great power. One who gives a blessing, however, is channelling divine energy through him or her and giving it out to someone saying: 'you are divine', 'you are a living human being, blessed to be alive, blessed by the love of greater powers'. A blessing should help the receiver feel connected to the divine forces of the whole.

EXAMPLE
Adapted Buddhist Metta Blessing
> *May you be well.*
> *May you be true to yourself.*
> *May you have your heart's desire.*
> *May you live in grace and love.*
> *And may you—be Gaiaed!*

Here the term 'Gaiaed' refers to the experience of feeling at one with the entire living Earth, a kind of mythopoetic spiritual-scientific sense of the sacred.

5. THE STORYTELLER GUIDES LISTENERS THROUGH IMAGINARY WORLDS

In centuries past stories were handed down through an oral tradition. This is where the power of heightened speech reached its zenith. Storytellers cast a light trance over their audiences, using elaborate descriptive passages to paint vivid pictures in the mind's eye of their listeners' ears. They engaged them emotionally on a journey to a parallel world, a once upon a time realm of the imagination. They used rhetorical runs to captivate, to engage and to enchant. You weren't there when it happened but the storyteller was, it seems. By dipping into that other world, even if only for a brief hour, you are bathed in Earth's oceans, enriched by Life itself.

EXAMPLES
Culhwch and Olwen
Here is an example drawn the earliest story to feature Arthur, 'Culhwch and Olwen' from the Mabinogion. This first selection shows the vivid use of visual imagery. Culhwch is riding to his cousin Arthur to ask

for help on his quest to make Olwen his bride. See the picture that is painted of the gilded youth floating on his way to the great king. Notice the Celtic knotwork imagery of crisscrossing greyhounds and clods of earth flying like swallows. This pairing of horses with birds is common in folklore. Horses are said to fly across the earth while birds gallop through the air!

Culhwch rode on a fine grey steed with sturdy shoulders and hooves like shells. Its bit was of gold; its saddle was inlaid with gold. In one hand he carried two silver spears, in the other a great battle-axe so sharp it could draw blood from the wind. On his thigh he wore a golden sword that glinted in the morning sunlight. From each corner of his crimson cloak hung an apple of red gold. Each apple was worth one hundred cows. In front of his horse ran his two white greyhounds crisscrossing from one side to the other, as four clods of earth from the horse's hooves flew about his ears like swallows. And as he made his way to Arthur's court not one strand of his hair moved, so light was the trotting of his horse.

Quest for Mabon

Later in the story Culhwch and his companions have to find Mabon son of Modron, the Great Son of the Great Mother. Mabon is the only one who can capture (from between the ears of the savage boar) the scissors, razor and comb needed to cut the hair of Olwen's giant father so she can be released to marry Culhwch. Neither Arthur, nor any of his warriors, nor the kings of Ireland and France, is up to this job. The quest for Mabon works as a kind of incantation. They have to ask the Ancient Animals, each of whom tells in turn how old they are. First they come to the Blackbird of Cilgwri. Gwrhyr, the Interpreter of Tongues who speaks all languages, asks the question:

"We are messengers of Arthur seeking Mabon son of Modron. Have you ever heard of him?" And the Blackbird said: "I am old, very old. When I was young there was an iron anvil here and every night I wiped my beak on it. Now it's no bigger than a nut. But in all that time I've never

heard of the man you seek. However there is one older than I and that
is the Stag of Rhedynfre. Go to speak to the Stag."

And so they come to the Stag who directs them to the Owl who
directs them to the Eagle. Each one is extremely old and yet has not
heard of Mabon. But the Eagle thinks he knows who will know. He says:

'I am old, very old. When I was young there was a great rocky crag here.
Every night I would stand on top of that crag and peck at the stars. Now
that rock is no bigger than a fist. But in all that time I've never heard
of the man you seek. However... once I went to the pool at Llyn Llyw
and there I saw a mighty fish that would feed me for many days. So I
flew down and sank my talons into its back. But it pulled me under the
water. It was all I could do to escape. Later I went with my kinsmen
to make war on that Salmon but the Salmon offered us only peace. I
drew fifty barbs from the back of that fish. If the Salmon doesn't know
about the man you seek I don't know who will.'

Of course it the Salmon, the oldest and wisest of the Ancient Animals,
who knows. Mabon is found and Arthur's warriors set him free. Soon,
riding the White Horse with the Dark Mane (symbolic of the Goddess)
the Great Son of the Great Mother overcomes the forces of darkness
(the Most Savage Boar and the Chief Giant) and releases Olwen, in
whose footprints spring up white flowers, and who is therefore the
Spirit of Spring.

This story could be the echo of an ancient ritual about the role of
the Goddess in overcoming darkness and bringing about the return
of Spring.

6. POETRY IS AN INFUSION OF INSPIRATION AND DEPTH

A poem may be narrative but more often is not. It may use compelling visual imagery but is more about enchanting with rhythm and unexpected rhyme, with cadence and the meaning of the words. It may surprise, shock or amuse. It may create an 'aha' moment. Often there is a density that repays familiarity: well-known lines may impart a feeling of wonder, pleasure, depth. Performance poetry is a contemporary example of heightened speech, empowered by the presence of the poet who delivers his or her words from the soul, as they were intended to be expressed. Here language is intensified. It is drinking an infusion of inspiration and beauty and depth.

EXAMPLES

Birth of Inspiration

There is a classic story from Welsh tradition about the birth of poetic inspiration in a culture where poetry is still granted high status. Ceridwen had gathered the ingredients to make an inspirational brew for her unfortunate son. But it was Gwion Bach who stirred the pot and after a year and a day it was he who accidentally swallowed the three drops of inspiration originally intended for his dark brother. Suddenly he was more awake than ever. He knew flowers and stars by name, remembered the past and could see into the future. He knew, too, that he had to run.

As Ceridwen chased him, they transformed through the elements. He was a hare, she became a hound. He was a salmon, she became an otter. He was a sparrow, she became a hawk. He was a grain of wheat, she became a hen—who pecked him up and swallowed him whole. Later she felt a quickening and in due course a boy was delivered, Gwion Bach reborn. Unable to slay him she placed him in a leather bag and pushed him out to sea where he floated for many moons, the waves of the world crashing over him, creatures of the deep whispering into his ear.

At last the bag was pulled from a fish weir by the unlucky son of a king. As he slit open the bag out stepped a young boy with light shining from his brow. 'Taliesin', the prince exclaimed, meaning 'Shining Brow'. Later, when asked by the king how he could speak when he was so little, he said: 'I am better able to speak than you are to question me.' 'In that case you'd better speak', said the king. And so it was that the young Taliesin spoke his first great poem.

I am Taliesin.
I make poetry of perfect meter and rhyme that will last till the end of the world.
I know why breath is black, why silver gleams, why liver is bloody.
I know why a cow has horns, why milk is white, why a woman is affectionate.
I know why ale is bitter, why brine is salt; why a kid is bearded, why cow parsley is hollow.
I know why the cuckoos complain, where the cuckoos of summer are in winter
I know what beasts there are at the bottom of the sea.
I know how many drops in a shower, how many spears in a battle,
Why a fish has scales, why a white swan has black feet.
I have been a blue salmon.
I have been a dog, a stag, a roebuck on the mountain;
A stock, a spade, an axe in the hand; a stallion, a bull, a buck.
A grain of wheat I grew on the hill.
I was reaped and placed in an oven.
I fell to the ground as I was being roasted.
A black hen swallowed me.
For nine nights I was in her crop.
I have been dead. I have been alive.
I am Taliesin.

This is an example of so-called 'I am' poetry, where the poet appears to remember many of the forms he has been in previous lives and many of the 'I know why's' he has learned. These kinds of insights may be familiar to those with psychedelic experience, where a window opens to memory that appears to go far beyond one lifetime. The inspiration associated with Taliesin and his poetry is widely known as Awen and is, arguably, the ultimate aspiration of all Welsh tradition.

7. THEATRE IS DRAMATIC PLAY WRIT LARGE

Theatre is ritual shorn of its explicitly divine intent. Rather, cleverly crafted words engage the audience's mind and hearts with ideas, characters, dramatic situations, a larger than life world to get lost in: the great passions and high dramas of the world are played out and ultimately resolved. Theatre can tell stories, be poetic, horrify, amuse and inspire awe. And sometimes passages reach out to lift the audience into the sublime, leaving the witness rinsed in Soul.

EXAMPLE

Here are just two examples that have meant a lot to me. Ted Hughes regarded this first piece from Shakespeare's *The Tempest* as the high point of western poetic literature.

> *Our revels now are ended. These our actors,*
> *As I foretold you, were all spirits and*
> *Are melted into air, into thin air:*
> *And, like the baseless fabric of this vision,*
> *The cloud-capp'd towers, the gorgeous palaces,*
> *The solemn temples, the great globe itself,*
> *Yea, all which it inherit, shall dissolve*
> *And, like this insubstantial pageant faded,*
> *Leave not a rack behind.*
> *We are such stuff*
> *As dreams are made on, and our little life*
> *Is rounded with a sleep.*
> *William Shakespeare*
> From *The Tempest*, Act 4 Scene 1

The Human Heart

George Trevelyan, in *Magic Casements* (subtitled 'The Use of Poetry in Expanding Consciousness'), says:

> *True imagination can blend with the being within form, and rediscover the miraculous oneness of all life... Poetry rightly used and rethought can become an instrument for awakening the atrophied organs of perception of the invisible worlds, the "magic casements opening on the foam of perilous seas and faery lands forlorn".*

Sir George often used to quote this passage from *The Sleep of Prisoners* by Christopher Fry. Though from a play it feels like a poem, a blessing and a prayer. It urges us to take 'the greatest stride of soul we ever took'. For me this is one of the finest examples of contemporary heightened speech.

The human heart may go the lengths of God.
Dark and cold we may be, but this
Is no winter now. The frozen misery
Of centuries breaks, cracks, begins to move.
The thunder is the thunder of the floes,
The thaw, the flood, the upstart Spring.
Thank God our time is now when wrong
Comes up to meet us everywhere,
Never to leave us until we take
The greatest stride of soul we ever took.
Affairs are now soul size
The enterprise is exploration into God.
But where are we making for? It takes
So many thousand years to wake,
But will we wake for the whole Earth's sake?

AND FINALLY...

There are many ways to experience an altered, or heightened, state of consciousness. My argument in this piece is that the spoken word, delivered with conviction and soulfulness, is one of the ways to achieve this end. I have tried to explain how, in different forms, this process works, and have given some examples. Prayer, blessing, poetry, story and more can lift a listener into sublime, divine and sacred realms that transfix the imagination and make life radiant with meaning. Even today it is still possible to experience the numinous through all these forms of heightened speech.

July 2018

PLANT MEDICINE CULTS: PSEUDO SHAMANISM, POWER, COERCION AND CONTROL

ELIZABETH JOYCE

In recent years, there has been a notable rise in the phenomenon of ayahuasca tourism, and with it, growing concerns about the existence of related cults. In October 2015, the *Daily Mail* published an article about 'suicides, sects, murder and insanity' in South American plant medicine retreats, which reported the recent deaths of two travellers in ayahuasca ceremonies. (Roper, 2015). This was preceded by a television show called *The Path*, which centres on an ayahuasca cult; the desire for belonging, and the psychic and social conflicts involved. (Jun, 2016). It is within this context that I became interested in the importance of ayahuasca cults, and collected the accounts of three 'survivors' of a cultic retreat centre in the Peruvian Amazon. This chapter focuses on the relational aspects of the cult experience, exploring issues of power, exploitation and subjugation within these stories.

The chapter begins with a definition of cults. It then analyses theoretical themes of conformity and belonging, and narcissistic bonding, interweaving the case studies of three women—two White European and one African American – who lived together in a new age plant medicine community in Peru, under the guidance of a White American male leader. The analysis reveals the dangers of coercive relational bonds formed with charismatic guru figures, and mechanisms of abuse. It is hoped that by illuminating the processes of brainwashing, indoctrination and coercive persuasion inherent in cults, this could raise awareness around the systems of control, allowing potentially exploited followers to find freedom.

DEFINING CULTS

The first thing to note about cults is that they very rarely define themselves as cults. Alexandra Stein (2017) defines cults as groups being led by a charismatic and authoritarian leader. They are governed by closed, isolating, hierarchical power structures, and exclusive totalising ideologies. Members are coerced into participating in isolating routines and an all-encompassing attachment to the leader, based on fear. Part of the reason members tend to remain in cults for so long—often lifelong—is because of unquestioned beliefs in the group's practices. This manifests in fundamentalism, an adherence to dogma and a monolithic identity (Singer, 2003). The closed, secretive nature of cults perpetuates systemic processes of psychological manipulation which keep followers in a state of confusion and entrapment. This form of manipulation, commonly known as gaslighting, creates a destabilising environment of denial and deception, which can lure victims further into a disorientating bondage cycle. Getting out then implies a collapse of the psychic and social structures that keep the idealised leader and powerful system of manipulation and thought reform in place, so the attachments, based largely on trauma and fantasy, endure.

There is a large body of research on the psychology of cult leaders, in which they are widely defined by pathological narcissism, a sense of personal uniqueness and entitlement, and absence of empathy. They often depend on their followers just as much or more than followers need them, but they disavow their own dependency, projecting it onto others, and building their identities around the admiration and fear of those they subjugate. In Daniel Shaw's (2014) account, the cult leader is a traumatising narcissist, who

seeks hegemony for his subjectivity by weakening and suppressing the subjectivity of the other for the purpose of control and exploitation.

The other is then left in grave doubt about the validity and even the reality of their own subjectivity. This sadistic, abusive aspect of narcissism stems from the belief, often held unconsciously, that the separate subjectivity of the other is a threat to the survival, literally and/or figuratively, of one's own subjectivity – and the other must therefore be captured and kept under control.

In order to defend against this form potential of coercive control, it is important to remember that leaders are usually charming and charismatic, but predatory. They isolate the group, operating in secrecy, and use techniques of manipulation and brainwashing to keep followers in a dissociative and confused state. They are deceptive and evade scrutiny, often encouraging followers to break contact with their families and friends. Other common dynamics of cult leaders (Shaw, 2014) may include controlling minds through 'purification of the ego'; demanding perfection and willingness to obey; a culture of hysteria or urgency and normalising a violation of boundaries. Cult leaders refused to be challenged or criticised, and require unwavering loyalty from followers, who in turn are indoctrinated into believing that their support of the leader's mission is life-affirming for them.

'GROUP MINDS', CONFORMITY AND BELONGING

The human need to belong is universal, but making sense of the social system to which we belong requires thought. Following Freud's (2005) analysis of Le Bon's work on the group mind, groups are impulsive, and whenever living beings gather together in groups, they instinctively place themselves under the authority of a master. When Franka, a twenty-eight-year-old White German woman, travelled to the Peru, her intention was to seek a spiritual experience through the use of ayahuasca. She found a retreat centre located in a remote part of the Amazon jungle, which promised ancient medicinal healing, community and ceremony. She was drawn in by the affirmation of a holistic lifestyle and the commitment to self-evolution and 'becoming whole'. When she arrived in the rainforest, the retreat was so far removed from her urban lifestyle in Germany, that she felt she could be 'reborn.' In Franka's words:

> *I was met by a member of the centre at the airport, who took me into the jungle by local transport. A shaman was waiting at the entrance and doused me in some potion which is used to cleanse the energy field, and then I was told to remove my shoes and join the group who were busy carving from the roots of plants, to make medicine. The whole place was geared towards medicinal healing, and some people referred to it as a hospital. I met some people who had done ceremonies the night before, and they looked dazed and confused. They told stories of healing and enlightenment, which scared and intrigued me.*

Up until that point, she said, she had not believed in the existence of spiritual entities or a 'higher power', but the group seemed convinced.

> *A woman told me my spiritual animal and said the plant medicine had gifted her with psychic abilities that helped people realise their "soul purpose."*

She met the leader, who shared his own story of struggle and the road he took to salvation and enlightenment.

Elise, a thirty-five-year-old White woman from Belgium, described the leader as 'charming and quite magnetic, but intimidating and narcissistic. Everybody seemed drawn to him but also feared him because there was a deadness behind his eyes. He used to go into the main town of Iquitos and when he was away, everyone in the retreat centre relaxed. And whenever he came back, we all had to be seen to be working or busy doing something. Some people were in isolation, doing medicinal treatments which lasted days or weeks. The volunteers and workers were always busy cleaning, cooking, working on the land and rushing around. He said he was creating a utopia and he didn't like us sitting around talking.' Visitors and residents would follow the leader's orders because they valued the structure and sense of belonging they created, but the rigid routine was also exhausting, and inhibited freedom of thought. Elise had joined the retreat centre as a resident, but then stayed on as a volunteer.

I didn't really question what I was doing there. I thought it was a good way to meet people, drink ayahuasca, and it was an ideal setting to build a community. Whenever I had a spare moment by myself, feelings of frustration and rage would come up, but I couldn't let them linger because there wasn't time.

Both Elise and Franka said they wanted to believe the leader's vision of paradise; and being in a remote part of the jungle with no access to technology or outsiders helped create a sense of new possibilities.

THE PROMISE OF A PERFECT WORLD

Each day on the retreat began at six o'clock in the morning with a meeting held by the leader, who assigned members a series of tasks—cooking, cleaning, running yoga and tai chi classes, talking to guests about ayahuasca's healing potential, facilitating 'sharing groups' for guests to open up about their difficult histories and surrender to the process of personal transformation and enlightenment. The leader's unquestioned belief that he was creating a perfect world laid the foundation of his authoritarian rule, which is common in cults. Shaw (2014) notes that when he participated in a cult, he portrayed to others 'an idealistic commitment to a noble spiritual path, dedicated to spiritual awakening and uplift in the world.' (Shaw, 2014, p. 44). Sabrina, a forty-three-year-old African American woman who worked in the Peruvian retreat centre for a year, described her commitment to the cause as

an entirely new way of life. When I first found ayahuasca, my mind was blown open, and I didn't know how to make sense of the new feelings of love and vulnerability I was experiencing. I wanted to help everybody, and I thought I'd found the answers to all life's problems. I thought if everybody could take this medicine—politicians, sick people—the world would be healed.

When she was offered an opportunity to live and work in the retreat centre, she imagined she would be part of a movement dedicated to the creation of a 'new paradigm', and if anything went wrong, it was because the creators were involved in new territory, under the guidance of unseen spiritual forces, such as 'plant spirits', and 'the universe.'

It was an exciting time. Everyone seemed to believe in the project, and we worked day and night trying to fulfil our vision. The more involved I became with the ideal of this perfect world, the less contact I had with the outside world. It was as though I was becoming a different person, and my old life no longer made sense or meant anything to me.

But the new self-identity, bound up with the 'perfect world' being created, was based on fundamentalist ideas fed down from the retreat's leader to its members. In Singer's (2003) book, *Cults in Our Midst*, cults are defined as having a charismatic leader, who is often worshipped and deified. They operate through the psychological processes of 'coercive persuasion' or 'thought reform', and leaders use patterns of manipulation and exploitation, which are idealised from below. Sabrina, Franka and Elise all described their desire to buy into the ideology of the retreat's leader, even when the reality was so different from their shared fantasy. The leader encouraged fear and suspicion of the outside world and a disavowal of member's previous lives, and used his own narrative of salvation to instil ideals that life inside the cult was the safest place to be and thrive. In Sabrina's words,

my memories of my life outside the jungle were tainted by this idea that when I had ayahuasca, I woke up and had returned to my true self, with nature, and before that, I was sleeping. I started to doubt that anything I'd been involved in before the "awakening" was even real.

The only reality afterwards centred around her adherence to the leader, and competitiveness with others who were also vying for his attention.

As Franka said,

the perfect world he kept talking about was all his world. The retreat was built with his money, and he was profiting financially from it. It was all his vision. I didn't know what it meant but really, I didn't even question it. After the ayahuasca, we were told the plants would guide us in everything. But that was dangerous. I just felt cut off and I missed home, but it was sometimes impossible to tell reality apart from fantasy. None of us knew we were in a cult. I don't think (the leader) even knew what he was setting up. We were all just going along with it as though our lives depended on it.

It was this shared vision of an imagined utopia that kept the followers closely enmeshed with each other, refusing to allow other realities, including that of the previous lives they had occupied outside the commune, to be given expression.

THE ROLE OF AYAHUASCA IN THE ACT OF COERCIVE CONTROL

Links between cults, the occult, and drug use have been recorded throughout history, venerated in the works of Aldous Huxley, William Blake, Arthur Rimbaud, as well as writers of the beat generation such as William Burroughs and Allen Ginsberg. Transcendental religious experiences and hallucinogenic drugs were popularised during the 1960s and 1970s, and many cultic groups have been formed on the use of certain mind-altering drugs, as well as the promise of curing drug addiction. As has been mentioned, cults operate within a closed structure, and followers are controlled by a sense of powerlessness, fear and dependency, thought reform, and system of reward and punishment. (Singer, 2003). Ayahuasca is an Amazonian indigenous brew comprising of two plants, *Banisteriopsis caapi* and another plant, usually chacruna (*Psychotria viridis*). It has a very powerful visionary effect, and some indigenous groups believe it produces the only true reality, whilst waking life is an illusion. (Fotiou, 2010). Ayahuasca is said to possess a spirit, with the ability to communicate and transmit knowledge through visions.

All of the participants in this study described their ayahuasca-induced experiences as profound and life-changing. But in the visionary state, their bodies became weak, they purged a lot, and their minds were opened. Franka said

> *I couldn't move for hours and at times I was so uncomfortable. It was worse than any nightmare. But then it shifted and [the plant] showed me something beautiful and comforting, and I stayed around for that because it was like nothing I'd ever known.*

This speaks to the fear and dependency, reward and punishment system inherent in cults. Sabrina gave a further account of her isolating and fear-inducing experience, 'after the fifth ceremony, I didn't even know what I was doing there. My mind was so warped, and my body felt so different. I was lighter, but also heavier, like more and more was coming up from inside, and it became an addictive process. I wanted to go deeper and explore what the plants were trying to tell me'. This quest for truth was mirrored by the leader's promises, which Elise said had maintained her dependency on the cult. 'Every ceremony was so powerful and each one was different, with new messages to absorb and try and process. There was no time to integrate what was being communicated though, because the leader told us not to think, and our days were so full, we didn't have any time to ourselves, so we were going from one intense experience to another, with the constant noise of the jungle around us.'

NARCISSISTIC BONDING AND SUBJUGATION

In a recent book by Janja Lalich, (2018) based on research on the children of cults, cult survivors said they had formed intense bonds with other members through shared trauma, which had left them feeling alienated when trying to form relationships with outsiders. The 'trauma bond' is a theory Shaw (2014) develops, when he notes that the kinds of bonds formed between cult members and leaders are narcissistic, as authoritarian leaders maintain a rigid sense of omnipotent superiority, infallibility and entitlement. The leader's fantasies of perfection and self-sufficiency have a cumulative effect of trauma and disempowerment on followers, who are ridiculed, humiliated or shunned if they resist domination. The leader's sense of omnipotent rule coerces the follower's into complying with his wishes and take on his disavowed feelings and fears of abandonment as their own. Discourse on mind control and brainwashing widely relates the personality of cult leaders to psychopathy. An absence of empathy encourages grandiose preoccupations with unlimited power, a tendency to treat others as objects to be manipulated and controlled, and a lack of guilt. Cult leaders are often thought to be outwardly charming and are deeply dependent on the attention and validation of others. They dominate followers by isolating them from their families and the outside world.

Volunteers, workers and guests of the Peruvian Retreat were being exploited by the leader from the moment they entered the centre, in many subtle and overt ways. The leader only employed attractive women to work in his team of housekeeping staff, counsellors, yoga teachers and so on. Two men were employed to work on the land, and they were described by Sabrina as passive or easily subjugated. After paying large sums of money to join the community, the new recruit's commitment was strengthened by their participation in regular 'sharing circles', in which they were asked to tell stories about their personal lives and the vulnerabilities that had led to them choosing to explore the 'medicine path' as a new way of life. Shaw defines cults as groups being led by a traumatising narcissist, in which members are subjugated largely through their objectification, and destruction of their subjectivity. Members are given validation only at the guru's discretion, and only to the extent that they comply to their demands. It is the kind of narcissism that leads a person to believe they are omnipotent and attracts followers who willingly and unconsciously submit to control.

The 'sharing circles' were designed to facilitate a 'breakdown of the ego' and build connections between retreat members. But the isolation and vulnerability left them open to being manipulated and controlled. Elise described a situation in which she had tried to challenge the leader and was publicly shamed.

He couldn't handle any criticism, and when I tried to tell him he was pushing us too far and making us work too hard, with no breaks, he lost it. It felt like I was a child trying to stand up to my father.

Sabrina said she had also interacted with the leader as an idealised father figure, who later became punishing and threatening. She blamed her lack of self-esteem for her identification with the leader's grandiosity and said that her submissiveness was met by his authoritarianism. Being in isolation in the jungle facilitated the creation of an intense and suffocating bond, which impeded her ability to think. The relationship quickly became sexualised, and although she insisted she was willingly participating in the beginning, she later learnt that the leader was having sex with some of the other women, and that many had previously left the retreat centre on grounds that they had been violated. Because the women were kept isolated, they were unable to organise or speak out. Shaw (2014) names these invisible violations 'murders of the soul.'

The relational configurations involved in traumatic narcissism are therefore based on subjugation. The cult leader is created and strengthened through the enslavement and debasing of the other, and these violent acts of exploitation and control are done in the name of love. (Shaw, 2014, p. 136). Convincing followers that they are being loved rather than abused, a process of gaslighting, participants get caught in an imaginary system, maintained through the erasure of subjectivity and reality. Breaking free and working through the allure of these bonds involves an understanding of power and a confrontation with mechanisms of objectification and submission, which can sometimes be too much to bear.

GETTING OUT

There is something captivating about the idea of relinquishing oneself to an omnipotent, infallible and self-sufficient paternalistic Other. The tendency towards domination and complicity is inherent in the matrix of human power relations, and to stand outside this may be to get lost and annihilated. As psychoanalysis tells us, we exist in the field of the other, but the fundamentalism of cult relationships should not, as Lifton argues, be seen as the final word. (Singer, 2003, p. xii). Rather, possibilities arise with the emergence of a more open, reflexive and ethical self, that rejects absolutism and dogma. Lifton calls this the 'protean self', after Proteus, the Greek sea god of multiple forms. Returning to the narratives of the three women who had been immersed in traumatic relational bonds with the leader of the retreat centre, all spoke about the difficulties they experienced in identifying the abuse of this charismatic but delusional form of control.

Sabrina was the first to leave, following another conflict with the leader, in which she was oppressed and her voice negated. The leader had also been trying to coerce her into a sexual relationship, and when she refused to concede to his domination, she was silenced and shunned, and forced to walk away. Although Sabrina said she felt only relief after months of living in a state of destabilisation and anxiety under the leader's control, Franka, who left the community a few weeks later, reported that she was still reliving the effects of the narcissistic abuse in her mind. Having forgone her individuality to become an object in the leader's world, she said she was still thinking and dreaming about him constantly, and struggling to embody a separate self. This was echoed by Elise, who was seeking counselling to help her make sense of her experience, and the loneliness and search for meaning in life outside the intensity and highly structured routine of the jungle.

All of these accounts speak to broader questions of self and otherness, negation and trauma. The phenomenon of cults illuminates our need to belong and connect. When we become objects of cult leadership and traumatising narcissism, our ability to act and think gets reduced to a reactive pattern of subjugation to the leader's demands. The leader's persistent denial of the other's subjectivity or right to exist as a separate self creates a contradictory and destabilising environment centred around his sense of omnipotent power. Seeking constant validation and excessive admiration, this power is maintained through fantasies of specialness and entitlement, based on the exploitation and devaluation of others. Breaking away from a cult involves a recognition of the relational systems of subjugation that keep targets trapped within a matrix of power, and an enduring process of recovery, as it is hoped the deep-rooted effects of relational trauma eventually become rewritten by mutuality, compassion and respect.

PSYCHEDELIC CEREMONY IN THEORY AND PRACTICE

JULIAN VAYNE

I'm going to talk about psychedelic ceremony. I'm going to give a range of examples of these practices and finish by considering the opportunities and challenges that face *us*, the growing planet-wide psychedelic community.

I suspect we the people at this conference (Breaking Convention 2017) have a broadly shared consensus of what we mean by 'psychedelic'. Our consensus would probably be around ideas like altered or extraordinary states of consciousness. The 'conscious' bit matters; these are states of awareness, they are the things we can recall, however imperfectly, when back in what we typically describe as our baseline or 'normal' states of awareness. The 'extraordinary' component of our definition reflects our subjective perception that these states are ones that are different, sometimes radically different, from the states of awareness that we are usually in. To use one of the latest descriptions for what the psychedelic state is, we can describe it as one in which the connectivity across brain regions is significantly changed, and increased (or perhaps more accurately, 'normal' cognition is downregulated and other connections emerge). We know that these mind states can be induced through a wide variety of practices: sex, dance, meditation, protracted periods of darkness, breathwork and of course by introducing various substances into our bodies.

But what is ceremony? When we think of ritual and ceremony, we may imagine military or civic rites, those of formal religious or public occasions. Celebrations of a particular event, achievement, or anniversary. We may imagine that words like 'ritual' or 'ceremony' indicate a series of actions performed according to a prescribed order. We might imagine a 'solemn act, formal and dignified, characterized by deep sincerity'. Equally we might imagine the wild bacchanalia or carnival. Ritual and ceremony are a broad church, but in the sense that I am using the terms here I'm interested in ceremony as *the intentional use of metaphor to affect the imaginal world.*

Ceremony for me is a natural activity for symbol-using meaning-making creatures such as ourselves. Sure, sometimes it may be formal in nature; at other times it may well up as a spontaneous gesture. Laying flowers at the site of a tragic event, wrapping presents, ritually disposing of our dead. These are things our species does. Ceremony then is the deployment of acts that are symbolic, often metaphorical, sometimes carefully planned, sometimes free-form and spontaneously arising in the moment.

In the context of the use of psychedelic drugs, psychedelic ceremony is the manipulation of sets and settings within which we might explore those remarkably potent and remarkably safe experiences offered by medicines such as DMT, ayahuasca, mescaline, LSD and all those other fascinating chemicals, the power and significance of which we are celebrating and exploring at this conference.

Why not 'psychedelic session'? Why use the religious-sounding word 'ceremony'? Well there are two reasons for this. The first is that I come to psychedelics as an occultist, an indigenous 'shaman' of the British Isles, and so I tend to think in those terms. Occultism is the study of that which is hidden, such as the relationship between matter and mind, a relationship that psychedelic drugs bring into stark relief. The practice by which this exploration happens is usually called 'magic' which we could think of as *the use of the imaginal world to extend the limits of our achievable reality.*

The second and bigger reason is that the sense of the sacred that these substances can generate demands the use of a word that goes beyond the apparently 'secular' expressions of 'session' or 'experiment'.

The word 'ceremony' itself derives from a Latin root that suggests ideals of holiness, sacredness and awe. Sure, many people eschew anything that sounds 'religious' but I feel that using this word shows both respect to those indigenous traditions who use entheogens, and reclaims the word from the dead hand of doctrinal belief. We need not throw the baby of the sacred out with the bathwater of dogma.

We are fortunate to be living in a time when knowledge about methods to hold, support and direct the psychedelic state is abundant. There is a great confluence of wisdom from 'traditional' practitioners, underground psychonauts and licensed scientific researchers. In the West, since the time of Tim Leary et al., we have known that the mental state and the environment can profoundly influence the way that our drug trip unfolds. Western culture itself has created ceremonial settings in response to the emergence of two widely available psychedelic drugs. Our first attempt at this was the creation of the music festival, our culture's collective response to LSD. Later we created the rave to hold the experience of MDMA. Our innate indigenous shamanic intelligence gave rise to the First and Second Summers of Love.

Psychedelic drugs are special, powerful things that by their very nature stimulate a feeling of 'the sacred' and this feeling runs deep. This feeling often inspires people not only to create specific environments and ceremonies for their psychedelic sessions, but also during the process of producing the drugs in the first place.

Whether we are mindfully rolling a joint, or singing as we stir the bubbling pot of ayahuasca, the preparation of these medicines that can evoke a sense of the divine is itself a sacred process.

There is, for example, some fascinating research to be done on the use of ceremony by contemporary clandestine chemists. I spoke with former psychedelic chemist Casey Hardison and asked whether he did anything he would consider to be a 'ceremony' when he produced, for instance, LSD. Casey told me that he used crystals, smudging with sage and other practices during some of this work. He had a practice of setting LSD to crystallize while music played, 'righteous Rasta music' structured to echo the pattern of the chakras in Asian esoteric anatomy.

Asked why, Casey said that his intention was that the molecule would somehow be affected by the music, helping those who took the drug to 'absorb the energy of loving themselves, allowing them to have the highest vibrational experience'.

Casey was by no means unique in his practice. To quote Cosmo Feilding Mellenin an interview about the film he directed, *The Sunshine Makers*:

The purity of different types of acids was an important part of psychedelic culture. People believed that the purer the acid, the better the trip. It was all very subjective, of course – Owsley would pay attention to the music they were playing in the lab at the point of crystallisation, and would then pray over the equipment to imbue it with positive vibes. Tim (Scully) was a rational scientist and initially thought it was all mumbo jumbo, but he eventually got sucked into it.

Information on the ritual preparation of acid was sometimes be provided direct to consumers. Torsten Passie in his book *The Science of Microdosing Psychedleics* recounts how 'Clearlight' LSD, which was distributed in the San Francisco Bay Area in the early 1970s, came with a leaflet explaining that it had been dried to the sound of bells and cymbals.

The unfortunately still incarcerated LSD chemist William Leonard Pickard mentions the ritualization of psychedelic synthesis in his wonderful book *The Rose of Paracelsus*. In a recent email to me he wrote:

Indigo [an LSD chemist] mentions Gregorian chant during synthesis or crystallization, often Amazonian shamanic, soft, gentle chanting. From my interviews of very high-level manufacturers in the 1980s– 90s for drug policy research, I recall most fondly one individual [who would] never dream of conducting a crystallization without Vivaldi's 'The Four Seasons' playing in one continuous loop, quite loud, for many hours from start to finish. He did so for years. Something about the beauty of the molecules finding each other, and the harmony of the seasons. The Vivaldi seems to be a lineage in certain groups.

In all these examples, leaving aside any parapsychological or subtle physical interpretations of what may or may not happen when one crystallizes LSD in the presence of music, what we can see is that these chemists are doing ceremony. They are creating a set of poetic, metaphorical relationships to influence their set by changing their setting (putting on certain music). They are doing so while in a psychedelically altered state (laboratory spillages, as even extremely thorough Swiss chemists know very well, can and do happen). They are using this poetic language of behaviour with a specific intention – that of making the best LSD, making good medicine.

Let's break down the idea of psychedelic ceremony in a little more detail and give a few examples of practices.

When we drink alcohol we say 'cheers'! We make an invocation to the spirit of happiness, perhaps a toast of greater or lesser complexity. So too in many traditions and approaches to psychedelics people will take a moment before they take the drug. That pregnant pause we have, sat before the awesome reality of the loaded DMT pipe. Some like to say a prayer over their drugs, some do this by offering their lover a pill in their mouth, ending the kiss with the words 'have a good one'.

Depending on the nature of the psychedelic adventure the location where the experience will unfold may have been specially prepared. The style may be very varied. From complex patterned fabrics and ready-to-undulate-when-the-mushrooms-kick-in wooden flooring, through to white walls and soft cushions, the point about the space is that it supports and directs the experience and therefore, in whatever way we choose, it demands our attention. Re-set your set by sorting out your setting. As we clean the room and place our power objects around us – pictures of our family perhaps, or of deities, or sports cars or kittens (if that's our thing) – we develop a deep sense that all is well. The mutual relationship of set and setting means any act of preparation (which could instead be about getting all glammed up if we are going out clubbing) is an instinctive ceremonial process.

Some spaces look very clearly like psychedelic ceremony. The beautiful crescent altar of the peyote circle, marked with the long glorious road that the participants take through the night together. Other ritual spaces may have a more modern look, with specially selected images projected upon the walls, sigils glowing in the blacklight and rotating dream machines. As psychonauts we make these chemical autonomous zones, these ceremonial spaces, in many ways. From spontaneously arising moments when we realise and respond to the sacred, through more formal group rituals, to gatherings so large we call them festivals.

There are many groups in many countries that meet to do these kinds of ceremonies: some are peer-led, others with more formal structures, often inspired by indigenous entheogenic cultures of the Americas. For some people their psychedelic ceremonies are solitary affairs, perhaps lone psychogeographical wanderings or night long solitary vigils, still others make pilgrimage to the temples where God is a DJ.

Once we are tripping we can use our skills to make the best use of our time in that space however it is constructed. While sometimes all we need is to lie down and let the experience take us, at other points we may like to do stuff; anything from contemplating the aeons-old architecture of our own hands, through to creative practices such as making art or singing and dancing. As the psychedelic state is so plastic we can make interventions here; in some contexts we might think of these as acts of psychological neurohacking, or perhaps sorcery, in any case they are examples of deploying symbolic activity with an intention.

For example. We can use mimetic magic also known as sympathetic magic. We create a psychological link; *as X happens so Y follows*, 'magical thinking' or perhaps 'thinking magically'. This works especially well when we are high and different (novel) parts of our minds are connected. The embodied psychedelic experience recalls the magicians' axiom 'as above so below, as within so without'. In psychedelic ceremony we are deploying symbolic action within the interrelated network of all things which, when not high, we experience as discrete objects.

Let's take a not too woo-woo psychological example of how this works: we might for example become aware that, when difficult memories of a failed relationship arise during the trip, that we screw our face up and hunch our shoulders. In the psychedelic state, where everything in the mind (and who knows, perhaps all things in the universe) is connected, we make a magical link; 'as I relax my tense muscles so I find a way to sit in equanimity with the pain of my past'. As we relax, passing through the journey of that intention, our state of mind while tripping, and our subsequent relationships with others after we come down, also relaxes and becomes easier.

Then there can be things that look more like spells in the proper witchcraft-pointy-hat sense. One might do a spell to encourage the conditions in society in which the benefits of psychedelic drugs can be widely appreciated. This spell could aim to find ourselves in a better relationship, as a species, with these divine medicines. One might do this by creating a magical sculpture, a physical form for a spirit, giving it a name and celebrating it as a god. Offering our psychedelic gnosis to it, desiring that it is empowered to carry this intention into the complex web of wyrd that connects all things. (You can see what we in magic call the 'material base' of such a spell, cast from within psychedelic ceremony, in the museum here at Breaking Convention.)

Display in The Psychedelic Museum installation at Breaking Convention 2017 [Izawa picture]

Let's consider another ceremony which can be deployed very easily by the psychonaut. We can think of this as a handy neurohack: We know that our bodies primarily get our conscious attention when things go wrong. We experience the alert of pain and discomfort when there is a problem. Most of the time we don't notice our left foot unless it hurts. We also know that cultivating an optimistic and grateful attitude has benefits on everything from the functionality of our own immune systems to our broader mental health, and that this well-being thereby affects others. It's a particularly powerful charm against depression, both individually and culturally. (Technically this is left-hand path *vajrayana*, fourth turning of the wheel of dharma shit we're talking here; check it out if you've not already grokked that stuff).

To cultivate this beneficial attitude we take a moment to thank all those things that are good. To deliberately take our attention away from the painful and the incessant human desire to solve whatever currently is 'the problem'. One way of doing this is by smoking in a ceremonial style.

Let's set the scene for this easy-to-do psychedelic ceremony; I walk away from the bonfire and the pumping sound system. I've got a pre-rolled joint or tobacco smoke in hand. I kneel down on the dry grass. I am here to pray. I ceremonially breathe the smoke of the joint up to the sky, then directly down onto the earth, I then blow it to the left and right and finally towards the moon above me. This metaphorical ritual process orientates me within the world. I use the joint to focus me in the moment and I pray, speaking about what I love, counting my blessings. There are many imagined locations to which we might address our prayer. Simply to 'The Universe', or for the those more theologically inclined 'the Great Goddess'. Personally, I rather like 'Great Spirit' and 'Great Mystery', and sometimes 'Baphomet'. We may silently formulate our prayer or it speak aloud (aloud is good since it folds the act of speaking through our surroundings, and back into our own ears, forming a new neural pathway). In our prayers we remember all those things we are grateful for; those who love us, our health, this life, these medicines, the cool of the night air. Whatever we really love and what fills us with joy and we take delight in.

When I'm done I bury the end of the joint in the earth, nod my thanks to the moon and return to the pumping sound of the party.

Our psychedelic ceremony, however we do it, unfolds…

Perhaps, towards the tail end of the trip, you decide to do some divination by consulting the tarot, using those obscure occult images to explore the relationships of things in your life that are important. Changing your perspective and looking on the problem as though from the outside, finding new possibilities. You can do something similar through the process that psychologists call a 'sculpt', using found or specially selected objects to represent characters or situations. Just as the psychedelic state joins up bits of our brain, so we can express and reflect internal processes through external symbol sets, in order to discern the novel interpretations and gain new understanding.

These techniques of divination can be usefully employed when we are high: from ones where a meaning is sought in what some claim is random stuff, such as the shapes of clouds or of fire or the first three runes picked from a bag. By interpreting these symbols, and perhaps manipulating them in some way, we open ourselves to new possibilities. It's also the case that, in my experience, what parapsychologists call 'hits' happen more commonly when we are in an altered state of awareness.

Whether simple or highly structured, lasting just half an hour or several days, eventually our psychedelic ceremony comes to an end.

As the dawn breaks we perhaps sweep clear the circle around the crescent altar and place the final sticks with impeccable care on the arrow fire. We tidy up after the party. We thank the spirits or the power of the time, the place, the medicine. We allow ourselves time to come down, to enjoy the shamanic return to a world renewed and full of possibility. To reflect, to eat, to sleep, to dream.

And, each of us a shaman, we bring back the insights from that trip into the ultraworld for the benefit of ourselves and community.

What insights might we gather from these psychedelic adventures? Too many to list of course, but considering the value of these substances in themselves, what might be learnt?

- That psychedelics have the potential to be amazing, fascinating medicines that feed our souls and inspire our spirits.
- That the benefits of these experience could be just the medicine our species needs.
- That we could live in a culture which nurtures settings in which the self-administered and autonomously interpreted psychedelic experience is open to all who seek it.

And to realise this possibility we know that in many ways, and many places, there is work to be done.

We are living in a time of increased licensed research and I'm deeply appreciative of the work of organisations such as the Beckley Foundation, MAPS, The Tyringham Initiative and others for their herculean efforts. But their work is hampered by both the laws and culture surrounding the prohibition of these substances. Both things that need to change.

As things are now, we know that the law relating to psychedelics is critical to our story. Most of us here, I would conjecture, took our first psychedelics in unlicensed and therefore possibly criminal circumstances. Given the severity with which some states punish the use of psychedelic sacraments, but for the Grace of God, we are all potentially the prisoners of prohibition.

For some people prohibition hits hard. I mentioned my chickens in an aside when writing an email to Leonard Pickard, who is in jail (serving two life sentences) for LSD manufacture. He told me in his reply that he'd not seen any creatures, besides humans, for 17 years. This is the real horror, the real bad trip – as we speak Leonard is shut away in his prison and we ourselves are only part-way free. So we must use all the strategies we have to transform this situation, even as these sacraments we have taken have changed us.

As a community of practice, we share our insights at gatherings such as this conference. Inspired, respectful and considerate of the teachings of contemporary indigenous psychedelic cultures, and informed by the discoveries of licensed and underground researchers.

We have a tremendous opportunity in this, the psychedelic renaissance. By sharing our collective wisdom I hope that we can build a culture suitable for a post-prohibition psychedelically upgraded world. More intelligent, more creative, more humane, more curious than perhaps ever before. Because, while it's easy to get messianic about drugs, we could really be onto something here.

Perhaps these substances really are that powerful, that important to our species. These are medicines for the mind and therefore for our culture, and we should not be afraid to use them.

Through deploying psychedelic ceremony we are learning to make our own medicine. 'The medicine' as a whole is the combination of the psychedelic experience within a set and setting designed to enhance its transformative and entheogenic potential. 'The medicine' is the complete psychedelic triangle of set, setting and substance.

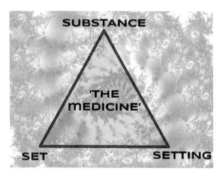

The Psychedelic Triangle (triangle)

Ceremony does not necessarily imply orthodoxy and I would like to see us maintain a variety of psychedelic spaces. Spaces for psychedelics as legitimate tools for healing, for research, for spiritual and for recreational use in our society. For there are many medicines and no one prescription.

The medicine of psychedelic ceremony can heal our souls by providing opportunities for revelation, rapture and fun. Used as medicines these substances offer opportunities to transcend our limitations, to problem solve, to heal, to resolve conflict, to dispel the illusion of separation.

Psychedelics employed in this manner can support our human search for meaning in a way predicated on personal spiritual inquiry rather than rote doctrine of any stripe. These are substances that entwine the scientific and the sacred, the religious and recreational, substances that can help make us whole.

With our wounded cultures and ecocidal behaviours it is clear that some wholeness and healing would not go amiss. We could do with this good medicine.

Stay high and stay free!

Ahoy!

DYING TO LIVE: THE POWER OF TRANSCENDENCE IN THE TREATMENT OF EXISTENTIAL ANXIETY

SAM GANDY

In Western society, death is a taboo subject and, from the perspective of medical science, is viewed as a defeat and a failure. Medicine is excellent at keeping people alive but is a great deal poorer when it comes to easing the passage of the dying. In a sense, society has actually regressed in terms of the integration of death and dying as medical science has grown in power, and death has become a less common part of our lives. Existential anxiety, which includes fear and anxiety centered on death and dying, is something often overlooked (Lehto & Stein, 2009), and there is a notable lack of effective treatments or therapies, with physicians likely to feel underequipped in treating the psycho-spiritual effects of death anxiety (Bates, 2016).

Despite the lack of currently integrated treatments, there are a number of avenues worthy of much more attention. Chief among them are the classical psychedelics, a group of substances long-used by humans in the context of healing and divination, which are currently experiencing a scientific research renaissance. Psychedelics may have a unique utility in their potential efficacy in the treatment of existential anxiety. While current research has focused on terminally ill patients, with respect to life we are all terminal, and it may likely be that the benefits of these substances are too important to limit to the treatment of sick people only, although this should be made a priority.

Valentina Wasson and Aldous Huxley were both early pioneers who perceived the potential efficacy of psychedelics for treatment of the dying. In 1957, in an interview printed in *This Week* magazine, Valentina Wasson described the potential of psilocybin for treatment of the terminally ill (among other potential applications), following her own psilocybin mushroom experiences with her husband Gordon Wasson in Mexico in 1955 (Grof & Halifax 1977). Aldous Huxley wrote a letter to pioneering psychedelic researcher Dr Humphry Osmond in 1958 about how lysergic acid diethylamide (LSD) could be used to treat terminal cancer patients so their dying could be a 'more spiritual, less strictly physiological process' (Huxley, 1999, p. 143). A few years later when Huxley—a man who talked the talk and walked the walk—lay dying from laryngeal cancer, he requested and received two 100µg dose injections of LSD from his wife Laura, who reported that his death was extremely beautiful and serene in a letter she wrote in 1963 to Aldous's brother Julian (Huxley, 1968).

A pioneering researcher and proponent of using psychedelics to treat the terminally ill was Dr Walter Pahnke. Pahnke joined the Maryland Psychiatric Research Center in 1967 and conducted psychedelic therapy with LSD and N,N-dipropyltryptamine (DPT) until his untimely death in 1971 (Coomber, 1998). He used LSD in the treatment of terminal cancer patients and wrote a number of papers and book chapters with colleagues on his research findings during this time. He studied the effect of the mystical-type experience on terminal cancer patients and the potential implications for psi research and explored psychedelic therapy utilizing LSD with terminal cancer patients. As in the case of Huxley, Pahnke was motivated in part by his own personal mystical-type experiences catalysed through his own psychedelic usage (Pahnke, 1964).

In central Africa, the oneirogenic ('dream-inducing') plant *Tabernanthe iboga* has a long history of use as a spiritual sacrament and medicine and is employed by a number of different groups, such as the Bwiti, in religious ceremonies. The Bwiti utilise a single large initiatory dose of the iboga plant, in the form of ingested root bark, consumed by the initiate to induce radical spiritual growth (Barabe, 1982). This induces an experience resembling a near-death experience (NDE) in which the initiate is instructed to go beyond the body to the spiritual realms to seek guidance and insight on life issues via communing with their ancestors (Barabe, 1982).

A number of recent studies have demonstrated both the safety and efficacy of classical psychedelics such as LSD and psilocybin in the treatment of existential anxiety and depression in the terminally ill. A pioneering pilot study by Grob et al. (2011) with psilocybin using a dose of 0.2 mg/kg reported safe physiological and psychological responses and no clinically adverse events. A reduction in anxiety was noted 1–3 months after treatment, with a long-term improvement in mood observed at 6 months. A study by Gasser et al. (2014) using LSD (at a dose of 200 μg) as a treatment for the anxiety associated with life-threatening diseases reported no lasting adverse reactions from LSD administration, long-term benefits sustained over a 12-month period following a single dose, and highly significant reductions in anxiety (in 77.8% of patients) and a rise in quality of life (in 66.7% of patients).

Larger scale studies using psilocybin in the treatment of anxiety and depression suffered by patients with life-threatening cancer have built on this previous research. One study conducted by Griffiths et al. (2016) at Johns Hopkins University using doses of 22 and 30 mg/70 kg found that 80% of patients reported lower depression and anxiety at a six-month follow-up, including reduced death anxiety and increased quality of life, life meaning, and optimism. Study participants reported improved attitudes towards life and self and improved mood, relationships, and spirituality, with over 80% of participants describing greater well-being and life satisfaction. It is notable that the mystical-type experiences occurring through psilocybin treatment mediated the long-term therapeutic outcomes. A study conducted by Ross et al. (2016) at New York University utilizing a psilocybin dose of 0.3 mg/kg reported similar results, with study participants reporting immediate, substantial, and sustained improvements in anxiety and depression, with decreases in cancer-related demoralization and hopelessness, improved spiritual well-being, and increased quality of life. Enduring clinically significant reductions in anxiety, sustained reductions in existential distress, increased quality of life, and an improved attitude towards death were each reported by a majority of participants. Again, it was noted that the psilocybin-catalysed mystical experience mediated the long-term therapeutic effect on anxiety and depression.

It can be seen from these studies that the mystical-type experiences, reliably catalysed through high-dose psilocybin, are a core part of their long-term therapeutic effect on depression and anxiety ratings, while enhancing life meaning and outlook. It seems, too, that the mystical experience is of great importance with regard to altering perceptions of death and reducing death anxiety. Facets of the mystical experience such as the sense of unity, perceived interconnectedness of all things, a deep sense of love, reverence, sacredness, and noetic quality (Griffiths et al. 2016) are very likely contributing to the uplifting attitudinal shifts towards death but also towards self, life, and others. A recently published study by Griffiths et al. (2017) utilizing high doses of 20 mg and 30 mg/70 kg psilocybin found that mystical experiences in synergy with spiritual practices produced significant large positive changes for a number of trait measures of prosocial attitudes, behaviours, and perspectives, among them death transcendence. This study is notable in that unlike all the aforementioned studies, study participants were physically and mentally healthy and not terminally ill. However, significant numbers of these participants reported death transcendence under high-dose psilocybin, suggesting that such a shift in perspective is something intrinsic to this experience.

Medicine and psychiatry operate under the paradigm of drugs affecting patients for the duration of time they are in a patient's system. The research described here demonstrates that a single dose of a classical psychedelic like psilocybin administered in a psychotherapeutic setting can produce highly beneficial long-term psychotherapeutic effects, lasting months to a year or more. This is an entirely novel, unprecedented, and potentially revolutionary finding which currently lacks a clear scientific explanation.

Treatment of rational suicide in the elderly is another unexplored frontier where psychedelics could hold promise. Rational suicide can be defined as suicide of the elderly to escape suffering or due to a weariness of living due to age-related losses. Psychedelic experiences in a psychotherapeutic context may help foster a sense of life-meaning and positive outlook and promote the perception that life is worth living, even in conditions of great adversity (Hendricks & Grob, 2016).

The mystical or transcendent experience catalysed through psychedelics seems to be a key part of their long-term therapeutic efficacy and to be strongly linked to the reduction of death anxiety. These experiences may allow patients to experience a sense of connectedness to the sacred, to enhance relationships with family and loved ones, to live fully in the moment with equanimity, and to make the most of their remaining time. Through their experience with the psychedelic, individuals may be able to transcend their primary identification with their physical bodies and experience ego-free states, which in turn may generate a new perspective and acceptance. It seems likely this facet of the psychedelic-induced mystical experience is a key factor linked to a long-term reduction in death anxiety. In the recent psilocybin studies described above, it was also noted that encounters with death or dying were common in people's experiences. Such experiences would vary widely in content between different individuals, with some feeling their consciousness as something separate from their physical body that will survive its demise (Pollan, 2015).

Whether the experiences reported by study participants are valid or illusionary is of secondary importance to the psychotherapeutic benefits these experiences have for the experiencer in question. To paraphrase pioneering psychologist and philosopher William James in his seminal book *The Varieties of Religious Experience* (1902), the value of mystical experiences can only be judged 'by their fruits' not 'by their roots' (p. 20). Furthermore, the psychological symptoms of existential distress share a great deal of overlap with those of a hyperactive default-mode network, a part of the brain that psilocybin is known to quiet (Carhart-Harris et al. 2012). Psilocybin may be particularly well-suited for use in palliative care scenarios. It doesn't carry the same political or cultural baggage of LSD and is shorter acting than the latter with less chance of yielding adverse reactions. It is non-toxic, physiologically well tolerated, and suitable for use by the terminally ill (Carhart-Harris et al., 2017). In the future, it could be administered in family groups in a supportive setting. Psilocybin is used in family settings by indigenous groups such as the Mazatec in Mexico (Munn, 1973) and, due to psilocybin's ability to lower psychological armour and facilitate communication, it could be an excellent catalyst for family groups to connect and say their goodbyes to loved ones with an openness that may otherwise not be easily accessible.

The psychedelic compound 5-methoxy-N,N-dimethyltryptamine (5-MeO-DMT) has received very little scientific research attention at the present time. It may, however, be well suited to treating death anxiety. 5-MeO-DMT treatment-provider Dr Geraldo "Gerry" Ruben Sandoval Isaac conducted a 10-year retrospective study with 1,699 participants and noted that 85% reported a mystical or religious experience and that 60% experienced some form of dying or death (Isaac, 2016). This is twice the 30% reported in the Johns Hopkins psilocybin trials of study participants reporting profound experiences of their own death. This is a notable result, as it can be seen from the aforementioned psilocybin research that the mystical experience that psychedelics can catalyse is a core component of their long-term psychotherapeutic effect in the treatment of existential anxiety. In addition, a simulated or hallucinatory experience of death or dying can be highly cathartic with regard to people's death anxiety. This study is suggestive that 5-MeO-DMT can induce both experiences with high levels of consistency, so it may be that this compound is particularly well suited for the treatment of death anxiety. The phenomenological effects of 5-MeO-DMT are somewhat atypical in comparison to other classical psychedelics and seem to more closely resemble NDEs in experiential content (Oroc, 2009). Luke and Kittenis (2005) found that reported death-related experiences (death, rebirth, or memory of a past life) tended to be more commonly associated with 5-MeO-DMT than any other substance. 5-MeO-DMT is a great deal more powerful than the other classical psychedelics such as psilocybin and LSD, so it requires careful handling, and session preparation and integration will be highly important to maximize experiential benefits. However, the experience is a great deal shorter than that yielded by the other psychedelics like psilocybin or LSD, so it would be much less taxing on treatment providers' time.

During a program of psychedelic therapy with terminal cancer patients conducted by Dr Stanislav Grof at the Maryland Psychiatric Research Center in Baltimore, a number of patients reported NDEs as their diseases progressed, and they reported their prior psychedelic experiences as being very similar to their NDEs and being an invaluable experiential training for dying (Grof et al. 2008). Both NDEs and psychedelics share a capacity for being able to change human personality in the long-term following an experience. This quantum change (C'de Baca & Wilbourne, 2004) in personality yielded by experiences catalysed via NDEs and psychedelics are distinct from one another but also share some interesting overlap. The personality changes yielded by a classic NDE can be considered as being deeper, more comprehensive, and more robust than those yielded by psychedelics such as psilocybin which tend to be more specific, in particular affecting the personality domain of openness (MacLean et al. 2011). Openness includes a hunger for knowledge, and this, too, has been highlighted by experiencers of NDEs (NDErs) as a long-term effect of their experiences (Sartori, 2014). An increase in well-being, life satisfaction, and sense of life-purpose or meaning are also commonly reported after-effects of both NDEs and psychedelic-induced mystical experiences (Noyes, 1980), and a negative relation between purpose in life and death anxiety has been observed previously by Drolet (1990).

An interesting property of NDEs is that simply learning about them can promote psycho-spiritual benefits and result in changes of outlook regarding death in people without a direct experience similar to one of an NDEr. Learning about NDEs through reading or hearing about them can result in such changes, but direct testimony from an NDEr seems to be the most powerful medium of transformation. A number of NDE researchers have noted such changes in outlook themselves, with Dr Kenneth Ring being one of the pioneering NDE researchers who first noted this phenomenon, describing it as a 'benign virus' (Ring, 1995) in reference to it being positively psychologically contagious. A number of independent studies such as those by Rominger (2009) and Tassell-Matamua et al. (2016) have further validated the existence of this interesting psychological phenomenon, and found that while it occurs in those at high risk of death, such as the terminally ill and those with suicidal ideation, it also occurs among clinically healthy populations. Thus, in learning about the NDE and people's experiences, one can reap much of the benefit of the experience without the inherent risk of being near death.

A core component of the NDE is the out-of-body experience (OBE). A common anecdotal side effect of OBEs is that people lose their fear of death, something noted by pioneering OBE explorer Robert Monroe in his book *Journeys Out of the Body* (1971) and others. Even a virtual OBE induced via virtual reality (VR) technology is capable of reducing death anxiety (Bourdin et al. 2017). This further suggests that it is the experience of being disembodied and transcending the primary identification with the physical body that is a common link and a core experiential and psychotherapeutic component shared by the OBE, NDE, and psychedelic experience and likely an integral part of its efficacy in reducing death anxiety. Moreover, there seems to be a great deal of reported phenomenological overlap between NDEs and OBEs in particular. Unlike the obvious risks involved in the generation of NDEs and the illegality of psychedelics, OBEs can, with practice, be induced voluntarily and safely.

As an aside to psychedelic therapy, NDEs, and OBEs, other consciousness practices such as holotropic breathwork have been found to reduce death anxiety (Holmes et al. 1996). Holotropic breathwork is an effective alternative and legal means of accessing transpersonal states that may have useful applications for the treatment of existential anxiety. Mindfulness meditation may also have potential in alleviating existential anxiety, with a mindful outlook showing efficacy in its ability to neutralize fears of death and dying (Niemiec et al. 2010).

So, there are a number of interesting avenues that warrant further attention in relation to direct experiences, consciousness-related practices, and simply learning about these experiences from others. Given that death is something shared by all, and given that it is an unavoidable and inevitable part of our lives, it seems there could be great potential benefit in giving these experiences the attention they deserve. It seems that these various experiences may all lessen death anxiety, but the benefits may transcend this alone. A simulated dying event before one's actual dying may serve not only to reduce death anxiety but also act to reinforce one's life priorities in a positive fashion while alive.

REFERENCES

Bates, A. T. (2016). 'Addressing existential suffering'. BC Medical Journal, 58(5), pp.268–273.

Bourdin, P., Barberia, I., Oliva, R., & Slater, M. (2017). A virtual out-of-body experience reduces fear of death. PLoS ONE, 12 (1), E0169343.

Barabe, P. (1982). 'The religion of Iboga or the Bwiti of the Fangs'. Medicina Tropical, 12, pp.251–257.

Carhart-Harris, R. L., Erritzoe, D., Williams, T., Stone, J. M., Reed, L. J., Colasanti, A., Tyacke, R. J., Leech, R., Malizia, A. L., Murphy, K., Hobden, P., Evans, J., Feilding, A. Wise, R. G. & Nutt, D. J. (2012). 'Neural correlates of the psychedelic state as determined by fMRI studies with psilocybin'. Proceedings of the National Academy of Sciences of the United States of America, 109, pp.2138–2143.

Carhart-Harris, R. L., Roseman, L., Bolstridge, M., Demetriou, L., Pannekoek, J. N., Wall, M. B., Tanner, M., Kaelen, M., McGoningle, J., Murphy, K., Leech, R., Curran, H. V. & Nutt, D. J. (2017). 'Psilocybin for treatment-resistant depression: fMRI-measured brain mechanisms'. Scientific Reports, 7, p.13187.

C'de Baca, J., & Wilbourne, P. (2004). 'Quantum change: Ten years later'. Journal of Clinical Psychology, 60 (5), pp.531–541.

Coomber, R. (1998). The control of drugs and drug users: Reason or reaction? Boca Raton, FL: CRC Press, LLC.

Drolet, J.-L. (1990). 'Transcending death during early adulthood: Symbolic immortality, death anxiety, and purpose in life'. Journal of Clinical Psychology, 46 (2), pp.148–169.

Gasser, P., Holstein, D., Michel, Y., Doblin, R., Yazar-Klosinski, B., Passie, T. & Brenneisen, R. (2014). 'Safety and efficacy of lysergic acid diethylamide-assisted psychotherapy for anxiety associated with life-threatening diseases'. The Journal of Nervous and Mental Disease, 202 (7), pp.513–520.

Griffiths, R. R., Richards, W. A., McCann, U. & Jesse, R. (2006). 'Psilocybin can occasion mystical-type experiences having substantial and sustained personal meaning and spiritual significance'. Psychopharmacology, 187, pp.268–283.

Griffiths, R. R., Johnson, M. W., Carducci, M. A., Umbricht, A., Richards, W. A., Richards, B. D., Cosimano, M. P. & Klinedinst, M. A. (2016). 'Psilocybin produces substantial and sustained decreases in depression and anxiety in patients with life-threatening cancer: A randomized double – blind trial'. Journal of Psychopharmacology, 30 (12), pp.1181–1197.

Griffiths, R. R., Johnson, M. W., Richards, W. A., Richards, B. D., Jesse, R., MacLean, K. A., Barret, F. S., Cosimano, M. P. & Klinedinst, M. A. (2017). 'Psilocybin-occasioned mystical-type experience in combination with meditation and other spiritual practices produces enduring positive changes in psychological functioning and in trait measures of prosocial attitudes and behaviours'. Journal of Psychopharmacology, 32 (1), pp.49-69.

Grob, C. S., Danforth, A. L., Chopra, G. S., Hagerty, M., McKay, C. R., Halberstadt, A. L., & Greer, G. R. (2011). 'Pilot study of psilocybin treatment for anxiety in patients with advanced-stage cancer'. Archives of General Psychiatry, 68 (1), pp.71–78.

Grof, S., Grob, C. G., Bravo, G., & Walsh, R. (2008). 'Birthing the transpersonal'. The Journal of Transpersonal Psychology, 40 (2), pp.155–177.

Grof, S. & Halifax, J. (1977) *The Human Encounter with Death.* New York, NY: E. P. Dutton.

Hendricks, P. S., & Grob, C. S. (2016). 'Classic psychedelics and rational suicide in the elderly: Exploring the potential utility of a reemerging treatment paradigm'. In: McCue, R. E. & M. Balasubramaniam, M. (eds.), *Rational suicide in the elderly: Clinical, ethical, and sociocultural aspects.* New York, NY: Springer, pp.203–210.

Holmes, S. W., Morris, R., Clane, P. R., & Putney, R. T. (1996). 'Holotrophic breathwork: An experiential approach to psychotherapy'. *Psychotherapy,* 33, pp.114–120.

Huxley, A. L. (1999). *Moksha: Aldous Huxley's classic writings on psychedelics and the visionary experience.* South Paris, ME: Park Street Press.

Huxley, L. A. (1968). *This timeless moment: Personal view of Aldous Huxley.* San Francisco, CA: Mercury House.

Isaac, G. R. S. (2016). *The god molecule: 5-MeO-DMT and the spiritual path to divine light.* Studio City, CA: Divine Arts Press, pp.148–155.

James, W. (1902). *The Varieties of Religious Experience: A study in human nature, being the Gifford lectures on natural religion delivered at Edinburgh in 1901-1902.* New York, NY: Longmans, Green & Co.

Lehto, R. H., & Stein, K. F. (2009). 'Death anxiety: An analysis of an evolving concept'. *Research and Theory for Nursing Practice,* 23 (1), 23–41.

Luke, D. P., & Kittenis, M. (2005). 'A preliminary survey of paranormal experiences with psychoactive drugs'. *Journal of Parapsychology,* 69 (2), pp.305–327.

MacLean, K. A., Johnson, M. W., & Griffiths, R. R. (2011). 'Mystical experiences occasioned by the hallucinogen psilocybin lead to increases in the personality domain of openness'. *Journal of Psychopharmacology,* 25 (11), pp.1453–1461.

Monroe, R. (1971). *Journeys Out of the Body.* New York, NY: Doubleday.

Munn, H. (1973). 'The mushrooms of language'. In: Harner, M. J. (ed.), *Hallucinogens and shamanism.* London: Oxford University Press, pp.86–122.

Niemiec, C. P., Brown, K. W., Kashdan, T. B., Cozzolino, P. J., Breen, W. E., Levesque-Bristol, C., & Ryan, R. M. (2010). Being present in the face of existential threat: The role of trait – mindfulness in reducing defensive responses to mortality salience. *Journal of Personality and Social Psychology,* 99 (2), 344.

Noyes, R. (1980). 'Attitude change following near-death experiences'. *Psychiatry: Interpersonal and Biological Processes,* 43 (3), pp.234–242.

Oroc, J. (2009). *Tryptamine palace: 5-MeO-DMT and the Sonoran Desert Toad.* South Paris, ME: Park Street Press.

Pahnke, W. (1964). 'First impressions of first LSD experience of March 30, 1964'. Purdue University Libraries Psychoactive Substances Collection. Available from: http://earchives.lib. purdue.edu/cdm/singleitem/collection/psyc/id/7 [Accessed 10th October 2017].

Pahnke, W. N. (1968). 'The psychedelic mystical experience in terminal cancer patients and its possible implications for psi research'. In: Cavanna, R. & Ullman, M. (eds.), *Psi and altered states of consciousness: Proceedings of an International Conference on Hypnosis, Drugs, Dreams, and Psi.* New York, NY: Parapsychology Foundation, pp.115–128.

Pahnke, W., Kurland, A., Unger, S., Savage, C., Wolf, S., & Goodman, L. (1970). 'Psychedelic therapy (utilizing LSD) with cancer patients'. *Journal of Psychedelic Drugs*, 3, pp.63–75.

Pollan, M. (2015). *The trip treatment*. The New Yorker. Available from: https://www. newyorker.com/magazine/2015/02/09/trip-treatment [Accessed 12th October 2017].

Ring, K. (1995). 'The impact of near-death experiences on persons who have not had them: A report of preliminary study and two replications'. *Journal of Near Death Studies*, 13 (4), 223–235. Available from: https://digital.library.unt.edu/ark:/67531/metadc799331/ [Accessed 14th October 2017].

Rominger, R. (2009). 'Exploring the aftereffects of the near-death experience: Brief summary of findings'. *Journal of Near-Death Studies*, 28 (1), 5–30. Available from: https://digital.library. unt.edu/ark:/67531/metadc461753/ [Accessed 14th October 2017].

Ross, S., Bossis, A., Guss, J., Agin-Liebes, G., Malone, T., Cohen, B., Mennenga, S. E., Belser, A., Kalliontzi, K., Babb, J., Su, Z., Corby, P. & Schmidt, B. L. (2016). 'Rapid and sustained symptom reduction following psilocybin treatment for anxiety and depression in patients with life-threatening cancer: A randomized controlled trial'. *Journal of Psychopharmacology*, 30 (12), pp.1165–1180.

Sartori, P. (2014). *The wisdom of near-death experiences: How understanding NDEs can help us to live more fully*. London: Watkins Publishing Limited.

Tassell-Matamua, N., Lindsay, N., Bennett, S., Valentine, H., & Pahina, J. (2016). 'Does learning about near-death experiences promote psycho-spiritual benefits in those who have not had a near-death experience?' *Journal of Spirituality in Mental Health*, 19 (2), pp.95-115.

'INTERSTICES OF UNREASON' AND THE IMAGINAL: AN EXPLORATION

WILLIAM ROWLANDSON

In the essay 'Avatars of the Tortoise' Borges cites Novalis:

> *The greatest sorcerer would be he who bewitches himself to the point of taking his own phantasmagorias for autonomous apparitions. Is that not our case?*

> *I conjecture,* [responds Borges,] *that it is our case. We, the indivisible divinity that operates within us, have dreamt the world. We have dreamt it resistant, mysterious, visible, ubiquitous in space and firm in time. But we have consented within its architecture tenuous and eternal interstices of unreason to know that it is false.*

We are the sorcerers, dreaming the world into existence, 'consenting' to beguiling 'interstices of unreason' (translated also as 'chinks,' 'crevices,' and 'cracks') that appear in the seemingly solid structure of this dream-world. As so often happens in Borges, this sequence, if explored with enthusiasm, spins into vertiginous loops, leading the reader into an unsettling yet entrancing state of confusion. The text itself becomes an interstice of unreason.

I have long been fascinated by these interstices of unreason, exploring many avenues of inquiry into these interstices. One is *mysticism*, another is *psychedelics*, and my contribution to the first Breaking Convention volume was a historical overview of the debate about the relationship between mystical and psychedelic states, a debate that bubbles on today. Another avenue is the *imaginal*. It is a word and network of associated ideas that vibrate at the heart of the mystical-psychedelic debate.

In my consideration of the imaginal, I share the fascination that Erik Davis feels for the *weird*. At the heart of psychedelic, he suggests, is something *weird*. The weird is present since earliest childhood, and so there is often a flavour of childhood fear and excitement in an adult psychedelic experience. He traces the word back from current machine-elf encounters through sci-fi comics, H.P. Lovecraft, Shelley, the Weird Sisters of Macbeth, to Beowulf and its Anglo-Saxon origins. Citing these historical sources, Erik peppers his chronicle with associated words that capture something of the weird: spectral, supernatural, creepy, disturbing, peculiar, strange, bizarre, wayward, spooky, irrational, thrilling, lowbrow, pulpy, not-for-polite-society, elfin, dreadful, ghostly, ghouly, crazy, zany, marvellous, odd, hoaxy, tricksy, uncanny, queer, deviant, wiggy, sticky, goofy. These weird words are the wyrd.

If, as Davis suggests, the weird is 'the uncanny's crass country cousin' (2017), the imaginal is the mysterious aunt, with a whiff of the exotic, the numinous, and, at times, the portentous. The imaginal, the psychedelic, the weird and the uncanny are kinfolk, sharing many an attribute; and the imaginal, like the weird, is present since earliest childhood.

Definitions of the word are variable, and its history reveals attempts to describe and explain something very difficult to describe and explain. In seeking the meaning I have explored some bizarre landscapes: the world of fairy and elves; daimons and numens of diverse hues, UFOlogy, Forteana (that's to say, the *damned facts* that Charles Fort so meticulously recorded), Swedenborg's angels, psychedelic psychotherapy, Borges and Julio Cortázar's troubling short stories, Magical Realism, semiotics, conspiracy theories, dreams, art and poetry.

It is an imaginal adventure to explore the imaginal. It is a little-known word that dances between discourses, and as such carries different baggage than some of its associated meanings, such as spiritual, mystical, oneiric, anomalous, paraphenomenal, psychedelic, weird.

In its current usage, we owe the word to Frederic Myers: poet, classicist, philologist, co-founder of the Society for Psychical Research and compiler of thousands of anecdotes about hauntings, spirit communication, precognition, telepathy, and other strange powers and phenomena, many of which he was the first to name. Myers inhabited that exciting period of Victorian cross-fertilisation of discoveries, disciplines and methods, of those lofty-named scientific and magical Societies, Institutes and Orders. He collected and collated with tenacity, building a solid base upon which to present his visionary theories, and he delved into the newly-blooming language of cellular biology and retrieved the word *imaginal* to refer to those spooky phenomena he investigated so avidly.

The imaginal is rooted in the biological matrix. Like the *imaginal disks* or *cells* that survive the grub's metamorphosis in the cocoon to construct the new insect, so humans have hidden powers that occasionally manifest and which demonstrate to us our greater potential.

The grub comes from the egg laid by a winged insect, and a winged insect it must itself become; but meantime it must for the sake of its own nurture and preservation acquire certain larval characters— characters sometimes so complex that the observer may be excused for mistaking that larva for a perfect insect destined for no further change save death. Such larval characters, acquired to meet the risks of a temporary environment, I seem to see in man's earthly strength and glory. (Myers 2011: 97)

There is an inspiring quality to Myers' vision of metamorphosis in a chrysalis towards the *imago* – the perfect insect. It has a flavour of baptism, spiritual emergence, death and rebirth, a narrative germane to many spiritual traditions. Yet Myers wove the term with the emerging discourse of evolution. 'We are watching the emergence of unguessed potentialities from the primal germ,' Myers declared. 'The mind is no walled plot which a diagram will figure; it is a landscape with lines which stretch out of view, and an ever-changing horizon' (2011: 98).

The analogy is problematic, not least because evolution means different things in different discourses, but it is stirring and optimistic, bringing into play an enticing teleological mythos. Metamorphosis, mutation, growth, adaptation, development, ascent, evolution. These words are great attractors. The grub-butterfly image has a simple parable quality to it that has ensured its survival.[1]

So why the *imaginal*? Why not the *imaginary* or the *imagination*? What is special about this word? Jeffrey Kripal writes in *Authors of the Impossible*:

> *Myers became convinced that in certain contexts, the imagination can take on genuinely transcendental capacities, that is, that it can make contact with what appears to be a real spiritual world, or, at the very least, an entirely different order of mind and consciousness. The imaginal is the imagination on steroids. The imaginary is Clark Kent, the normal. The imaginal is Superman, the supernormal. Same guy, different suits. The Human as Two.* (2010: 83)

The mutant, superhero feel is wonderfully appropriate to Kripal's love of comics and pop culture heroes and villains, a place alive with magic and archetypes. The imaginal is central to Myers' conviction that the human personality greatly exceeds the vessel it inhabits, that it has prodigious talents and can perform prodigious deeds, that it is not restricted to localised space-time, that it may survive bodily death. Yet our language and educational models do not equip us appropriately to acknowledge, investigate and enact these imaginal capacities. Hence we remain shy of our true potential, the caterpillar unaware of butterflyhood.

Whilst the word *imaginal* is not prominent in the vocabulary of Carl Jung, there is much of the imaginal in his explorations of that peculiar interpenetration of the physical and the psychical.

Depth psychology, animated by the languages of myth, archetypes, the numinous, the unconscious, the psyche, synchronicity and individuation, is a profound exploration of the imaginal. Indeed, Jung's practice of Active Imagination is a method for extending the reach of the imagination into its Superman capacities and thus engage in the process of healing.

Henry Corbin, friend of Jung and co-guest at the Eranos gathering, theologian and professor of Islamic Studies in Paris and reader of Swedenborg, discovered in his readings of Sufi poetry and in particular the Andalusian poet mystic philosopher Ibn 'Arabi, the idea of *ālam al-mithāl*. He translated this expression as *mundus imaginalis*, with which, writes Angela Voss, 'to designate the psychic space in which the "super-sensible" reality of dreams, theophanies and spiritual beings are manifested, in a visionary sense, to the individual' (2009: 1). In Corbin the imaginal is less psychical, less paraphenomenal, than for Myers, yet it retains that idea of latent power activated by the imagination where the spiritual and the material interact. In Corbin the experience is sacred, elevated, divine.

The imaginal is meaningful if meaningfully experienced. To begin with, a threshold needs to be crossed in understanding, quite simply, that weird stuff happens. Myers, Charles Fort or Colin Wilson are perfect reading here. Can one reach the end of Wilson's *Mysteries* or *Beyond the Occult* and maintain that weird stuff does not happen?

Perhaps.

One might maintain that all such experiences may be explained rationally, somehow. Statistically, precognitive dreams are *bound* to happen sometimes. Whilst improbable, there is nothing *impossible* about the apparition of a relative on the eve of his or her death in another land. It is simply remarkable coincidence. UFOs are secret military aircraft, or tricks of the light, or photographic double exposure, or hoax, or just plain delusion. Alien encounters and abductions are overactive dreams. DMT entities are culturally-conditioned brain-blips, wild hallucinations. Nevertheless, in order to produce such rational explanations, one would have to recognise that something *odd* had occurred in order to warrant studying it in order to refute it. Sceptics are keen explorers of the weird. Scepticism is a very useful tool.

The second threshold is recognising that the tools of sceptical inquiry, whilst useful, are clumsy in the fluid and often fragile architecture of the imaginal.

We can consider this in the light of divination. It is inevitable and wholly appropriate that a book of wisdom such as the *I Ching* should provide meaningful responses to questions posed. It is a book of wisdom. That is what it does. The 8 trigrams are symbols of archetypal resonance: *Heaven*, the Creative, *Lake*, the Joyous, *Fire*, the Clinging, *Thunder*, the Arousing, *Wind*, the Gentle, *Water*, the Abysmal, *Mountain*, Keeping Still, *Earth*, the Receptive. Their arrangement within 64 hexagrams provides interesting dramas of these principles, which have received commentaries from such luminaries as King Wen, Confucius, Ricard Wilhelm and Carl Jung. These hexagrams then spin their own narrative depending on the arrangement of inner trigrams and the changing lines (yin to yang, yang to yin) that in turn change into new hexagrams.

How could this *not* be meaningful? Wonderful, but not impossible.

The *I Ching*, however, has the capacity to respond to the querent with such precision that a peculiar resonance is felt, something addressed, uncannily conscious in the response, something certainly impossible: a reader can know a book, but how can a book know its reader?

Likewise the Tarot. Each of the 22 cards of the major arcana drips with symbolic meaning. It is inevitable that one may derive meaning from an emergent story that moves from, say, *La Lune* to *L'amoureux* to *Le Chariot*, to the unnamed and unnumbered card of *Death*.[2] How could a reading *not* be meaningful in some capacity?

It is precisely this inevitability of meaning that has granted divinatory systems such power and durability over the centuries. They spell out mythic narratives of essential aspects of life, germane to all people, translatable into languages and cultures across time and geography. This is the mythic power, but it is not necessarily the imaginal power.

There are times that the Tarot winks back. That peculiar resonance again, that uncannily conscious response. This is the imaginal. The layers are blurred. We enter a fiction. An interstice of unreason, briefly felt, then passing, and we begin the long work of understanding and incorporating the response. This is the hidden pulse of divination. It is the same with Jung's synchronicity. Random events of a similar timbre *can*, however improbably, occur. For the occurrence to become synchronicity, there must be the will to perceive meaning. The events flood with psyche. Mechanistic explanations, however plausible, are unsatisfactory.

This is the hidden pulse of art and of literature. As a young man, Allen Ginsberg entered a state of reverie while reading William Blake's poem 'Ah! Sun-flower!' in his New York apartment. The atmosphere changed and he heard the voice of Blake read out the verse. He spent his life trying to recapture that feeling through poetry, altered states and spiritual practices, recognising in India that Blake was his guru.

Borges explored interstices of unreason, those moments that reveal the dream-aspect of reality. Odd moments, strange experiences, brief encounters with the numinous, with the numens. He experienced them. He created them in his fiction, playing curious literary games where the layers intermingle, where the boundaries between the author, narrator, character and reader become blurred.

'I don't write fiction,' declared eighty-year-old Borges in interview, 'I invent fact' (1982: 117). That reads like a zen koan, a profoundly imaginal puzzle making sense on one level, nonsense on another, without either layer being neatly identified. Borges presents himself as the narrator and character in tales that inevitably become truly weird. Locations inside and outside the text are hard to separate.

Things seep through. The fiction-within-fiction-within-fiction worlds of Mlejnas and Tlön affect the fiction-within-fiction of Uqbar. Objects from Uqbar start appearing in the real world of the tale, which is our world as it is narrated by Borges, in Buenos Aires with his *compadre* Adolfo Bioy-Casares. These apports are called *hronir*, and one that Borges witnessed was a metal coin so heavy it could scarcely be lifted.

Things seep through. *El mago* of 'The Circular Ruins' heads off to the wilderness to dream a son, and having eventually dreamt his son into sovereign, autonomous, existence, understands 'With relief, with humiliation, with terror, that he also was an illusion, that someone else was dreaming him.' Wait – if he thought himself real but finds out that he is fictional, what about the reader, what about me? Who is my author?

Things seep through. In 'Borges and I' he separates himself into two, the popular Borges: 'the other', and the private: 'I'. The known and the unknown, the revealed and the hidden, the persona and the self. Yet they both borrow from each other. They intermingle. They're hard to distinguish. He ends with the typically Borgesian line: 'I do not know which of us has written this page.' We're back at the beginning – a snake eating its tale.

In the poem 'Ajedrez' the lively chess pieces are unaware that they are pieces in the game. The players do not know that they are pieces in God's game. (Borges being Borges does not end there): God does not know that he is a piece in another god's game, etc. etc. ad infinitum.

It is a dizzying vision, unfolding fractally. I find it everywhere in Borges. It is an intellectual riddle at one level, a labyrinth that can be viewed from above. But enter the labyrinth and you lose orientation. Events from the fiction start unfolding in the reader's world. *Hronir* are everywhere. Things seep through.

This blurring of the layers between actor, character, playwright and audience is at the heart of theatre. Velázquez the painter paints his own reflection painting his own reflection in Las Meninas. M.C. Escher's hand draws the hand drawing the hand. Neo enters the Matrix armed with the knowledge that it is all computer coding. Dan Milligan, the hero of Spike Milligan's *Puckoon*, lambasts the author for writing him terrible legs: 'Wot are dey?' he repeated angrily. 'Legs.' 'Legs? LEGS? Whose legs?' 'Yours.' 'Mine? And who are you?' 'The Author.' 'Author? Author? Did you write these legs?' 'Yes.' 'Well I don't like dem. I don't like 'em at all at all. I could ha' writted better legs meself' (2003: 28). Italo Calvino draws the reader into the plot of *If on a Winter's Night a Traveller*, reaching through the textual separation. Cervantes fucks with these layers constantly in *Don Quijote*. Characters become their own fictions in dialogue with the chronicler, narrator, translator, author, and reader. Untying the knots is impossible.

If explained as mere trope then it remains as mere trope, a nice depiction of a riddle, cunning literary artifice. But if pursued, then the reader is drawn into the plot and enters the fictional landscape. That is imaginal reading.

This is where authors can uncannily communicate with their readers, as the readers understand that the author addresses *them!* Something is activated through the text that allows the author, narrator, character and reader – separated across space, time and layers of artifice – to vibrate together, to communicate mutually. This is where art performs its magic. This is where great learning can occur.

Corbin emphasised that 'The organ of this universe is the active Imagination; it is the place of theophanic visions, the scene on which visionary events and symbolic histories appear in their true reality.' It is the imagination that enables and hosts the experience, yet Corbin distinguished between Imaginal and the Imaginary: 'The word imaginary will never be used, because with its present ambiguity this word, by prejudging the reality attained or to be attained, betrays an inability to deal with this at once intermediate and intermediary world' (2014: 4)

Corbin emphasised this intermediate quality of the imaginal – both real and not-real, intrinsic and extrinsic, psychic and physical. Kripal eloquently seizes this conundrum, referring to the imaginal as 'that *tertium quid* or third space between fantasy and reality, apparition and appearance, subjectivity and objectivity, through which folklore and mythology and much magical and mystical experience appear to be mediated' (2007: 179).

This strange middle ground, both imaginary and not imaginary, is what I find so appealing about the imaginal. A useful hermeneutic tool in appraising odd phenomena in all their forms. The imaginal is meaningful engagement with the imagination without fixation on whether it is real or not.

It is a persistent ontological question. W.B. Yeats pursued Swedenborg's spiritual journeys with sympathy, recognising their profound validity, whilst quipping that Swedenborg's heavens, with their immaculate gardens and lack of the wild or rugged, were very much a product of Swedenborg's pre-Romantic age. The voyages are thus temporal and a-temporal, culturally-conditioned and a-cultural, real and imagined.

It is a persistent question. Given that so many people have reported encounters with entities in DMT-space, what does this say about the ontology of the entities? Are they real like us: intelligent, self-aware, autonomous, sovereign, mortal and determined by form, or are they figments of our imagination, collective visions from the collective unconscious. In short, are they *really* real or make-believe? The answer: yes!

The encounter is imaginal: it is the place where consciousness pushes out to interact with other consciousness—both inner and outer. It is, as Corbin writes, intermediate and intermediary.

This is why psychedelic therapy can be so effective. The imagination can be animated by the particular medicine, by the set and setting, and the explorer can enter landscapes of such *realness* that the important work of healing can take place. Memories, dreams, events, people and beings can be encountered and engaged with. Knotty traumatic blocks may be untangled. Fragmented aspects of the self, visible and tangible in this radically altered state of consciousness, may be harmonised and integrated. Destructive patterns of behaviour may be modified.

The imagination could be dismissed as fantasy, illusion or delusion, but what happens in imagination can ripple into empirical reality, showing not only the reality of the imagination, but the imaginary nature of reality. Things seep through.

It can be terrifying.

Paranoia is imaginal. Not because it is mere delusion but because the state and its corporate commercial arms have the capacity to gather data of every thought, communication and activity in our lives. 'Just because you're not paranoid,' Bob Anton Wilson reminds us as in *Everything is*

Under Control, 'doesn't mean they're not plotting against you' (2009: 17). Conspiracies, he insists, are occurring all the time, some conspiracy theories are proved by history to be correct, others bat-shit crazy. The fears are not implausible.

Corbin warns that the realm of the imaginal is 'not to be entered by housebreaking,' that one must overcome the will-to-power. He reminds us that 'the very idea of associating such concepts as "power" and the "spiritual" implies an initial secularization' (2014: 16). When ruled by the power principle, the imaginal can be exploited to nightmarish ends. Wilson rapped about Operation Mindfuck, a discordian revolution of cultural chaos in which nothing is quite what it seems. It is manifesting with terrifying force in the figure of the 45th US President and his feedback loops of conspiracy and fake news. An unwitting mindfuck operative taking power. Nothing is what it seems. Things fall apart.

The imaginal is also enchanting. It is also re-enchanting, because it gives us again that sense of potential felt as a child – the world as an extraordinary place. The world is wider and weirder than we suppose. We have astonishing potentials.

So the first threshold does not disrupt any ontological certainties. Weird stuff does happen but rational answers, however clunky, can be wheeled out to explain it. At the second threshold things get a bit wobbly. Yes, it may have been a trick of light or hallucination, but something truly weird happened, something beyond the rational answer. This is where things seep through, interstices of unreason sparkle in strange corners of books and plays and paintings. The statue is more than mere representation of the numen; it hosts the numen. This is where magic occurs. Spells and incantations, blessings and curses, prayers and offerings, are affective. The healing prayer offered to a revered saint is heard by the saint.

Or not. Because the imaginal is at work. The saint must be revered in order to hear. Without reverence there would be no saint. The prayer is the meeting between pray-er and prayed-to. Intermediate and intermediary. This final threshold opens dizzily into the wider, mythic, reaches of the imaginal: it is all real and all fictional. Consciousness flows into form, whether a biological system like a human, a statue of a saint, a child's teddy bear or a fictional character like Don Quijote or Borges. How to distinguish ontological substance, self-awareness, autonomy? The question is ultimately a distraction: we are all imaginal beings, encountered through the ebb and flow of consciousness.

This is why Jung is so useful. Over the course of his enormous career he paid great attention to the creatures and landscapes of the psyche without passing judgement on their ontological status. A passage I refer to repeatedly is from the (very) posthumously published *Red Book*, with the Prophet Elijah rebuking Jung for calling him a symbol. It's not that Elijah is *not* a symbol, it's that he is no more nor less symbolic that Jung himself. It is a beautiful reminder that we are all creatures of the imagination, imaginary beings, and that the contours of our reality are variable.

We flash into existence – into this body form – and from the body form send images of ourselves spinning into the matrix of reality. We are consciousness, and we far exceed the boundaries of our body, name or personality. We are part of vast networks of flowing information, interacting and engaging with other conscious forms.

The imaginal is the reminder that language is fluid, categories are not fixed, structures are flexible and logic is not always logical. 'The world is full of many maybes,' Robert Anton Wilson reminds us, operating on the system of maybe-logic. The story is written in the act. If you can't find a good leg-writer, write your own legs.

WORKS CITED

Borges, J. L. (1982) *Borges at Eighty: Conversations*: Indiana University Press.

Corbin, H. (2014) *Creative Imagination in the Sufism of Ibn Arabi*: Princeton University Press.

Davis, E. (2017) 'The Weirdness of Being.' Talk delivered at *Breaking Convention*: https://www.youtube.com/watch?v=x1hGqQ2mG6c

Jodorowsky, A. (2008). *The Spiritual Journey of Alejandro*: Simon and Schuster.

Kripal, J. (2007). 'The Rise of the Imaginal: Psychical Research on the Horizon of Theory (Again)' *Religious Studies Review*, 33:3, pp. 179-267

Kripal, J. (2010). *Authors of the Impossible: The Paranormal and the Sacred*: University of Chicago Press.

Milligan, S. (2003) *Puckoon*: HarperCollins

Myers, F. (2011). *Human Personality*. Cambridge: Cambridge University Press.

Voss, A. (2009) 'A Methodology of the Imagination', *Eye of the Heart Journal* issue 3, 37-52.

Wilson, R. A. (2009) *Everything Is Under Control: Conspiracies, Cults, and Cover-ups*: Harper Collins.

ENDNOTES

1. Alejandro Jodorowsky writes of his zen training with Ejo Takata: 'Ejo silenced me with a blow of his flat kyosaku. "Intellectual, learn to die!" I was offended. This was the first time he had said this to me. Then he struck me again. "Awakening is not a thing. It is not a goal, not a concept. It is not something to be attained. It is a metamorphosis. If the caterpillar thinks about the butterfly it is to become, saying 'And then I shall have wings and antennae, there will never be a butterfly. The caterpillar must accept its own disappearance in its transformation. When the marvellous butterfly takes wing, nothing of the caterpillar remains...' (2008: 62).

2. Whilst the minor arcana of the Marseille deck are more distant, a subtle meaning may be revealed through the number and the suit, the shapes and colours. It just requires a little more work.

ACKNOWLEDGEMENTS

AIMÉE TOLLAN

Wow what a journey it has been, the fourth Breaking Convention did not disappoint. Firstly I would like to thank all of the attendees of the conference. We run Breaking Convention entirely from ticket sales (and a small amount of sponsorship), so without you the conference would not happen! Secondly to the speakers, I think the unique thing about BC is that people from all stages in academia get to share the stage, from undergraduate students all the way up to the old guard and the pioneers of the psychedelic community. I am always blown away by you. To our volunteers, without whom the conference would not function, we are so grateful for the extra mile all of you go to.

Furthermore, I would like to send a huge thank you to the BC committee members. The executive directors Ben, Cameron, Dave K, Dave L and Nikki, who are, quite frankly, inspirations. To the wider committee, who never cease to amaze; Cara, for the difficult job of organising the filming of the lectures, it is so important that we have a record of this important research for us to disseminate online. Hattie, for keeping everything running smoothly. Adam, for always putting on a great after-party, especially when up against the countless rules and regulations of the university's licensing. Rob and The Psychedelic Press for providing the psychedelic poetry anthology, and also for The Psychedelic Museum. Julian, likewise for your efforts with The Psychedelic Museum and for your uplifting presence. Andy, for your help with the BC merchandising and always taking great photos. Stuart, thank you so much for your curation of our visionary art gallery, especially considering the lack of space in the building. Ashleigh and Ali, for obtaining the extra sponsorship we so need, for the Speakers' Drinks and the organisation of the stalls. Maria, for bringing the much-needed feminine energy to the conference line-up. Stephen Reid, well done for pulling off a successful press conference, where the message was spread outside of the psychedelic echo chamber. Paul, for the curation of our cinema track, and last but definitely not least, Mark, for providing us with your amazing IT skills; you truly are a great asset to the organisation.

All of the team work voluntarily, so thank you for all of your extra work in your already busy lives!

A shout out should also go to the University of Greenwich for giving us a beautiful environment to hold the conference, and providing an awesome backdrop for our infamous group photo! And to Anton Bilton who hosted us in his beautiful home for our big committee meeting.

Lastly to my family, who continue to provide a solid foundation for me.

BEN SESSA

Like an all-knowing ecotoplasmic soup of DMT-firing neurons, the Breaking Community continues to reach its tendrils into all aspects of culture and society. 2017 was, as always, yet another epic year. Gone are the white coats and gone is the tie-dye. Instead we now have a multidimensional mixture of informed, engaged and educated professional psychedelic connoisseurs. It's all about the accessibility. These fascinating chemicals are just too damn good to remain the playthings of the rich and privileged—or arrested and maligned—few. Go forth Breakeroos! Take the message to the masses. It's time to mind your altars and leave no left turn unstoned.

CAMERON ADAMS

My family is very important to me and continue to provide the support and love that I need to go on. My mother, brother and his family never question my integrity and have accepted this crazy drug thing as reasonable and important; something uncommon among conservative Christians, and proof that stereotypes and expectations are poor models of reality. I am always in awe of Zoë, who is growing into an amazing woman and keeps me optimistic about the future. It is challenging being an immigrant. I am so happy to have found my adoptive local family in the Breaking Convention executive and wider crews. You guys are a special bunch and I love you all. Thank you to everyone who participates in any way because without you, there is no Breaking Convention. Some of you have become good friends and I hope many more of you will in the future.

DAVID LUKE

Breaking Convention continues to grow and amaze me each time, and 2017 was no exception. The whole event was literally vibrating and levitating by the Sunday, and then the afterparty, and then the unofficial after afterparty. Wow! I can't even begin to list all the people that made it happen, you know who are and I am deeply grateful to be a part of the whole fantastic stochastic elastic multidimensional mind-gasm that is BC. Special thanks to the executive committee, the entire wider crew, my family for supporting it and everyone who contributed. Love long and perspire!

NIKKI WYRD

Breaking Convention has changed my life. Words cannot express the deep sense of connection, community and enthusiasm for life that this organisation has brought to me; I am so grateful to my partner, my friends (above all, the other BC Committee members) and the wider community who put so much time, effort and energy into co-creating this marvellous event. In particular, the amazing volunteer team, whose capable and cheerful presence generates a special atmosphere. Research into psychedelic consciousness leads us along some interesting paths, and I am happy to walk so many of them in such amazing company.

CONTRIBUTORS

TIM HARDWICK

In 2002 I was awarded a First Class Bachelors Degree in Literature and Philosophy for my dissertation, titled 'On Being God – Romanticism and Transcendentalism: A Mystical Approach', which was subsequently published in *Lila: The Journal of Transpersonal Psychology*. In 2005 I was awarded a Master's Degree with Distinction, for my dissertation, 'Effing the Ineffable: Non-conceptual Discourse and Literary Subversion in The Doors of Perception and The Joyous Cosmology'. For the past 10 years I have pursued a career in technology journalism, and have written tutorials, articles, reviews and features in numerous specialist magazines and online publications.

MATTHEW CLARK

Since 2004 Dr. Matthew Clark has been a Research Associate at SOAS, University of London, where he taught Hinduism from 1999 to 2003. He has published books and articles on Indian ascetics (sadhus) and yoga. Since 2002 he has been lecturing worldwide on the history and philosophy of yoga. He has also designed research units on various religions and several branches of philosophy. Matthew is also a musician, singer and songwriter. He makes records as Mahabongo.

CHRISTOPHER LETHEBY

Dr. Chris Letheby is a philosopher working on issues related to the therapeutic and transformative potential of classic psychedelic drugs. His doctoral research, conducted at the University of Adelaide, presented the first systematic analysis of psychedelic experience within the framework of twenty-first-century philosophy of cognitive science. In his thesis Letheby argues that an 'entheogenic conception' of psychedelics as agents of epistemic and spiritual benefit is both consistent with philosophical naturalism and plausible in light of current scientific knowledge.

LINDSAY JORDAN

Lindsay Jordan is a full time senior lecturer at the University of the Arts, London, where she leads a postgraduate course in the philosophy and practice of higher education. She is also a doctoral candidate at Oxford Brookes. Her thesis explores different ideas of the university, and considers how higher education and research might recover from the disenchantment of secularisation and specialisation. Lindsay is interested in altered states of consciousness and their contribution to human flourishing and fulfilment. Her autoethnography of psychedelic experience and doctoral study won the 2017 Breaking Convention student essay competition. She also makes organic artisanal chocolate.

NADIA VE

Nadia VE has an MSc from the London School of Economics in Gender, Policy and Inequality and has worked in a number of diversity-related organisations. Their work is primarily concerned with addressing damaging power dynamics. They were previously the Head of Diversity and Inclusion at the Psychedelic Society and ran the Psychedelic Society of London for over 2 years. Their MSc dissertation 'Cognitive Dispossession: Entheogens, Ecofeminism and Neuroqueering Drug Policy' won the Breaking Convention 2017 Social Science Research Award, a condensed version of which has appeared at conferences (Breaking Convention 2017, Theorizing the Drug War 2017) and in the book *Psychedelic Mysteries of the Feminine* (Papaspyrou et al, 2019) and they have worked closely with Breaking Convention in creating its Safer Spaces Policy. In 'Psychedelic Kyriarchy: Subhumanization, Feminist Reflexivity & Transformation in Paradox', they explore how damaging power dynamics intersect with UK drug policy, within the psychedelic community and show the critical insights that are grained through queer theory and ecofeminist analysis.

NIKLAS SERNING

Dr Niklas Serning is a doctor of counselling psychology and a child psychotherapist. He is the Consultant Psychotherapist of Bristol's award-winning young person's charity Off the Record, a Senior Lecturer at the University of the West of England (UWE), on the MAPS register, and sees clients and supervisees in his private practice. He teaches psychotherapy, ethics, therapeutic uses of psychedelics, and sexualities at doctoral level, and also brings extensive experience from managing several United Nations operations in complex international emergencies.

OLI GENN-BASH

Oli Genn-Bash, MA, is a co-founder of the University of Kent Canterbury Psychedelics Society and Kent Cannabis Social Club. He has undertaken postgraduate research primarily within the field of politics, with a specific focus on the philosophy of resistance, mysticism, religion, psychedelic experiences, and stand-up comedy – in particular the work of the late American comedian Bill Hicks. He is particularly fascinated with Gnostic traditions, along with the philosophy of Taoism and Judaism.

ELI LEE & NINA LYON

Eli Lee is Fiction Editor at Minor Literatures. She has written for *Delayed Gratification*, *The Quietus*, *Strange Horizons* and the *Financial Times* and has recently completed her debut novel.

Nina Lyon is a writer with an interest in philosophy, nature, culture and psychedelics. She is the author of *Mushroom Season* (Vintage, 2014) and *Uprooted: On the Trail of the Green Man* (Faber, 2016), for which she was recipient of the 2015 Roger Deakin Award. She is currently working on a PhD thesis on Lewis Carroll as metaphysician and trying to get her head around the world when not (and sometimes when) looking after her children. She lives near Hay-on-Wye in Wales.

LUKE GOAMAN–DODSON

Luke Goaman–Dodson is a musician and writer based in Canterbury, UK. His academic background is in Comparative Literature, and his postgraduate work focused on the use of language as a tool of occult practice in the work of William Burroughs and Jorge Luis Borges. Since then, his interests have veered towards parapolitics, conspiracy narratives, and Jungian psychology.

MICHAEL MONTAGUE

Michael Montagne is an independent researcher in Boston, Massachusets. Educated in pharmacy and sociology, he then received postdoctoral training in psychiatric epidemiology. He is the author of over 300 research publications, book chapters, and books including: *Searching for Magic Bullets: Orphan Drugs, Consumer Activism, and Pharmaceutical Development,* 1994. He has written for the Psychozoic Press, Psychedelic Monographs & Essays, Integration, and the Psychedelic Press. He has taught and performed research for 40 years on the social, cultural, and historical aspects of the drug experience.

THARCILA CHAVES

Tharcila Chaves is a pharmacist with a masters degree in medicine and the sociology of drug abuse. Currently, she is a PhD student at the University of Groningen (Netherlands) and also an editor of the OPEN Foundation. In her master's degree, she conducted a qualitative study about cravings in crack cocaine users in the city of Sao Paulo (Brazil). The use of ketamine to treat pain and depression is the focus of her current research.

JOSIE MALINOWSKI

Josie Malinowski is an oneirologist (dream researcher) and oneironaut (dream explorer). She conducts both academic and personal experiments uncovering the secrets, patterns, meanings, absurdities, profundities, joys, and terrors of dreams. She completed a PhD researching the Continuity Hypothesis of dreams in 2013, and is currently employed as a lecturer in psychology at the University of East London. Her academic research projects mainly investigate the nature and possible functions of dreaming. On a personal level, she is interested in the more enigmatic aspects of dreaming such as dream lucidity, telepathy, and precognition. She is currently working on projects investigating how suppressed thoughts return in dreams, and how dreamwork helps us understand ourselves through uncovering connections, metaphors, and personal insights. In her spare time she is also preparing her book *The Psychology of Dreaming* which is due to be released by Routledge in 2019.

REGINA U. HESS

Regina U. Hess, PhD, works internationally as a clinical psychologist, integrative psychotherapist, researcher, lecturer, and has authored various international journal articles and co-edited books. She is on the Board of Directors of the European Transpersonal Association. Regina is a member of the Swiss Medical Society for Psycholytic Therapy, and is lead of the Amsterdam Office, NL, of the MIND European Foundation for Psychedelic Science.

DAVID LUKE

David is Senior Lecturer in Psychology at the University of Greenwich where he teaches the Psychology of Exceptional Human Experience. He was President of the Parapsychological Association between 2009-2011 and has published more than 100 academic papers on the intersection of transpersonal experiences, anomalous phenomena and altered states of consciousness. He has co-authored/ co-edited four books on psychedelics and paranormal experience, directs the Ecology, Cosmos and Consciousness salon at the institute of Ecotechnics, and co-founded Breaking Convention.

GEORGE ERVING

George Erving is Professor of English and the Susan Resneck Pierce Professor of Humanities and Honors at the University of Puget Sound, where he teaches European intellectual history and British Literature from the mid 17th to the mid 19th Centuries. He is the author of scholarly essays on the works of Samuel Taylor Coleridge, British Romantic Period Theatre, and the literary theories of Rene Girard. His current work is on formulations of selfhood during the Romantic period and the psychology of desire in William Blake's major works, The Four Zoas, Milton, and Jerusalem.

LUKE WALKER

Luke Walker has published articles in journals including Romanticism and Comparative American Studies, as well as book chapters in *Rock and Romanticism: Blake, Wordsworth, and Rock from Dylan to U2* (2018) and *The Routledge Handbook of International Beat Literature* (2018). He has taught at the University of Roehampton and University of Chichester, as well as at the University of Sussex, where he completed his PhD on 'William Blake in the 1960s: Counterculture and Radical Reception'. He lives in Brighton, UK.

SAM KNOT

Sam Knot performs a kind of psychedelic (super)naturalism across a variety of media, with a particular focus on his work as a poet and illustrator. After many a year playing around in the poetry sections of various psychedelic forums, while keeping up his day job as a mental health care assistant, he self-published his first book of illustrated poetry, *Being Psilly*, in 2011. You may have seen him performing his poetry in somewhat spontaneous outbursts when the flow of a party or festival seems to permit it, awe deep in the magic of night around the odd (very odd) campfire. He currently lives in relative poverty and rich rural bliss somewhere nowhere in northwest France, poised between self-study in the twin arts of earth gardening and computer programming. Meanwhile he tries to keep www.fleshprism.net up-to-date.

ERIC MADDERN

Eric was born in Australia and educated in England. After graduating in social sciences he spent ten years travelling round the world seeking a deeper understanding of humanity and himself. This culminated in working as a community artist in the Aboriginal communities of Central Australia, an experience that influenced him profoundly. After returning to Britain he chose to settle in North Wales. There, with much help, he has created Cae Mabon, a unique eco-retreat centre in the foothills of Snowdonia. Since 1990 Eric has been a professional storyteller working in a wide range of venues but specialising in natural and historic sites. For English Heritage he wrote *Storytelling at Historic Sites*. He has also written eleven children's picture books (published by Frances Lincoln) and *Snowdonia Folktales*, published by The History Press.

ELIZABETH JOYCE

Elizabeth Joyce, PhD, is a psychotherapist, researcher, and mental health activist, working in the area of psychosis. Her published research has focused on trauma, kinship, narcissism and power relationships. She is currently working with people with lived experience of the psychiatric system in London, exploring the ways in which visual arts, community gardening and local kitchen projects can be used to connect people and facilitate belonging. She has a Master's degree in counselling and psychology and a PhD in Psychology.

JULIAN VAYNE

Julian Vayne is an occultist and the author of numerous books, essays, journals and articles in both the academic and esoteric press. His work is informed by the post-modern style of chaos magic as well as his lineages within Wicca and Uttarakaula Tantra Julian is a co-organizer of the psychedelic conference Breaking Convention, a founding Trustee of TransformDrugs.org and of The Psychedelic Museum. Julian facilitates psychedelic ceremony as well as providing one-to-one psychedelic sessions and integration support. He is the author of the celebrated *Getting Higher: The Manual of Psychedelic Ceremony*.

SAM GANDY

Dr Sam Gandy has a lifelong love of nature and wildlife and a PhD in ecological science from the University of Aberdeen. He currently works at the forefront of psychedelic research as scientific assistant to the director of the Beckley Foundation and as a collaborator with the renowned Imperial College Psychedelic Research Group. Sam savours inner and outer world explorations, and has been fortunate enough to conduct field research in various parts of the world including the UK, Kefalonia, Almeria, Texas, the Peruvian Amazon, Vietnam and Ethiopia. He has a particular interest in the capacity of psychedelics to reconnect us to nature.

WILLIAM ROWLANDSON

William Rowlandson is Senior Lecturer in Hispanic Studies at the University of Kent. He is the author of *Sartre in Cuba–Cuba in Sartre* (Palgrave 2018), *Imaginal Landscapes* (Swedenborg Society, 2015), *Borges, Swedenborg, and Mysticism* (Peter Lang, 2013), and *Reading Lezama's 'Paradiso'* (Peter Lang, 2007); and he is co-editor with Angela Voss of *Daimonic Imagination: Uncanny Intelligence* (Cambridge Scholars, 2013). He has published widely on Latin American cultural and political history, and has published various translations from Spanish into English. He plays drums as often as he can.

STRANGE ATTRACTOR PRESS 2019